CHINA AND IMPERIALISM

CHINA AND IMPERIALISM
(During the Nineteenth Century

TAN CHUNG

Abridged and Ediied
by
D.N. GUPTA

GYAN

China and Imperialism
(During the Nineteenth Century)

ISBN: 978-81-212-0207-7

Published in 2013 in India by
Gyan Publishing House,
23 Main, Ansari Road, Darya Ganj,
New Delhi-110002
Phones : 23282060, 23261060
Fax : 011-23285914
E-mail: books@gyanbooks.com
Website: www.gyanbooks.com

Lasser Type Setting by: Quick Media, Delhi
Printed at : G. Print Process,Delhi

To my Colleagues and Students,
Past and Present,
in Delhi University and Jawaharlal Nehru University,
and all those whose Endeavour is
to Develop Chinese Studies in India

Contents

IV–REFORMATION

Preface

It was in the early years of the 1980s that I made a request to my teacher, Professor Tan Chung, to publish the collection of his already published articles on 19th century China in China Report, Indian Economic and Social History Review and Bodhi-Rasmi in a book form for the benefit of university teachers and students interested in the study of Chinese history. My persistent efforts ultimately convinced him about the academic value of such an anthology for all those who have been interested in the study of colonialism/imperialism and national movements. But soon he expressed his reservations about such a collection on the ground that despite his long-ago made promise to his readers, he had not contributed any article on certain important rubrics like "Commercial and Finance Imperialism", "Christian Missionary Activities" and "The American Policy of Open Door". We genuinely felt that without the inclusion of these vital aspects in the new Collection, it will remain incomplete and lop-sided. Therefore, we decided to write three fresh articles for the book. Two of these were written by Professor Tan Chung and I contributed one on the "American Policy of open Door". The result of these efforts was 'Triton and Dragon' published by Gyan Publishing House in 1986. As Tan Chung has explained:

> It (Triton and Dragon) is particularly the driving spirit of Mr. D.N. Gupta, my former student and a long-time friend and colleague, which has made it possible to make my articles appear in public in the present form. D.N. has also forced me to write two more articles on "Commercial and Finance Imperialism" and "The Christian Missionaries" which I had promised to write several years ago but failed to produce earlier. He himself has contributed a short piece

on "The Open Door" to make this volume covering all major aspects of the history of nineteenth century China.

Why was there a need for me to persuade Tan Chung to publish his articles in a book form? The most important reason obviously was that during over 15 years of my teaching of courses on Chinese history both at the graduate and post-graduate levels at Delhi University, I had noted that it was pargely the Fairbankian framework (propounded by Jonh K. Fairbank in his innumerable writings and uncritically accepted by his disciples and students) that was followed in the class-rooms. But this was precisely the framework that was inadequate with its illogical reasoning that required a critical assessment.

The Fairbankian understanding of 19th century China was mainly guided by the dichotomy between 'tradition' and 'modernity'. He, in his works, divided the entire Chinese history into 'Great-Tradition' and 'Modern Transformation'. The two related aspects of this schema are: (*a*) that China was so tradition that it was difficult to modernise her, and (*b*) that whatever 'modernity' China achieved had been a gift of the West. As Tan Chung has pointed out that the Fairbankian structure, "always conceives China as an outmoded, stagnant and reactionary culture and the West as a modern, dynamic and progressive culture." This raises a pertinent question: Do 'modernity' and 'tradition' exist as two separate and independent phenomenon in opposition to each other, or is 'modernity' the monopoly of the West? Tan Chung has totally rejected 'tradition-modernity' schema in the following words:

> Tradition and modernity are related concepts. They co-exist like carbon dioxide and oxygen. Transformation had long been a regular phenomenon in Chinese history before the advent of modern West in China. Tradition always lives (more than dies) hard in modern China.

As against the Fairbankian formula for the understanding of nineteenth century Chinese developments, Tan Chung has suggested the role of internal and external forces that influenced each other in shaping nineteenth century history.

As he observes:

> Nineteenth century China received dosage of aggression, reduction, killing, construction, destruction, mobilisation, diplomacy, reform, conspiracy, bankruptcy etc.
>
> It was a brisk period of grouping and re-grouping, alignment and re-alignment of political forces. It was a period of unprecedented activities, crimes, miseries which pushed China into a pre-destined course-revolution.

In short, Fairbankian framework which has basically been guided by the nineteenth century 'white mans's burden dictum', fails to explain "the specificity of China's confluence of internal and external forces which had influenced one another."

It may also be pointed out that Fairbank has backed up all his arguments with the misinterpretation of Chinese terminology. Words like Tien-hsia (All Under Heaven), Tien-tzu (Son of Heaven), Yi (Eastern Barbarians) and Chunggho (Middle Kingdom) have been misinterpreted in order to create an impression that Chinese tradition has always looked down upon foreigners. All Fairbankian concepts: 'Tribute-System', 'Treaty Port System', 'Dynastic Cycle Theory' and most important of all, 'Sino-Centrism, are the outcome of his tradition-modernity schema. In its perspective and final analysis the interaction between China and the Western world could only be a one-way traffic with the West at the giving end and China at the receiving end. China becomes a "Whipping boy for the wrongs committed by the prince of Western imperialism" and, therefore 'the theory of Sino-Centrism' owes much to the holier than thou attitude of the nineteenth century, 'Old China Hands' who took away China's wealth on the one hand and used the other to point out an accusing finger against China's outmoded system. Opium was sent to China because Chinese were considered to be unworthy people. Unequal treaties were forced upon the Chinese government because it had no inkling of International equality. The ghost of Sino-centrism served to justify Western imperialist aggression on China.

Fairbank has extended his concept of Sino-centrism to the understanding of the causes of the opium wars and the peasant rebellions during nineteenth century China. According to him opium was only the 'Occasion' and not the 'Sole Cause' of the Opium wars. The British went to war with China "to secure privileges of general commercial and diplomatic inter-course on a Western basis of equality". In support of his thesis he has cited the provisions of the treaty of Nanjing that did not have any clause about the opium trade in future. Fairbank's arguments that "Occasion-is-not-the-sole-cause of the war" and "Settlement-is-the-cause-of-war", have been questioned on a number of grounds by Prof. Tan Chung. First of all he points out that, "Fairbank harps on Cultural conflict and thinks that troubles began with the Chinese cultural superiority. The Chinese could never respect foreign intruders". How could England, the first workshop of the world accept this situation? According to Tan Chung this was not the case at all. Secondly, he is of the view that the treaty of Nanjing was an event different from the outbreak of the war. So motivations for the latter could be different from those of the former. Thirdly, is it not a fact that the treaty settlement contained a clause for the payment of indemnity for the opium confiscated and destroyed by Commissioner Lin? Could China still try to control opium smuggling or even its free trade in future? This was simply to kill the desire of the Manchu government to suppress the Opium traffic at all. That was the reason why the volume of opium increased tremendously from 20000 chests in 1840 to 50000 chests in 1850.

At the same time Tan Chung has also criticised the theory that the industrial bourgeoisie looked upon "the Chinese market of 350 million population" as the solution, "for the crisis of over-production". He has noted a few shortcomings in the Marxist formula of "Capitalist-Over-Production-leading-to-crisis and crisis-leading-to-aggressive-wars". First, it has been observed by Tan Chung that Marx merely talked about the chequered history of the textile industry and never established a direct link between the crisis of over-production and the opium war. Secondly, Marx mentioned only one crisis of 1825. "If the opium war were the direct result and a solution to the crisis of the British textile industry," argues Tan Chang, "the picture of the latter's performance would have been one of deepening depression and crisis from 1836 to 1839 and one of prosperity from 1842 onwards."

Undoubtedly, Tan Chung has argued his case convincingly, but his thesis does not take into consideration the fact that the industrial bourgeoisie threw its entire weight behind the British aggressive/forward policy in China. Why did the leading Chambers of Commerce of big cities of England pass resolutions in favour of such a policy? Is it also not a fact that the industrial bourgeoisie, being a forward-looking class always looks for protecting its future interest in the present? One crisis of 1825 was enough to convince this class that such crises in future could impact its interest adversely.

As against cultural conflict and trade war theories, Tan Chung has advanced "Opium Imperialism" thesis. His most important contribution is that he has analysed opium trade as an imperialist device of international exploitation. As he observes, "Britain's China trade was no ordinary international trade. It was colonial exploitation, remittance and smuggling...The triangular trade (Britain, China and India) with opium as its linch-pin was not only consolidating the Indian colony, but was also converting China into a "semi-colony". Three articles: 'The Britain-China-India Trade Triangle,' 'Opium war' and 'Foreign Mud on Good Earth, British Opium Enterprise vis-a-vis China' that have been included in the present Collection, examine 'Opium Imperialism' thesis in all its complexities.

Tan Chung has also offered a critique of the Fairbankian 'Dynastic Cycle' theory. The details of 'the theory have been worked out by Franz Michael in his book-The Taiping Rebellion: History and Documents'. According to Michael, "The origin of the Taiping Rebellion can be found in these conditions of decline that characterised end of a dynastic cycle, aggravated by special factors of population growth and the new Western impact". Thus 'conditions' fall within two categories: (a) General category of woeful situations which appeared, as a rule, at the end of any dynastic cycle and (b) Category of particular circumstances which gave rise to the Taipings.

Tan Chung does not accept the 'dynastic cycle theory' as an adequate explanation for the outbreak of the Taiping movement. He has put forward the following arguments:

(*a*) That the dynastic cycle theory reduces the study of Chinese history to simple geometry. Scholars who have expounded it have never made it clear whether this dynastic cycle is an unalterable course of China's historical development, or whether it is just a historical co-incidence that the decline of every Chinese dynasty was attended by identical phenomena.

(*b*) That the dynastic cycle theory smacks of the long-standing Western intellectual prejudice about China's historical changelessness. Every dynastic decline in China was characterised by the particularity of its historical circumstances, and not by the generality of the dynastic cycle which exists only in the scholar's imagination.

(*c*) That it is more correct to say that the Taiping was a cause of Manchu dynastic decline rather than vice versa. Also that the Taipings challenged a dynasty which still had a powerful image and vitality... The real cause of the Taipings war must, thus, be differently conceived from the theoretical framework of the dynastic cycle.

Tan Chung's articles have perhaps been the only articles that offer a full-length and point to point critique of the Fairbankian framework which is supported by its *i.e.* logical reasoning and misinterpretation of Chinese terminology. Fairbank does not raise the basic question: Was China 'modernized' or 'colonialized' semi-colonialized? Of course, this is not to deny the fact that Fairbank does use terms like "imperialism," "domination," "hegemony and "gun boat-diplomacy" but he not only negates the theory of imperialism which is generally understood as a system of colonial oppression and capitalist exploitation of foreign peoples but also does not apply these terms to the understanding of concrete events of 19th century China. Instead the central perspective is that of 'cultural conflict' between China and the West which transformed the contradiction between 'trade' and 'tribute' in the Chinese scene in recent centuries.

Most of Tan Chung's articles were published in journals which were not easily accessible to the large number of teachers and students of Chinese history as the 1980's were yet to see e-revolution. This motivated us then to bring out 'Triton and

Dragon' in 1986 which was supported by exhaustive use of English and Chinese language sources thus enhancing the academic value of the book. 'Triton and Dragon' not only received an overwhelming response but also generated a need to bring out a reprint or a revised edition of the book which had to wait for the time being. However, once work on the book commenced, suggestions were taken from a cross-section of teachers and students interested in studying imperialism and colonialism and national movements in the nineteenth century China which guided us to bring out an abridged and edited volume of 'Triton and Dragon' so that it could be used as a much neeed textbook on the history of nineteenth century China. However, the thrust and basic arguments of 'Trigon and Dragon' have not been interfered with. I am sanguine that this new abridged and edited volume will serve the purpose for which it is published.

—D.N.G.

Acknowledgements to Triton and Dragon

This book is brought out under the urge of many well wishers whose number is too large to be mentioned by name. They have seen in my articles published in different journals from time to time some new materials and fresh ideas for the study of nineteenth century China, and urged me to bring out the book for the benefit of a wider readership. It is particularly the driving spirit of Mr. D.N. Gupta, my former student and a long time friend and colleague, which has made it possible to make my articles appear in public in the present form D.N. has forced me to write two more articles on "Commercial and Finance Imperialism" and "Christian Missionaries" which I had promised to write several years ago but failed to produce earlier. He himself has contributed a short piece on the "Open Door" to make this volume covering all major aspects of the history of nineteenth-century China. In this sense, the book is a joint product of both of us. The Bibliography is also our joint baby. Being himself a teacher on these topics in Hindu College for two decades, he has much more direct contacts with the learners than I, and has made various suggestions on the production of this book. He has also a good rapport with Gyan Publishing House which has done an excellence job in bringing the book out in a short time of four months. My thanks to D.N. Gupta and all those in the publishing house who have co-operated to produce my articles in such a fine volume.

I also thank Mr C.R.M. Rao, Editor of *China Report,* and Professor Dharma Kumar, editor of *Indian Economic and Social History Review,* for permitting the republication of my articles. I should also thank Professor S. Bhattacharya for valuable suggestions on my article on “Commercial and Finance Imperialism”.

New Delhi **Tan Chung**
2012

Introduction*

The history of 19th century China was a great inventor. It invented the "Gunboat Diplomacy", "Treaty Ports", "Most-Favoured Nation Clause", "Extraterritoriality", "International Concession", "Spheres of Influence", and "Open Door" for the treasury of international diplomacy. Many Chinese names, particularly "Taiping" and "Yihetuan", have become international lingua franca. Mass legend also contributed by creating the most indelible term of "Opium War" much to the dismay of many a politician and scholar. The amount of ink spilled to obliterate the crime and misfortune created by British opium imperialism can match that spent on glorifying any greatest human achievement.

In this book, readers may find a bit of a "Fairbank-watching". He, being the guiding light of the modern comments on nineteenth-century China, no one who studies the subject can bypass him. I don't know whether not having been a student of Fairbank is a liberty or liability. Ignorance certainly offers courage to be outspoken, if not critical. But, there might be short-comings on my part to understand the patriarch of China-watching as thoroughly as his own students could have. I must hasten to add that I admire him as much as I do my guru.

I think it inadequate to regard Fairbank as an institution. He has been at the head of a school of thought on nineteenth-century China. I should further think this Fairbankian School as an extension of the Traditional Society School which wages war against the World Economic Development School led by Myrdal, Prebisch, Frank etc. in the theoretical field of economic developments. What the Fairbankian School has done amounts to flogging the Chinese tradition as a whipping-boy to chastise the crimes committed by the prince of Western imperialism.

---

*It is an abridged form of introduction that Prof Tan Chung originally had written to his collection of articles, *'Triton and Dragon'*. For the full text see Tan Chung, *Triton and Dragon (Delhi, 1986).*

Indeed, all students of nineteenth-century China have to deal with the Fairbankian "laws", such as "Sinocentrism", "tribute system", "Canton system", "treaty-port system" etc. which figure quite prominently in the chapters of this book. The law of Sinocentrism is invented to transform opium from a "cause" into an "occasion" of the first Sino-British War of 1840-1842. Hsin-pao Chang expands this to a law of "cultural conflict" with social science genius to define the war as an X-War with the algebraic "X" replaceable by a host of commodities ranging from opium to rice. This is one example of the "multidisciplinary manner" in which the Fairbankian School responds to the challenge of anti-imperialist historians.

I do not think Fairbank and like-minded historians have been obsessed with imperialism, much less the defence of it. But, they have been too overwhelmed by the Toynbean law of "challenge and response" to see China as it is, rather than as what the West has made her. By saying this I do not deny that there has been significant impact of the West on China. The crux of the issue lies in whether we should treat China as a part of the inseparable process of human evolution or as if she had come to the modern world from a stream totally different from that of the Western civilisation. China's challenge and response *vis-a-vis* the modern West has always been, and shall always be, an integral part of the global development.

The Challenge-and-Response theory, it should not be understood as a simple formula with the West representing the challenge and China representing the response. Within China herself there was the contradiction between a decadent government which could not cope with the external aggression and the suffering masses who wished to come out of the rot. The internal challenge against the Manchu government was built up by the Taiping Rebellion. It was also an indirect challenge against British opium imperialism. Britain and other imperialist powers responded to this challenge promptly by lending a powerful hand to destroy the rebellion. From that time onwards Western imperialism had been internalized into China's own contradictions. The equation was no longer drawn between China on the one hand and the Western powers on the other. It was, as Mao Zedong and his comrades have clearly fomulated, a battle between the Chinese masses on the one hand, and Western imperialism in alliance with the reactionary forces within China on the other.

The greatest weakness of the Fairbankian School is to isolate China into a water-tight compartment unrelated to the world-wide development. The scholars in this School have been blinded to the historical reality of not only the internalisation of Western imperialism into China's internal developments, but also the internalization of China into the world development. Was China not a part of the two World Wars? Surely she was. Did China not figure in the internal contradictions within the imperialist camp? Surely she did. If so, there should have been far more laws and equations than what the Fairbankian School had offered. China was equally influenced by the internal and external dynamics which were shaping the developments of other countries. It is anti-historical to treat China as a separate category altogether.

Fairbank, himself, shows us the way that a thorough understanding of the Chinese problem involves an overall understanding of Chinese history in its totality. The course of history is an on-going development. Historical events never consciously synchronize with the turns of decades or centuries. We cannot discuss any century in isolation. The time boundary of this book is meant to be crossed. And the setting of the boundary serves to highlight the importance of a certain historical juncture.

This book is conscious of the existence of the half-truths and un-truths about the history of nineteenth-century China and their great harm done to the understanding of the modern Chinese development. More scholarly attention is therefore necessary to probe into the happenings of this crucial period. A basic understanding of the nature and significance of the history of nineteenth-century China is very essential for viewing modern Chinese developments in proper historical perspective.

First of all, we must break away from the Fairbankian framework of dividing the entire Chinese history into a period of 'Great Tradition' and another of 'Modern Transformation'. Tradition and modernity are related concepts. They always coexist like carbon dioxide and oxygen. Transformation had long been a regular phenomenon in Chinese history before the advent of modern West in China. On the other hand, tradition always lives (more than dies) hard in modern China. The speciality of nineteenth-century China was highlighted by an unprecedented confluence of internal and external forces which had influenced one another. 19th century China received a concentrated dosage of aggression, revolution, killing, construction, destruction, mobilization, diplomacy, reform, conspiracy, bankruptcy, famine, etc. It was a period of brisk grouping and regrouping, alignment and realignment of political and social forces. It was a period of unprecedented activities, crimes, miseries which pushed China onto a predestined course—revolution.

The dilemma of the Fairbankian pespective on China is that on the one hand, China was so traditional that it was difficult to modernize her, and whatever modernity China achieved has been a gift from the West and on the other hand, Fairbank seems to have suddenly lost his confidence in the moral power of the modern West in the hypothetical contest with future China. This only implies that modernity is never the monopoly of the West.

The second thing to deal with the history of nineteenth-century China is to treat the entire period as the labouring period for the birth of a new nation. What must be emphasized is the intensity of the birth pangs—an aspect which is consistently overlooked by the Fairbankian School.

On the contrary, the Maoist School holds that a major impact of the modern West on China was the creation of two more mountains over the heads of the suffering masses of China who had already been languishing under the mountain of repression of the combined tyranny of feudal lords and the ruthless government backing the latter. Mao's "Three Mountains" theory—Chinese masses being crushed under the weight of feudalism, imperialism and bureaucratic and comprador bourgeoisie—was one of the winning cards in the Chinese Communist revolutionary ideology. The theory sees that imperialism has accentuated the miseries of the Chinese people who had already been condemned to acute traditional exploitations.

The sufferings of Chinese masses have always evaded the attention of the Fairbankian School, but occasionally noted by other American scholars. Richard Henry Tawney wrote as early as 1931 about the poverty of the Chinese peasants based on field surveys. His findings were that in the beginning of the twentieth century many rural Chinese families lived well below the "minimum income needed to support a family in China" which was estimated to be between U.S. $100 and 150 per annum. According to the International Famine Relief Commission in 1922, 62.2% of the peasant families of Shandong and Hebei provinces had income of less than $50 a year. Tawney's evidence made him conclude that "a large proportion of Chinese peasants are constantly on the brink of actual destitution. They are, so to say, a propertied proletariat, which is saved— when it is saved - partly by its own admirable ingenuity and fortitude, partly by the communism of the Chinese family, partly by reducing its consumption of necessaries and thus using up its physical capital."[1]

With such fragile economic foundation resulting from cruel exploitation the Chinese masses easily perished in times of natural calamities. Tawney gathered estimates that during the famine of 1849 nearly 14 million Chinese peasants perished, and during the famine of 1878-1879 nine to thirteen million Chinese peasants lost their lives.[2] "Calamity is more frequent in China than in the West," observed Tawney.[3] The Maoist theory can be strengthened by Tawney's data. Under the three repressive mountains, the Chinese peasants in the nineteenth century were among the most miserable living beings of the world. The nineteenth-century Chinese peasants had been mercilessly exploited by the landlords, who were, in turn, exploited by British opium imperialism. In this telescopic structure of semi-feudal and semi-colonial exploitation the peasants were bled white. It was not that the Chinese peasants had not suffered cruel exploitation in earlier times, but they suffered even more during the nineteenth century under additional imperialist exploitation. The poverty and misery wrought by external and internal forces from the Opium War till the eve of liberation can claim the highest record in Chinese history.

The third salient feature of the history of 19th century China was its clear manifestation of the revolutionary potential of the Chinese people. Wherever the land level is the lowest maximum water flows to it. And wherever human living standard sinks to the nadir maximum revolutionary spirit dawns on the human lives there. Since the Three Mountains had reduced the majority of Chinese masses to the status of proletariat, the latter had little fear to overthrow the *ancien regime* which had given them nothing but the chains on their bodies.

This book is a collection of articles written with different vintages. Most of them were published in journals earlier, for which reason it has been difficult to make them available to all those who have been interested in studying imperialism and colonialism and national movements in nineteenth-century China. By bringing them together into a book, they can reach a much larger readership, especially the university teachers and students. The book also fills in the void by adding three new articles on (1) Commercial and finance imperialism (2) Christian missionary activities in nineteenth-century China, and (3) the "Open Door" (which is written by D.N.Gupta).

All the articles in the collection are the result of a history teacher's intense reflections and extensive data-hunting on the topics which they deal with. As each article is marked by a date, no attempt has been made to revise them and update them. This not only observes a respect for historiocity but also helps to reveal the various stages of a thinking process. As almost all the articles are written in the scheme of in-depth discussion, certain basic knowledge on the part of the reader has been taken for granted. However, readers can always go back to the authors mentioned in the references to regain what they have missed before reading this book. An attempt has been made in these articles to synthesize the parallel historiographies existing in English and Chinese languages by comparing and contrasting different shades of opinions and schools of thought.

T.C.

References

1. R. H. Tawney, *Land and Labour in China* (Boston, 1966), pp. 69-73.
2. *Ibid.,* p. 76.
3. *Ibid.,* p. 73.

PART—I

Orientation

1

On Understanding Nineteenth-Century China*

For the history of the world in general and that of China in particular, the 19th century, particularly its second half, was a period of unprecedented international cultural interaction with fierce confrontations as well as passionate cross-fertilization between eastern and western cultures. It was a period of Europe making Asia and Asia making Europe. The history of 19th-century China was a microcosm of this world scenario.

I think that the history of 19th-century China was made both by international and domestic forces. Not only was there the dimension of western (plus Japanese) imperialism versus China, but developments within China were results of interaction between domestic and foreign elements, both materially and spiritually. It is easy to see that if there were no opium the Chinese internal development would have been vastly different. The growth of the Taiping movement, cannot be separated from the introduction of Christianity to China. The "Self-Strengthening" movement, the "Hundred Days" reform and the "Boxer uprising", all had their share of foreign stimulants. It was as though 19th-century China was made by Europe. Yet, this was not all.

I have gathered the impression during my previous research that China was an important element in the making of modern Britain. Modern scholars are in the habit of tracing the genesis of the events of the 19th century to the Industrial Revolution, and even further back to the Reformation and Renaissance in

---

*The article is the summary of the text of a speech that was delivered to the History Society of Lady Shri Ram College, New Delhi, on 21 November 1983 and was published in *China Report* (Delhi) Vol. XX, No. I, (January-February, 1984)

European history. Even the cause of the Opium War has been linked with the British Industrial Revolution—a problem which I shall take up a little later. If one likes to jump into the fray of such cause-addicted scholarship in historical studies, one might stretch one's imagination further back to the Chinese invention of paper and printing without which European Renaissance would not have taken place at all, let alone the Industrial Revolution. But let us refrain from such a meaningless exercise. The support for my assertion of China being a creative factor in the making of modern Britain is not abstract. It is a tangible material. I mean tea.

There is no single vegetation which has contributed so much to the making of modern Britain than the Chinese herb, tea. Some research needs to be done to ascertain the beginning of Britain's romance with the Chinese beverage. I have a hunch that the British aristocrats (including the royalty) were at first fascinated by the oriental tea culture with its mannerism and the delicate charm of the porcelain tea sets. Gradually, tea drinking had its civilizing effect on British alcoholism, and a new culture of public debate-minus-brawl emerged from coffee-house gatherings over a cup of tea. King Charles II, one of the last of the Mohegans of British despotism, was frightened by this growth of democratic culture and contemplated closing down the coffee-houses.[1] Would it not be appropriate to acknowledge the contribution of tea, an exotic leaf from China, to the promotion of Britain's democratic way of life?

If Chinese tea revolutionised British life, Britons also revolutionized tea drinking. The Chinese started drinking tea as a purgative, but under Buddhist influence they turned it into a popular beverage served and drunk with some elegance. The Britons turned the beverage into a food by adding milk and sugar to it. This beverage-to food revolution in tea-drinking occurred more due to the dictates of economic developments than to the British mood for innovation. The Industrial Revolution increased not only the capitalist's expectation of profit, but also the worker's duration of daily toil. Tea with milk and sugar provided a food item for the industrial workers to refresh their energy during intervals of their long working day. Thus came the "tea break", an important part of life routine which has come down to us from the Industrial Revolution, thanks to the British transformation of the oriental beverage into an energy-giving food. Tea is the major Chinese intrusion into the lives of modern Britons, Indians and many other peoples who have assimilated British cultural influence.[2]

You would think that I have made the most unexpected, if not fantastic, revelation by dramatizing the influence of tea on British democracy and Industrial Revolution. This revelation dawned upon me when I was searching for an answer to Britain's 'cost-what-it-may' mood in her attempt to obtain monopsony of Canton trade which was the only source of supply of tea before the Opium War. But I did not want to dramatize, let alone distort historical facts. The London India House's "cost-what-it-may" instructions to its Canton agents in 1720[3] was a significant clue to the understanding of the British expansion policy. A near-complete control of the source of supply of an important international commodity like tea enabled Britain to fulfil her age-old mercantilist dream of making Britain the entrepot of colonial products that tea would first be shipped from Canton to London before being distributed to all its markets in the world. In this manner not only the revenue from tea contributed to one-tenth of British Government income during the first half of the 19th century, but there was a great fillip to the growth of British Shipping Industry and naval power while the Chinese tea chests embarked on round-the-world trips courtesy of Britain. This makes clear why tea became an issue in the movement for American Independence. Can we then ignore the importance of Chinese tea in Britain's colonial expansion?

Many western scholars have smelled Sinocentrism in Chinese culture. This may be undeniable, much as I would be the last person to admit it. But Eurocentrism as a historial phenomenon is even more undeniable. Western intellectuals just take this charge in their stride. Although I do not necessarily believe that ethnical prejudices are inborn, even people who have the most generous international outlook could become victims of parochial bias.

I have criticised some Chinese historians for over-emphasizing the effect of the British "Industrial Revolution" on the events of Chinese history.[4] I fail to understand how Britain's annual production of one million tons of pig iron and thirty million tons of coal could make Britain so uncouth and aggressive as to wage an Opium War against China. During the time of Karl Marx these statistics might have meant something, but they cannot frighten the intellectuals of even the least developing Asian country today. I am even prepared to buy the so-called Marxist perspective on the Opium War (by linking the war with the inevitable history course as charted out by historical materialism) if statistics could show that 20 per cent, or even 10 per cent of the British pig iron and coal were so much in excess for the smooth functioning of British economy that they had to be consumed in a war so far away so that Britons would not be waken up from their sleep by the merry booming of British guns and heart-piercing cries of injury from Chinese soldiers and civilians.

Here, I may plead innocence against the charge of committing anti-Marxism in my Opium War studies (a charge which I hear has been levied in Delhi University history classrooms). Marx was one of the first intellectuals of the world to advance the Opium-War-due-to-opium proposition which I have reiterated. If Marx was not himself the creator of the vivid term "Opium War", his forceful advocacy has definitely contributed to the perpetuation of the stigma which shows no sign of fading even after so much effort to whitewash it.

A thorough understanding of the 19th century requires' the elongation of our historical projection. Why I have strongly objected to the onesided view of modern China being created by the West alone is because China was not born in the 19th century. China had many thousand years of civilization before the westerners appeared on her shores. A nation, a culture, and a society which had lasted for so long must have had its internal dynamism and vitality. If we have no knowledge of China's past, our understanding of modern China would surely suffer. Any study of 19th-century China without the insights of pre-19th-century China would at best be fractured scholarship.

This opens up new vistas for our study of 19th-century China, and our search-light must now turn onto the Chinese society itself. Instead of focusing on how the West has made China, our focal point should be the inner Chinese vitality which has enabled China to stand the onslaught of the West and China's emergence from her past ordeal as a new nation.

References

1. Tan Chung, "Civilizing Influence of Tea", *The Statesman,* 1 February 1970, (Magazine Section, pp. I-IV).
2. J.C. Williamson in his *Short History of British Expansion* (London, 1958) asserts that without the new food of the mixture of tea, milk and sugar "the poor diet of the factory-workers should not have kept them going" during the Industrial Revolution (p. 38). Perhaps this was the reason why the Britrons always preferred to have the stronger black tea rather than the fragrant green tea.
3. Faced with some competitors known as the "Ostenders" the Court of Directors of the East India Company instructed: "We give this order thus large, that the Ostenders may be disappointed of Tea, and if they are we shall esteem it an excellent piece of service done the Company, for which you shall not want our encouragement... Cost what it will we must try to make these Interlopers sick of their voyages for Tea." See H.B. Morse, *The Chronicles of the East India Company Trading to China* (Oxford, 1926), p. 162. Not tolerating any competitor for the Chinese tea and keeping all competitors away at any cost was the prevailing British mood in obtaining monopsony in the Canton trade, *i.e.,* monopoly of the buyers' market.
4. Tan Chung, "Imperialism in 19th-century China (I) : Foreign Mud on Good Earth : British Opium Enterprise *vis-a-vis* China" *China Report.* Vol. XVII, No. 2, March-April 1981, p. 14.

2

On Sinocentrism : A Critique*

I

The theory of Sinocentrism is founded on the premise of Chinese "culturalism" in contrast to Western nationalism. I Culture has been hyperbolized into an omnipotent monster which allegedly swallowed up both individuality and national identity in traditional China. This premise, however attractive, betrays a superficial understanding of Chinese history.

First of all, one must not take a static view of the *Chineseness* in Chinese culture. A well-known Japanese historian Tomi Saeki has developed the theory that the early Chinese not only imported bronze but also culture (including the imperial system) from West Asia.[1] According to a renowned U.S. scholar William H. McNeill the neolithic culture in ancient China had received beneficial influence from that of Mesopotamia, echoing a theory which was popular among Western scholars a couple of decades ago.[2] It is well known that the people of Qin (from which name came the Indian word *Cheena* and the English word China) who lived first on the western fringe of the Chinese mini-world and later unified it into a centralized empire, had strong cultural affinities with the peoples of the West.[3] Being the first ruling group of imperial China, they surely played the catalyst's role in introducing West Asian and European ingredients into Chinese culture.

A fashion was the use of powder for make-up by both Chinese men and women from the Han Dynasty onwards.[4] Another fashion among the court ladies of the Tang Dynasty was the V-shaped collar which half-exposed the bosom—an

---

*This article is the revised version of paper which was originally presented to the 29th International Congress of Orientalists, Paris, July 1973 and published in *China Report*, Vol. IX, Nos. 5 & 6 (Sept.- Oct. & Nov.-Dec. 1973).

imitation of female fashion in Central Asia, if not further beyond. Many Tang women also wore the European-style folded collar.[5] Imitation cf foreign fashions can be traced back even to the time of Han emeror Wu (140-87 B.C.) whose places were said to have been filled with imported jewels and novelties, including ivory-mats and bead-screens.[6] A jewel-studded saddle from India was said to have created a vogue of saddle-decoration among the aristocrats in the capital Chang'an during his reign.[7] The emperor also started a new fashion in China, the use of aromatic substances as perfume or in fumigation. Since then foreign perfumes have been an inevitable item of China's import trade.

The Chinese fondness for perfumes not only shows their materialistic outlook on life, but further strengthens their admiration for foreign lands. Perfumes even influenced Chinese politics. An insignificant official in the foreign trade department was promoted straightaway to colonel's rank by the Han government for his contribution to the importing of perfumes. This earned him the nick-name of "Perfume Colonel" *(xiangwei).* A thousand years later, during the Song Dynasty (960-1279), a dismissed official from Canton worked his way up to reinstatement and dramatic promotion to governorship of Canton by supplying perfumes to imperial courtiers. He is remembered in Chinese history as the "perfume Governor".

Moreover the Chinese writers always maintained a rather objective attitude in reporting what they heard about other countries mostly from boastful foreign visitors. They were ignorant, no doubt, but they had also curiosity, imagination and admiration, and no superiority complex. It was this attitude which led to the rage of buying exotic goods and imitating foreign fashions.

We have already touched upon the foreign-ization of Chinese dress. Chinese food habits changed as greatly as their dress. When we now look at the ingredients of Chinese cuisine, we find a host of things which are non-Chinese in origin, notably, soya-bean, broad-bean, cucumber, spinach, amaranth, lettuce, lily-bulb, rape, white mustard, caraway, pumpkin, sponge-gourd, bitter-gourd, snake-gourd, brinjal, potato, sweet-potato, tomato, pepper, sugar, sesame, garlic, onion, anise, cumin, grape, walnut etc.[8]

Chinese literary taste underwent equally drastic changes. Rhyming entered literary styles after Chinese writers had discovered the initials and finals in their sound-system with the aid of Indian phonological analysis. Drama and novel developed, thanks to enthusiastic Buddhist preaching among the masses,[9] and nomadic culture being integrated into Chinese life. The Chinese air had been constantly fumigated rather than polluted by exotic incense. The Chinese lantern festival, which used to be a red-letter day for millions of pleasure-loving Chinese, was originally a Buddhist festival and may be regarded as a Chinese version of the Indian *Diwali.* In the exquisite ancient artifacts which have been unearthed recently and are now continuously excavated in large quantities in China we see unmistakable non-Chinese figures, motifs and styles.[10] The famous Dunhuang, Longmen, Yungang and Datong and innumerable other caves in China, which are rich repositories of art treasures, owed their original ideas to the people of Afghanistan and India.[11] Foreign influence on Chinese music throughout the ages has been even greater than that on Chinese art. The seven musical notes along with a host of wind and string instruments are joint gifts from the peoples of Central Asia and India.[12] Even the Chinese seasons have been rotating according to non-Chinese calculations after two major revisions of the Chinese calendar, first during the Tang and then during the Ming Dynasty (1368-1644), under the guidance of Indian and European expertise respectively.[13] Practically, there is no aspect of Chinese life which has not been foreignized. From the 14th century onwards, the traditional Chinese fibres, names were replaced by (Gubei) *i.e.,* cotton which was the Indian gift to China as silk was a Chinese gift to India.

All this, of course, essentially belongs to the material life. Let us now examine the "Chineseness", or the lack of it, in the spiritual outlook of Chinese culture. We must begin by saying that a great number of Western scholars, particularly those obsessed with the proposition of sinocentrism, tend to overlook the immense impact of Indian culture on Chinese spiritual life.

First, these scholars do not realize or deliberately refuse to recognise the important role played by China in disseminating the *Buddadhamma* in the world. This blindness arises from prejudice. They say that the success of Buddhism in China provides another classical example of sinicization, as if the Chinese embraced the Indian ideology just for the fun of acculturating another barbarian phenomenon. Only historical facts can help us argue against such unreasonableness.

Those who went on pilgrimage were fewer in number than those who were converted in China. In the 6th century, there were about 60,000 monasteries and more than two million monks and nuns in China.[14] From the seventh century onwards almost all Chinese owned the Buddha and other *Bodhisattavas* as their deities. Buddhism thus became the national religion of China. There is an outstanding example of this historic conversion in the life and reign of the Liang emperor Wu (502-549), who styled himself "Bodhisattva-emperor" *(Pusa huangdi)*. He turned his ancestral house into a Buddhist temple, and soon after his enthronement repatriated all women in his palace to their respective homes. He was the only monarch in the world who could boast of not having once touched a morsel of meat or shared the roof with a woman at night throughout his forty odd years' reign. He spent most of his time studying scriptures and participating in religious ceremonies, and also exhausted his treasury building Buddhist temples and other monuments, and offering patronage to Buddhist organisations. Three times he sold himself to a Buddhist temple, causing his courtiers to spend money to ransom him back to the throne. At another time, he even sold all his subjects to the temple.[15] This marked the maddening climax of conversions to Buddhism in China.

The Chinese had collected all Buddhist scriptures available in the world and translated them from Sanskrit and Pali into Chinese. These have become the best preserved Buddhist documents, while the Sanskrit and Pali texts of most of them are not extant.[16] The Chinese Buddhists earnestly tried to develop the Buddhist philosophy, and in a solemn and responsible manner helped the Japanese, Koreans and

Vietnamese to acquire Buddhist teachings. All this shows the outward look of Chinese culture. It serves to show that Chinese culture has always been a synthesis of native and foreign elements. Chinese culture absorbed foreign ingredients from time to time to adopt itself to changing circumstances.

Therefore, the fundamental weakness of the theory of culturalism lies in its refusal to regard economic interest as the fundamental issue of any social problem. When the Chinese gentry willingly and loyally served alien rulers, they also served their own socio-economic interests. Culture was the means not the end. When Zeng Guofan (1811-1872) and other Han Chinese helped the Manchu government to suppress fellow-Han rebels under the banner of Taiping, it was not because the Taipings had imported foreign culture while the Manchus resisted it. Zeng's real motivation was different. First, he had already tied his own fortune to the Manchu chariot. If the latter was over-thrown his personal interests would have suffered. Secondly, the Taipings were bent on destroying the *ancien regime* in China and establishing a new order in which Zeng's social group would be down-graded. Thus, the instance cannot substantiate the hypothesis that the Chinese tradition was pro-cultural and anti-national in character.

II

Sinocentrism as a hypothesis is a powerful appeal to the kind of scholarship that excels in generalization. In recent years, some social scientists, have entered the fray to establish the Chinese "Middle Kingdom Complex", defined as an "unquestionable" and "unshakable identification with historical greatness". It is further said that "merely to be Chinese is to be a part of the greatest phenomenon of history," and everyone of the many hundred million Chinese is entitled to a "sense of personal association with a glorious and self-contained history that encompasses all of merit and greatness in the human experience."[17]

These assertions seem to argue that the degree of national pride is directly proportional to (a) the size of the nation, and

(b) the length of the nation's recorded past. But such an argument leaves many important aspects of national life out of consideration. We know that psychological contentment springs from economic satisfaction, social security, political participation, physical fitness, spiritual enlightenment, and even aesthetic appreciation. To be one of the teeming millions does not necessarily evoke a sense of pride.

The contention that every Chinese is born a proud creature because of his being a part of Chinese greatness (great in size of her population and length of her history) has a topsyhturvy historical perspective. A great nation has always great problems which, in turn, impair the people's attachment to the land of their birth. China was one of the two super empires under the Han Dynasty which extended to a couple of centuries both before and after Christ (the other being Rome). Were the people of Han obsessed with the Middle Kingdom complex? We have really no proof that they were.

Moreover, too much is made of the "hierarchical nature" of Chinese society. It is even suggested that equality is alien to Chinese cultural tradition because it is asserted that the Chinese world-order was always a hierarchical system. Such contentions have confused the Confucian tradition of decorum which rather rigidly observed a senior-junior relationship in social intercourse with the guiding principles of Chinese political thought. When we examine the latter, we do not find the spirit of equality lacking. Confucius's exposition of the ideal of *Datong* Grand Equality is a unique piece among the noble and enlightened writings of the world. China was also one of the first countries to place law above the individual. The rule of law worked as a social safeguard for equality between man and man.

The so-called Chinese world-order being maintained by the tribute-system is but a myth created by modern scholars imagination. The Son of Heaven in pre-imperial China was given a universal image because he was the tutelary leader of a loose confederation—the Chinese mini-world. The imperial government of China inherited the narcissism of *Tianzi* for reasons other than establishing a sino-centric order. Anyone who had a part in shaping imperial China's destiny would easily see that, first of all, the mere size and heterogeneity of China, could breed enough centrifugal forces to disintegrate the empire. Secondly, there was glaring disparity in the distribution of social wealth, and the discontentment of the populace provided a hot-bed for revolution. Thirdly, the country's boundaries were too long to be easily defended. Sheer military might could not ensure the safety of the ruling dynasty. Cultural and political weapons had to be employed to reinforce the repressive machinery. The glorification of *Tianzi's* respectability and supernatural image formed a part of this reinforcement. Internally, he was depicted as the benevolent father and sagacious teacher of the people, and the custodian of moral values and social order. Externally, he was deemed the cynosure among the illustrious heroes all over the world. But all this was just propaganda aimed at scaring away the contenders to the throne—the secessionists, revolutionists, and, to a lesser extent, the foreign aggressors.

The superman image of the Son of Heaven symbolised the totalitarian political system of traditional China. To vindicate *Tianzi* was to support this system. And the system was to ensure the economic, social and political domination of the ruling elite. In Marxian terms, the narcissism of the Son of Heaven was a part of the superstructure which served the interests of the base. But where there is repression there is rebellion. Call it class struggle or not, the drama of Chinese social upheaval was no tame affair. The tide of peasants rebellion witnessed at the end of the Han and Dang dynasties had few parallels in world history. Such fierce struggle between the oppressors and the oppressed inevitably reflected itself in the superstructure. A kind of war was always going on on the ideological front. All dominant political and philosophical theories of traditional China can be viewed as an endless apology for the totalitarian system.[19] Special pains were taken by the ruling elite to mend fences on the ideological front, and an elaborate system of rituals evolved around the person of the emperor.

The tribute-offering ceremonies formed an important part of this system. Once a year, all people of significance within the country offered tributes to the emperor on his birth day, and the imperial treasury sank a substantial part of its annual savings in the fanfare to boost the morale of the ruling family. More tribute-offering meant more prestige for this family and reinforcement of the political system. Tributes from abroad were an additional prop, even eagerly sought and awaited.

It is clear that the real motivation behind the so-called tribute-system, or rather the tribute-offering ceremonies, was to safeguard the political system in imperial China. It was an internal game, a part of the Chinese order rather than that of the world order. Of course, since the external aspect of the fanfare had become a part of China's internal politics, and since the foreign tributary envoys were given audience by the Son of Heaven in front of all significant personages from all parts of China, the names of foreign countries became involved in the elaborate Chinese campaign of vindicating the Son of Heaven. They were listed in Chinese official documents as "tributary states" to enhance the reputation of the Chinese ruling regime, especially in the eyes of the Chinese masses. Judging from this, the "tribute system" was by no means a "Sino-barbarian system".[20]

True, the 1818 Statutes included Britain as a tributary state along with Portugal, Holland and a few other European states. But France and U.S.A. were among the important omissions. It is easy to see that the Chinese discrimination was based on the other consideration that Britain and other countries had sent a kind of tributary mission to Beijing while France and U.S.A. had not. The three British embassies to China, Cathcart's in 1787, Macartney's in 1793 and Amherst's in 1816, were, of course, not meant to be tributary missions. But they were made to appear so (to join other tributary missions in the gala celebrations of the Chinese emperor's birth-day) in order that they could be received without difficulty. Neither Macartney nor the Foreign Office in London protested against the flags on the yachts provided by the Chinese hosts for the 1793 embassy, bearing the inscription "The English Ambassador bringing tribute to the Emperor of China".[21] This having been noticed, London not only sent another embassy to Beijing in 1816 which exactly followed the proceedings and beaten-tracks of its 1793 predecessor, but also dispatched to the Chinese emperor two additional consignments of tribute-like gifts (without envoy) in 1796 and 1804.[22] Beijing thus had no lack of excuse to brand Britain a "tributary". Yet the initiative was not China's. The Chinese knew nothing about the Cathcart mission as the ambassador died before entering the China waters. And Beijing was informed about the Macartney and Amherst missions only after the latter had already sailed from London. But, it took a couple of years for the British government decision to send an ambessdor to materialize. In other words, London never thought it necessary to seek China's prior permission, but only created a *fait accompli* for the Chinese. Judging from any standard, the British courtesy to the Chinese government was not commendable. The Chinese could not be blamed for any kind of imposition of tributary status on Britain. Rather it was the latter who imposed a pseudo-tributary mission on the former.

Actually, neither London nor Beijing took the tributary relationship seriously, and it was certainly not "the insulting and degrading form of relation between lord and vassal" as it is alleged.[23] Of course, here the reference is made about the kowtow issue. But, in traditional China, as in many other cultures, prostration was a ritual rather than an insult. While every Chinese was supposed to kowtow to the emperor, he in turn had to kowtow to the empress dowager. When the Chinese prime minister (who himself kowtowed to the emperor) asked the British ambassador (who was lower in position than the prime minister) to conform to the Chinese formality and ceremony, he meant no insult to the British nation. Dr Morrison justly pointed out a century ago that if the ritual was reciprocal, it would not "interfere with the idea of equality".[24] When the Chinese urged Macartney to kowtow to Emperor Qianlong, they did not reject Macartney's suggestion to reciprocate the same courtesy before the British crown.[25] And the Chinese envoys kowtowed to the Russian Tsar in 1729 and 1731 when they went to St. Petersburg for negotiations.[26] Even London did not instruct the ambassadors to fight shy of Chinese ceremonies.[27] If it was legitimate for Macartney and Staunton Jr. (who was the deputy to ambassador Amherst) to react sharply to the Chinese demand for kowtow,[28] the Chinese government had even stronger reasons to feel insulted by such foreigners who had themselves come to pay tribute but would not observe the rules. The Chinese emperor's loss of prestige owing to such British arrogance could have led to serious consequences, had Emperors Qianlong and Jiaqing (1796-1820) not exercised self-restraint. In any case, the Opium War which broke out in 1840. 24 years after the last British tributary envoy had been graciously sent off after a lavish banquet from Canton, could not have been due to either the tributary affair or the kowtow issue.[29]

III

In conclusion, we find that the theory of sinocentrism has very much exaggerated China's cultural eccentricity, and overlooked the basic fact that she has existed, under different sociopolitical systems, as an economic, social, political and cultural entity like any other nation state. Those who harp on this theory lack deeper understanding of the dynamics of China's internal development. The most glaring example of this is the ease in which many scholars cite the letter from Emperor Qianlong to King George III of Britain in 1773 to substantiate a number of charges ranging from China's cultural arrogance to her lack of interest in trade and other contacts with the outside world. Actually, the emperor's sentiments were grossly misunderstood.

Emperor Qianlong already knew about Britain's richness, technical advancement and military power. He was much flattered when he heard of the impending arrival of the Macartney mission. Not only did he overlook the lack of courtesy in Britain's short-notice but also permitted the British to violate his own order (that all foreign ships should anchor off Canton) to sail directly towards Tianjin. He also created quite a stir in all coastal provinces by asking for an early report about the whereabouts of Macartney's ship, by ordering all famous monuments on the route along which Macartney was to travel to be renovated, by reminding his subordinates that the British mission was not an ordinary tribute mission like those which arrived every year from Burma, Annam and other countries, and by giving specific instructions to the viceroy of Zhili (who was one of the few top imperial officers in China) and the Salt Commissioner to personally attend to the affairs of reception, which "should not be simple and moderate". The emperor's excitement can be seen from the fact that he issued ten edicts in one month (the 6th moon of the Chinese calendar) which exclusively dealt with the details of the reception. Never did a Chinese emperor pay so much attention to a foreign embassy. He also extended a special invitation to Macartney and party to meet him in his summer resort in Jehol, and cancelled his hunting programme to return to Beijing to see the special gifts which were brought by the British.[30] Macartney indulged in elaborately explaining the intricate mechanism of the British presents and aroused the emperor's curiosity greatly.[31] On top of his disillusionment, the emperor was displeased by Macartney's refusal to kowtow, and by the latter's various demands for concessions and facilities for trade. The emperor knew that Britain was the major trading country at Canton and the chief contributor to China's maritime customs revenue. He had already heard from his subordinates and from the British guests about the importance of British trade. But his *normal* (not sinocentric) pride reacted strongly against yielding to British pressure. His letter to the British king reflects such sentiments. That Qianlong and his courtiers were not arrogant in treating the British embassy can best be testified to by Macartney's writings.

The lack of understanding about Chinese historical developments cannot be made up by superficial quotations of Chinese maxims or terminology. It is uncharitable enough when one fails to appreciate another people's true sentiments and intentions. It is positively unfair to impose one's subjective judgements on another culture. The theory of sinocentrism owes much to the holier than thou attitude of the 19th century 'Old China Hands' who took away China's wealth with one hand and used the other to point an accusing finger against China's outmoded systems. Opium was sent to China because the Chinese were unworthy people.[32] Unequal treaties were forced upon the Chinese Government because it had no inkling of international equality. But all this has done no credit to Western civilization. Sir Robert Hart, who was China's Inspector General of Customs for four decades (1863-1908) and who was likened to a part of the trinity that ruled China in the second half of the 19th century (along with the Empress Dowager, Cixi or Tz'u-hsi, and the super minister, Li Hongzhang), had these words to compliment a Christian Westerner's behaviour in China :

> He knows that such and such is the way of doing things at home—therefore he condemns all Chinese otherness...his doxy is orthodoxy, and everything else is heterodoxy, and so intercourse, instead of being mutually beneficial, is the reverse, and instead of fastening and cementing friendly relations, is producing discord, ill feeling, and even enmity.[33]

Half a century after this, one still hears Western scholars blaming the Chinese for their hatred of the Westerners.[34] And the blame is exactly on "Chinese otherness", viz. sinocentrism. Hatred and enmity could not have been a one-way traffic, while resentment against external repression and even national pride are not the same as ethnocentrism. The Chinese may have been victims of conceit. But they have never gone as far as those who carried the white man's burden all over the world. Sinocentrism or no sinocentrism, they had in the past revered three Indians, Buddhacinga Kumarajiva and Amoghavajra in the 5th to 8th centuries as *Guoshi* or "National Teachers".[35] Though history has not repeated itself, the way in which the modern Chinese revere Karl Marx (1818-1883), Frederick Engels (1890-1895) and V.I. Lenin (1870-1924) is something phenomenal. Never had these three Europeans' works been so keenly and seriously studied by so many hundreds of million people as they are now studied in China. After his first visit to China where he saw huge portraits of Marx, Engels, Lenin and Stalin, an American reporter recently commented : "I doubt if there's ever been a nation that has so idolized its spiritual founders, four men of other race and countriess."[36]

The ghost of sinocentrism served to justify Western imperialist aggression on China. It also served the U.S. cold-war politics before Richard Nixon's visit to Beijing. Many of the exponents of this theory have followed in Nixon's footsteps to the ramparts of the Great Wall which was so often regarded as a symbol of Chinese isolation and insularism. This raises hope that the theory of sinocentrism may be thoroughly revised, if not totally discarded.

References

1. My interview with him at Kyoto University on October 13, 1973.
2. William H. McNeill, *The Rise of the West* (Chicaco, 1963) pp. 34-40; Wang Teh-chao, "Makeneier xifangde xingqi", in the Journal of the Institute of Chinese Studies of Chinese University of Hong Kong, II : I (1969) : 24.
3. Fang Hao, *op cit.,* I, 20; Liang Qichao, "Zhongguo lishishang minzi zhi yanjiu", *op cit.,* p. 17 (p. 51).
4. *Cihai,* VIII, 188, "Hufen".
5. Zhuang Shen, *loc cit.,* pp. 2-4.
6. *Gujin tushu jicheng,* Vol. 788, pp. 32B-33A, citing Guoxie. *Dongming ji,* Vol. 799, p. 12A, citing *Shiyuan.*
7. Zhang Xinglang, *Zhongxi jiaotong shiliao huibian,* (reprint, Taipei, 1962), VI, 29.
8. Evidence from the Herbal *(bencao)* literature.
9. Such preachings developed a new literature called "Bianwen". Cf. Zheng Zhentuo, *Zhongguo suwenxue shi* (Beijing, 1954), I, 180-191, 207-213.
10. The most striking article is a ceramic tri-colour object depicting a band of five musicians on a camel's back, which was recently unearthed from the grave of a Tang aristocrat in X'ian. Two of the musician have Chinese faces, while the other three, including the leader, have typical foreign features—big eyes, sharp noses and exuberant beards. See *Archaeology in New China* (Beijing, 1961), photo CX.
11. The earliest work in China to carve out Buddhist shrines on rocks was started in the beginning of the 5th century or even earlier at Binglingsi, a place not far from Lonzhou after the vogue of grottoes had spread from India to Afghanistan and to other Central Asian states upto Dunhuang right on ancient Chinese border.
12. Practically all important musical instruments now used in China originally came from foreign countries. Leaving out the modern western ones, those imported to China in ancient times were *Huqin* (fiddle), *Di* (flute), *Gu* (drum), *Konghou*

(*sitar,* the Indian harp), *Suona (Sirnai,* the Persian trumpet) etc. See *Taipino yulan, juan* 567, p. 9; Hayashi Kenzo (tr. by Kuo Mojo), *Sui-Tang Y nyuediao yanjiu* (Shanghai, 1936), *passim. Wenxian tongkao,* p. Kao 1208. *Cihai,* II, 107, "Suona", VIII, 21, "Konghou".

13. Fan Wenlan, *op. cit.,* II, 506; Kenneth Ch'en, *Buddhism in China* (Princeton, 1964), p. 136.

14. Fan Wenlan : *op. cit.,* II, 382-3; *Taiping yulan, juan* 654, pp. 3-4.

15. Beginning from the Liang emperor Wu in the first half of the century, the Chinese imperial governments used to collect, compile and print Buddhist scriptures. These collections were added by private collections published by monasteries and other pious organizations. In recent decades, the Japanese have taken keen interest in reprinting Buddhist scriptures in Chinese language which the Japanese Buddhist scholars still read. And the best collection of these is *Taisho Daizokyo* (the Taisho edition of Chinese Three Pitakas) which is indispensable to all libraries of Buddhist studies all over the world.

16. Lucian W. Pye, *The Spirit of Chinese Politic's* (M.I.T. Press, 1968), pp. 50, 53.

17. *Ibid.,* p. 78.

18. The exposition is contained in *Liji,* chapter 20. His idea of *Datong* as expounded by many enlightened modern Chinese intellectuals, Kang Youwei. Liang Qichao, Guo Moruo etc.

19. The entire traditional Chinese philosophical teachings are summed up in this light in Yong Guorong (ed.), *Jianming Zhonggno Zhexue Shi* (Beijing, 1973).

20. Cf. Fairbank, Trade and Diplomacy, p. 23.

21. Cranmer-Byng, *op. cit.,* p. 88.

22. Morse, *Chronicles,* II, 275-76, 431.

23. Remark by John Quincy Adams (1767-1848), the 6th President of USA and Harvard professor. See *John Qincy Adams Memoirs,* II. 39, Tyler Dennet, *Americans in Eastern Asia* (reprint, New York, 1963), p. 107.

24. Morrison's *Memoir on Lord Amherst's Embassy* cited in George Thomas Staunton, *Miscellaneous Notices relating to China* (London, 1822), pp. 122-23.

25. Cranmer-Byng, *op. cit.,* p. 100.
26. I.C.Y. Hsu, *China's Entry into the Family of Nations* (Harvard, 1960), p. 14.
27. Cf. Morse, *Chronicles,* II, 236; III, 281, wherein London's instructions to Macartney and Amherst are appended.
28. Lord Amherst would not have declined to perform kowtow had Staunton not opposed it strongly. See *ibid,* III, 262-63.
29. As soon as he had dismissed the Amherst embassy without granting an interview, Emperor Jiaging recored from his fit of fury and sent repeated orders to various viceroys to see that the embassy was treated with courtesy and hospitality in their inland journey from Beijing to Canton. The "tributary" presents from England were accepted and reciprocated. This was done in a solemn ceremony at Canton attended by the viceroy, followed by a banquet. See *Qing Jiagingchao waijiao shilao,* I. 57, 62; VI, 8-37.
30. *Qing Gaozong Shilu, juau* 1421, pp. 5-7; *juan* 1423, pp. 11-3; *juan* 1426, pp. 3-4; *juan* 1428, pp. 9-10, *juan* 1429, pp. 8-9, 25-26; *juan* 1430, p. 1, 9-11; *juan* 1431, pp. 1-2, 3-4, 5-6, 8-11, 12-14, 15-17, 17-19, *juan*1432, pp. 4-6, 7-8, 10-12; *juan* 1434, pp. 7-8.
31. One of the aims of his mission being "to impress" the Chinese's minds "of the wealth and power" of Britain as his government instructions clearly stated, Macartney was seized by the issue of the presents upon his arrival in China. "It appears" wrote he, "that the expectations of the Chinese have been raised very high, by the manner in which the Embassy was announced, of the presents which it is to be accompanied with." The emperor's reactions to Macartney's boast of the intricasy of the presents were expressed in some of his edicts in which he said : "I read the translation of the list of articles, and find it not free from exaggeration. This shows that the foreigners are narrow-minded. They think they monopolize the secret of making them, thus they boast about the intricacy in manufacturing them." Again, he said in another edict : "The tributary envoy is indulging in boasting the intricacy (of the presents). If the installation of them takes one month, it would have to take years to manufacture them." Later, after visiting the pavilions of the emperor's summer palace in Jehol, even Macartney was surprised at the treasures therein, and felt that "our presents must

shrink from the comparison and 'hide their diminished heads'." See Morse, *Chronicles,* II, 239-240; Cranmar-Byng, *op cit.,* p. 69, 126; *Qing Gazong shilu, juan* 1431, pp. 17-19; *juan* 1432, pp. 4-6.

32. Sir Henry Pottinger, British plenipotentiary in the negotiation of the 1842 treaty between Britain and China, told his Chinese counterpart: "If your people are virtuous, they will desist from the evil practice (of opium-smoking); and if your officers are incorruptible and obey your orders, no opium can enter your country. The discouragement of the growth of the poppy in our territories rests principally with you... " In other words, Britain imported opium to China just because the Chinese deserved such a treatment. See S.W. Williams, *The Middle Kingdom* (London 1883), II, 550-551.

33. Robert Hart, *These from the Land of Sinim* (London, 1903), pp. 123-124.

34. Pye, *op. cit.*, pp. 67-84.

35. Tang Yongtong, *Han Wei liang-Jin Nan-Beichao fojiao shi* (reprint, Chongqing, 1944), I, 139; *Gaoseng zhuan* in *Taisho Daizokyo*, L, 331, 334, LI, 80; *Cefu yuangui, juan* 51, p. 9.

36. James Michener, "China Diary" in *Reader's Digest* (August, 1962), p. 161.

3

Foreign Mud on Good Earth : British Opium Enterprise Vis-a-Vis China*

I

In the existing scholarship on British opium trade and the Opium War, there are two tendencies: some scholars minimise the predatory nature of the opium affairs; others underplay the importance of opium by over-emphasizing the dynamic force of British Industrial Revolution.

The overemphasis on Sino-British cultural conflict and Britain's industrial-commercial expansion prevents the scholars from seeing the predominant factor—opium—which led Britain to war against China in 1840, and also shaped British colonial exploitation of China throughout the 19th century. By saying this I am not denying the fact of British industrial expansion and its impact on the development of Sino-British relations. The important thing is to gauge the dimension of this expansion, and grasp the salient features of this impact.

II

Britain in the 19th century had the distinction of being "the Factory of the World" and "the Nation of Shopkeepers"—the first epithet being a self-compliment, and the second, by courtesy of Napoleon. British economy thrived by the so-called "free trade imperialism". Although there was an inner linkage between being "the factory of the world" and "the nation of shopkeepers", it was not entirely due to Britain's industrial power that she scored the highest in commerce. Britain had far greater a commercial infrastructure, particularly in overseas trade, than

---

*The article that was written in 1980 and published in *China Report*, Vol. XVII, No. 3 (March-April, 1981), has been abridged for this edition of the book.

her western rivals. She had the largest fleet of merchant ships, the richest capital in trading transactions, and the largest army of personnel employed in institutions servicing her trade in the whole world. There were enormous earnings from British trading organizations in addition to the equally impressive gains from "invisible" items like shipping, insurance, brokerage, etc. Her industries were still in infancy—still far from becoming an independent self-generating system, still heavily dependent on commerce and trade to supply the much-needed investment income.

Opium on the other hand was an international instrument linking Britain's colonialisation of India with Britain's economic exploitation of China. Like a milch cow which transforms worthless fodder into valuable milk, China turned out her treasure after taking in opium. The advantage of opium in milking China lay in its double action. On the one hand, the input in the production of opium was low, neither consuming much natural resources, nor involving any technology—merely requiring some land for poppy cultivation, which India had enough to spare. But, its profit was high. Every dollar paid for it became almost net income, revenue and profit. According to a recent Chinese study, this payment was to the tune of 163,384,164 Spanish dollars (equivalent to £39,212,197 in the decade from 1830 to 1839)[1]. Moreover, as a trade offensive, opium had no rival. With the free flow of opium unchecked, it zoomed past previous export records of all prized Chinese goods to create an adverse balance for China, for which China had to pay in white silver to the tune of five to six million taels a year on the eve of the Opium War[2]. Both the British and the British Indian treasuries coveted this outflow of silver from China.

Opium was a part and parcel of the Indian empire—the mainstay of Britain's predatory colonial mainstream. Yet, there was a division of labour between opium and other institutions of British India. Opium's one target was China, or, more precisely, Chinese money. This resulted in another division of labour between India and China in their colonial service to Britannia. Britain's export policy in cotton textiles clearly indicates that she preferred to clothe the India with cotton rather than China. This explains why in the third and fourth decades of the 19th century for every yard of British piece-goods shipped to China there were more than three yards of the same reaching Indian destinations. Britain obviously found it more profitable to sell her cotton textiles to the Indian consumers than to their Chinese counterparts. Not that the Indians were worse bargainers; the British Raj predestined that they be Manchester's favourites. As for the neglected Chinese, by consuming opium they would help the British cotton industry develop faster than by wearing British cotton cloth. Manchester was always confidently looking forward to the receipt of Chinese money either through the hands of the British opium sellers, or through the hands of the Indian consumers of British manufactures. For the larger part of the 19th century, China had a little more than 400 million people. Each of them had a share of more than half pound of Indian opium as a gift from British colonialism. Fortunately, the Chinese did not take opium orally as half an ounce of such intake could kill a life. If they had done so, the entire Chinese population would have been wiped out many times over.

The estimate shows that for each pound of Indian opium which British colonialism thrust into Chinese hands, there was gold valued at 95 per cent of a pound sterling. In other words, for every pound sterling which Britain could not earn from China *otherwise* there was 1.05 lb of Indian opium for China. Hsin-pao Chang has credited the British trading community with the achievement of destroying the outmoded Chinese tribute system. Here in opium, an inverted tribute system came into being, with China paying more than £10.5 million a year as tribute to Britain, during the thirty years, 1851-80.

The question which we should ask is how such a gigantic international traffic in narcotics could go on smoothly without the knowledge of China's imperial government. Half of the answer to this question lies in the lacunae of the Chinese imperial system. The other half lies in the manoeuvres of the East India Company. The fact was that not only had the EIC seized monopsony in the Canton trade, it had also gained complete control over the *hong* merchants, who are often described by scholars as the monopolist twin-brother of the EIC.

Some scholars even suggest that the exit of the EIC's monopoly from the China trade in 1834 caused the loss of balance in the Sino-British equation-with Chinese "monopolists" face to face with British "free traders". This lopsided situation, many felt, was the root cause of the Opium War. This is totally untrue.

That the *hong* merchants were far from being powerful "monopolists" is borne out by the fate of Shi Zhonghe (Pidgin English spelling "Shy Kinqua") who used to ride in sedan-chairs in and out of the East India Company's factory to convey Canton government orders. But suddenly, one day, he was brought before the EIC officials in chains and prostrated before the president of the EIC Canton Committee.[3] William Jardine wrote to partner J.H. Gladstone in 1830 that all the Canton *hong* merchants except two were financially bankrupt. He added that in reality the Canton trade was "carried on by European or rather English capital", meaning that the *hong* merchants survived on British financial support[4].

Due to government squeeze, mismanagement, and, most important of all, the want of modern credit facilities and liquidity of money, most of the *hong* merchants were indebted to foreign traders, particularly to the East India Company. It was an open secret that the EIC was protecting many *hong* merchants from declared insolvent and meeting the fate of Shi Zhonghe. A corollary to this protection was the Company's winning the allegiance of the *hong* merchants. It was this *EIC-hong* collusion which had made the narcotic traffic so smooth at Canton until 1820.

The Manchu government gave "monopolist" role to the *hong* merchants not only because it trusted their loyalty, but, even more important, because it wanted them to insulate the foreign traders from the Chinese masses—both being potential trouble-makers in the eyes of the Manchu rulers. The irony of the Canton System lies in the fact that while the *hong* merchants were the Chinese government's watch-dogs *vis-a-vis* the British traders, they were beholden on the East India Company and were secretly serving the EIC's interest. The insulator between the potential foreign troublemakers and Chinese trouble-makers had actually turned into the insulator between the international opium traffic at the mouth of Pearl river and the ears of the

Beijing government. Every Britishship heavily laden with Indian opium was certified by a "security merchant" (the senior *hong* merchant whose responsibility was to guarantee lawful behaviour on the part of foreign traders) for having carried no contraband. The Canton prohibitory authorities' palms were greased through the good office of the *hong* merchants. Although both the EIC's Canton officials and the *hong* merchants did not handle opium by themselves, both played the vital role in promoting the narcotic traffic. Being the custodian of British colonial interests and the producer of opium, the Company was the commander of the opium operation in China. At the Company's command, the *hong* merchants ensured smooth narcotic traffic on the one hand and kept the imperial government in the dark on the other.

By 1820, opium trading activities had gone beyond the means of secrecy. The Canton government, under the leadership of an able Viceroy, Ruan Yuan, made the Canton port too hot for the drug racket to operate. The British responded to Chinese challenge by starting the "Lingding era" of opium operation. From 1821 down to the outbreak of the Opium War, opium ships nick named "hulks" were stationed in the area of the Lingding sea which was the outer-anchorage for British naval ships as they were prohibited from entering the Canton harbour. Around this floating storage of opium the British staged a show of open, armed smuggling of the contraband in collaboration with Chinese smugglers. British ex-servicemen and naval deserters were employed to deliver the drug to secret coastal points in armed schooners. A British consul said later, in 1843, about these British desperadoes: "I do not believe that there is a Gang of Burglars and Highway Robbers in England more relentless, more unfeeling and more cruel... than these British semi-pirates upon the Canton River."[5] A band of these daredevils after returning from a delivery mission in the summer of 1839 called at a small harbour in Fujian province and kidnapped native women on board and raped them. Some women died on the spot during the outrage; others who had survived committed suicide in shame.[6]

These episodes show that long before the outbreak of war in 1840, British naval might had already held China in ransom.

In a sense, the Chinese were held under duress to accept opium and pay tribute. Even if the Chinese officials were non-corrupt, China could not have extricated herself from the extremely unequal situation. To say that Manchu officials connived at the opium traffic does not show any appreciation of their situation. They had no choice when deterred by British power.

We cannot, of course, exonerate the Chinese for allowing the opium habit to spread unchecked. But we cannot also explain British actions in terms of demand and supply as Pottinger saw them. We must clearly distinguish essential and non-essential commodities and non-essential narcotics. Essential commodities are needed for sustaining human life. They are not only constantly demanded by consumers, but the demand is for a constant quantity. The law of demand and supply operates within this parameter of two-way constancy. The consumer's demand is also conditioned by his purchasing power. In the case of non-essentials, the demand is elastic. It is even more conditioned by availability of purchasing power and by prices.

When purchasing power is limited, demand for essential commodities holds primacy over demand for non-intoxicants. But, the demand for intoxicants can upset the normal consumption pattern and interfere with the demand for essentials. An addict places the demand for the narcotic over and above the demand for other goods, even essentials. In his consumption scheme, the narcotic becomes a constant, while the essentials become a variable. Opium addicts in 19th-century China persisted in smoking opium even when their children suffered from hunger and their wives had no trousers to wear.[58] Canton was full of beggars who were opium addicts; they had seen better days but had lost everything else except their addiction.

The narcotic supplier is no ordinary trader; he is a victimising monster, a slave catcher and ultimately, a killer. Paradoxically, in the vicious game he is helped by his very victims. An opium addict not only sticks to his own sin, but converts others, and expands his ranks. In 19th century China, there were innumerable addicted families, inclusive of domestic servants and even pet animals. One remarkable feature of the opium traffic was that it went on expanding till China's resources got exhausted at the end of the 19th century. The demand for opium did not reach any saturation point as British woolen and cotton cloth had experienced. It is only after the British decision to reduce and eventually stop the supply of opium at the end of the 1910s that Chinese demand for the drug fell.

Pottinger's was imperialist logic, while his aim was to blackmail the Chinese to legalize the opium trade. This he did on instructions from London. When he took over charge from his predecessor, Rear-Admiral George Elliot, Pottinger also became the addressee of letter from the Foreign Secretary, Lord Palmerston dated London, 26 February, 1841, originally addressed to Elliot. The letter urged the British envoy to pressurise the Chinese side to legalize the opium trade: "Her Majesty's government having taken into consideration the circumstances connected with the China opium trade, I have to instruct you to endeavour to make some arrangement with the Chinese government for the admission of opium into China as an article of lawful commerce."

However, after stating this, Palmerston thought it too blatant a demonstration of London's pro-opium policy to go without camouflage. He hastened to add: "In bringing this matter before the Chinese Plenipotentiaries, you will state that the admission of opium into China as an article of legal trade is not one of the demands, which you have been instructed, to make upon the Chinese government; and you will not enter upon the subject of it in such a way as to lead the Chinese Plenipotentiaries to think that it is the intention of Her Majesty's Government to use any compulsion in regard to this matter."[7]

The duplicity of the British Foreign Secretary provided the touch of grace to the Opium War; opium was totally kept out of the Treaty of Nanking thus helping to promote an ambiguity about the nature of the Opium War. As A.J. Sargent has put it, "because in its settlement, no allusion whatever is made to opium", therefore the name Opium War is a misnomer.[8] Sargent has overlooked two facts. First, Palmerston did wish the legalization of opium to be a part of the treaty settlement. It was she stubborn resistance of the Chinese side plus

Palmerston's reluctance to force the issue which spared the first Sino-British treaty from the stink of opium. Second, the *de facto* legalisation of the import of opium to China was conceded by the Chinese government by its capitulation to the British, whether the Treaty of Nanking mentioned it or not.

It has been my thesis that Britain waged the Opium War in response to China's anti-opium war led by Commissioner Lin in 1839. (This theory has been described by a student as an anti-anti-opium-war theory.) This conclusion I have arrived at after analysing various Sino-British tension areas and the nature in Sino-British relations. Because of the overriding importance of opium and the multiple gains in the triangular trade in which opium was the keylink, other Sino-British tension areas receded to the background in British strategic calculations. The pre-Opium War British mood *vis-a-vis* China can best be summarized by the following observation of Sir James Graham, First Lord of the Admiralty: "Trade with China is our only object; conquest there would be as dangerous as defeat. Our grand object is to keep peace, and by the mildest means, by a plastic adaptation of our manners to theirs to extend our influence in China with the view of extending our commercial relations."[9]

However, my proposition should not be taken as seeking to reduce British imperialism to opium imperialism, although I do believe that the latter was an important constituent of the former. The Opium War and the Treaty of Nanking show that British aggression against China far exceeded the scope of opium imperialism. What I have argued in my book is against underestimating the significance of British opium imperialism. It was unique, extraordinary, unprecedented, longest lived, and not committed by any other brand of imperialism.

We can now diagnose the nature of the Opium War. Since the focal point of Sino-British conflict was the opium trade, the war was the consequence of the tension generated by this. The despatch of Commissioner Lin to Canton signifies the end of the "flowing poison" and the "seepage" of Chinese resources. On the British side, London had long decided to recognise the illicit child of the East India Company—the opium enterprise—as a lawful part of Pax Britannica. This can be illustrated by three events:

(*a*) The withdrawal of the earlier offer of a package deal with China (stopping opium operation in exchange of Chinese concessions pertaining to trade, etc.) from the instructions to the third British ambassador-designate to China, Lord Amherst, in 1816;

(*b*) British Foreign Secretary Palmerston's instruction to the first British Chief Superintendent of trade in China, Lord Napier, not to "interfere", nor "prevent" the British maritime activities on the coast of China (*i.e.* the opium operation) and

(*c*) Palmerston's despatch of Rear Admiral Maitland's fleet to the China waters in 1837 to deter the Chinese authorities from suppressing coastal smuggling activities. The Opium War was the corollary of the hardening of attitudes on both sides towards the opium traffic.

Second, the war was a search for a permanent Sino-British relationship. By this, I do not mean the overthrow of the so-called tribute diplomacy and the sinocentric order, nor was it for what is called China's entrance into "family of nations". All these to me are meaningless cliches. We have seen earlier that the opium trade had tied China to the bandwagon of British colonial exploitation when China remained substantially a sovereign state. Such a Sino-British equation was obviously unsatisfactory to Britain. But, it was unthinkable for Britain to establish a second Raj in China. A permanent Sino-British relationship to avail of colonial benefits from China without Britain's shouldering colonial responsibilities had all along been the British strategy *vis-a-vis* China. The opium trade offensive itself was the very manifestation of this strategy. Britain was concerned about preserving the health of India while polluting China with opium because of the Great Divide between areas of responsibility (like India) and areas free of any responsibility (like China). Conquering China and making a second Raj would have meant taking on responsibility for the exercise of a moral rule there. In that case Britain would have had to give up opium which was the most handy way of colonial exploitation and the most important mechanism in materialising Britain's Inverted Colonial Dependence on India and China.

Paradoxically, the Opium War had an anti-war element in it. It was fought to open negotiations. The boom of British broadside was meant to register a louder threat than banging the table. That this strategy proved effective is borne out by Emperor Daoguang's following edict deciding to capitulate to the British: "The English foreigners are like whales and crocodiles of the sea, coming and going in an unpredictable manner. But seven of our provinces have to be alerted to face the menace... Can there be any justification for our wasting the energy of the military and the civilians as well as the resources of the nation in this manner?...Is it not far better to use a word and a sheet of paper than to deploy millions of troops?"[10] In making this decision, the Manchu government fell into a trap. China could well afford a protracted war with Britain and register a bigger Waterloo in British military history than could the French. Returning to the negotiating table and signing agreements according to British terms was just what Britain expected from her opponent from the Opium War operation. It was also in the Opium War that Britain discovered another type of colonial control over China. Instead of assuming sovereignty, just sabre-rattling could make China yield to colonial exploitation.

The Opium War whetted Britain's colonial appetite. But the Chinese were unable to satisfy it. When China became defiant once again in the 1850s, it was time to refresh her memory of the first Opium War. Thus came the second one in 1856-60. The British government disapproved of the nickname second opium war much more than they did the first. It vehemently denied that the legalization of opium trade by the Sino-British Treaty of Tianjin (1858) was the result of British pressure. But the British defence of this is all too thin. We have already seen the abortive effort of Britain to get the opium legalization inserted into the Treaty of Nanking. How would Britain not pursue it when the second opportunity cropped up and when opium was assuming greater and greater importance in Britain's Inverted Colonial Dependence? Besides the legalization, the second war waged by Britain on China was of the same nature as the first, viz. sabre-rattling to force the Chinese government to conclude a treaty on British terms. The term opium war has actually acquired the connotation of "gunboat diplomacy" or "opium diplomacy" which are synonymous.

From 1821 onwards British opium diplomacy in China had taken the form of gunboat diplomacy. The two opium wars may thus be regarded as the high tide of the opium policy. In essence, forcing the Chinese to take opium and to pay tribute amounted to waging war on the Chinese nation. It may be said therefore that an invisible war was started against China the moment the EIC's factories at Patna and Benaras turned out "provision opium" for Chinese consumption. In that sense, the two Opium Wars were but the bloody manifestations of the invisible opium war which Britain had waged on China from 1773 till 1919. This makes the terms opium trade, opium war and opium imperialism synonymous. My opium war perspective is not merely a simple war-due-to-opium formulation. It characterizes the very peculiar British mode of colonial domination in China.

In short, Britain's China wars in the 19th century were Opium Wars. London's decision for these wars was not actually taken in 1840. It was taken much earlier, some time at the beginning of the 19th century when Britain decided to withdraw her offer to abandon the government sponsored Indian opium export to China. Britain was determined to demand its pound of flesh from the Chinese by giving them opium to redress the remorseless drain of Britain's 'Inverted Colonial Dependence' on India and China throughout the century. Whether the Chinese realized it or not, resisted it or not, these wars had been foisted on them. Every opium ship was a part of the war machine, and every sailor on board, a member of the vanquishing army. The Union Jack was always there—in China waters—to inspire new conquests. Victory singals were transmitted in the form of prized Chinese goods and shining silver ingots. The war proceeded quietly without gunshots when the Chinese did not offer resistance. World opinion hardly noticed it but, the boom of guns came loudly in 1840-42. World opinion was shocked. Even conscientious British statesmen disapproved it, as William Evert Gladstone was to voice it: "A war more unjust in its origin, a war more calculated to cover this [British] nation with permanent disgrace, I do not know, and I have not read of."[11]

The tragedy, however, was that in the last decades of the 19th century and having been four times British Prime Minister, Gladstone was unable to bring this disgrace to an end. The truth then dawned on him that British colonialism could not survive without opium imperialism.

It must be said to the credit of the Manchu government that although it capitulated to British imperialism, it never surrendered its opposition to the opium traffic. This was expressed persistently through whatever means it had at hand. Generally, it sought to persuade Britain against opium trade. Although such anti-opium persuasion did not have gun-boats as its spokesmen, it was supported by the moral force of humanism and humanitarianism. The anti-opium war which the Manchu government first waged without success in 1839 was, thus, continuously carried on at the diplomatic and psychological levels. This put Britain on the defensive. Eventually, she had to face defeat. In 1909, the British government at long last agreed to the gradual reduction of the cultivation of poppy in India and by 1919 there was no more *official* export of Indian opium to China. Thus concluded the inglorious chapter of opium imperialism in history.

The world has long forgotten the crime of opium imperialism. Hence the academic confusion which obtain today. But China has still not recovered from her losses in economic vitality and popular health. On top of it, China also earned permanent disgrace by acquiring the image of a Nation of Opium Smokers. The stigma would have stuck even to this day had not Mao Zedong and his comrades overthrown the *ancien regime* in China. So, while everything is forgotten, there is no villain left on the stage any longer. In the human drama there has come a happy ending. To the students of history, however, it remains the job to clean up the junk in the historical cupboard of the modern stage.

References

1. Li Boxfang *et. al.*, "Guanyu shijushiji sanshi niandai yapian jinkou he baiyin wailiu de shuliang" (On the quantities of opium import and silver outflow in the thirties of the 19th century) in *Lithi yanjiu* (Journal of Historical Studies), (Beijing), No. 5, October 1980, p. 82.

2. *Ibid.*, p. 87.
3. H.B. Morse, *Chronicles,* II, 270.
4. Tan Cbung, *Brave New World,* pp. 64-65.
5. *Ibid.*, p. 163.
6. *Ibid.*
7. *Papers Relating to the Opium Trade in China, 1842-1856,* House of Commons, 1857, in *IUPP,* Vol. 31, p. 279.
8. A.J. Sargent, *Anglo-Chinese Commerce and Diplomacy* (Oxford, 1907), p. 87.
9. Tan Chung, *Brave New World,* p. 136.
10. *Ibid.*, p. 220.
11. *Ibid.*, p. 215.

PART—II

China and Imperialism

4

The Britain-China-India Trade Triangle (1771-1840)*

The Opium War (1840-42), which was an important milestone in Chinese history, was the consequence of China's trade with Britain and India. To understand the economic and political significance of this triangular trade, we must study its commodity-structure and grasp its external and internal rhythms.

I

British interest in China began with the woollen textiles, the glory, great wheel and one of the pillars of England, which urged the 16th century English to search for the large, wealthy, densely populated but climatically cold country described by Marco Polo and others as "Cathay" *i.e.* north China. It was believed that once British "home spun" gained access to such a market, the key to British prosperity would be found. According to Sir William Foster, it was not spice-hunting, as generally held but actually the quest for the Chinese market for woollen cloth which led Britain into the "Brave New World".[1]

Two centuries later, British merchants in the East had a different perspective. The East India Company which had inspired King Charles II (1660-1685) to make tea a British national drink,[2] went on a tea-buying spree as soon as it had settled down in the China market. The court of directors instructed their Canton supercargoes in 1720 to make their European rivals "sick of their voyages for tea" at any cost.[3] This set both the pattern and the pace of Britain's "China trade". The East India Company's tea investment increased from 6 million

*This is an abridged version of the article that was written in 1973 and published in *Indian Economic and Social History Review* (Delhi), Vol. XI, No. 4, (Dec. 1974).

lbs per year in the decade 1771-1780 to 35 million lbs per annum during the period 1831-1837. While in the 1770s Britain took 33% of the total tea exports from Canton (the only Chinese port open to maritime Western nations), this share increased to 54% in 1781-1790, to 74% in 1791-1800, and reached the highest point of 80% in 1801-1810.

This investment expanded nearly five times in seven decades without developing a corresponding expansion of the Chinese market for British manufacture. British exports to China obviously occupied a secondary position in the East India Company's China trade policy, which was import-oriented. Initially, the generating force behind the triangular trade was the expansion of Britain's tea imports, which were sustained by exporting silver and goods from Britain on the one hand and by sending Indian goods to China on the other. After the turn of the century, there was a rapid expansion of Indian exports to China, which made it unnecessary to export British silver to China to foot a part of the tea bill. In this new situation, British exports to China still remained a static force, and Britain's China trade maintained its import orientation.

First, India was the starting point of the trade triangle and Britain was the ending point. The dynamic force behind the trade was the India interests (who consisted of those Englishmen who were closely associated with the Indian Empire), not the British manufacturing interests. Second, Chinese tea was utilized by the India interests as an instrument to expand Indian exports. That is why Indian exports to China grew at a faster rate than Chinese exports to Britain, and the quantum of the former out-stripped that of the later after the turn of the century. The East India Company played a dual role as the architect of the triangular trade and the founder of the Indian Empire under the British Crown, as "merchants" and "sovereigns".

It was good strategy for the East India Company to show profuse enthusiasm in a Chinese commodity in the initial stage. By their wise manoeuvre, the E.I.C.'s Canton supercargoes not only established themselves as the favourite customers of the semiofficial Chinese hong merchants, but also succeeded in using the good offices of the latter to grease the palms of the Manchu customs authorities for the smuggling of Indian opium into the forbidden Chinese kingdom. The expansion of Indian exports to China would not have been so smooth and rapid without the apparent tea-obsession of the East India Company in the 18th century.

Even when tea was utilised as a catspaw, the Chinese herb served the British national interest well. It acted as a moderate and harmless stimulant, and when accompanied by milk and sugar, provided a good refreshment, "without which the poor diet of the factory-workers would not have kept them going" during the hectic days of the Industrial Revolution.[4]

Secondly, despite the myth about the Company's losses, there was good lucre in the tea trade. The Company's gross profit in importing Chinese tea always stood much higher than 10%, and never fell below s 1/8 per Ib. during the three decades from 1781 to 1810. It was this bright prospect which had made the British traders so enthusiastic in importing Chinese tea.

Thirdly, the British exchequer used to get as much as one-tenth of Britain's total revenue from the tea consumers, collecting, in 24 years between 1814 and 1837, a total of £82,640,531—an average of £ 3,443,355 per annum.[5]

Fourthly, tea played a pivotal role in British economic development. It made round trips all over the world via London on British bottoms, making England the entrepot of tea in the world on the one hand and developing British shipping on the other. Tea also brought a boom for another important British colonial enterprise, as every handful of it invariably went down the pot with several spoonfuls of West Indian sugar. Both tea and sugar were the two most highly taxed articles in British, the per capita consumption of which doubled during 1843-1857, four times as fast as the growth in population in Great Britain.[6]

With such advantages, tea provided the Indian interests with a good instrument for converting British money in India into British money at home. When tea was purchased at Canton, the Company paid to the hong merchants what it had received from private British traders who had came from India and had the proceeds of their Indian goods. Before leaving India, they had signed bonds with the Indian government which obliged them to remit their proceeds to the Company's Canton treasury. The latter, after receiving the proceeds, issued them bills of exchange with which they could draw cash from the Company's London office. The exchange rates (between the tael and the Spanish dollar in which the Company's Canton receipts were registered, and with the pound sterling, in which the bearer of the bill was to be paid in London) were generally generous. In the late 1820s, a tael of silver was offered from s 6/3 to 6/7, while in 1787, when the Company's Canton treasury needed replenishment urgently, it absorbed £ 1.3 million from private Englishmen at as high as 7s. $7\frac{1}{2}$ d. per tael.[7] Another important form of remittance was the commanders' cotton-bonds. The bond was signed by the commanders of the East Indiamen at an Indian port (usually Bombay) where they loaded cotton (supplied by the Company) onto their privilege tonnage and later they were required to pay the proceeds of cotton to the Company at Canton. There was no lack of ingenious mechanisms to first convert Indian opium, cotton and other goods into Chinese silver, and then, convert the silver into pound sterling through the instrument of Chinese tea. Tea was an important commodity in the trade triangle, but not of prime significance to the Indian interests.

II

What was of prime significance to the Indian interests was Indian opium. The British-Indian opium enterprise had two components: the Bengal opium and the Malwa opium. The former was a real child of the British Raj, and the latter, of illegitimate origin, an adopted child. The Company's Bengal opium monopoly took shape as soon as Englishmen arrived at Patna after the Battle of Plassey. In 1773, the Company, officially took over it. From then on, East India was developed into the leading opium-producing country, surpassing Turkey, the land of Afyon.

Malwa opium, the produce of a wide area from Rajasthan down to the Deccan, rose as a non-Company enterprise, emulating the example of the Bengal opium and competing with the latter in the China market. The Board of Customs, Salt and Opium of the Bengal government inquired into the matter and discovered in 1820 three advantages of the Malwa over the Bengal in the China market:

(1) The Chinese could get 75% of pure extract from the Malwa and only 57% from the Bengal moister;

(2) The Malwa cakes were small and flat, thus easier to smuggle into China than the large and globular Bengal cakes;

(3) The Malwa chest adopted the Chinese picul system (a picul weighing $133^1/_2$ Ibs., which was the weight of opium in a Malwa chest), thus was more convenient for Chinese counting than the two-factory-maunds (weighing 149 Ilbs) Bengal chest.[8]

This discovery coincided with a change in the Company's attitude to the Malwa opium. It gave up its earlier dog-in-the-manger policy and flung open the gates of Bombay to facilitate the export of Malwa opium to China. Subsequently, the Malwa opium enterprise was brought under the Company's monopoly. In 1820, Malwa opium valued at Rs. 32,15,317 passed through Bombay on its way to China. In the next two decades, Bombay's average annual export of Malwa opium to China was Rs. 41 lakhs in 1821-1830, and Rs. 1 crore plus in 1831-1840.[9]

The year 1820 was significant not only for the Company's new patronages for Malwa opium, but also for its decision to expand poppy cultivation in the Bengal presidency, leading to a spectacular increase in the production of Bengal opium. The effect of all this on the China trade was evident. The export of Indian opium to China during 1821-1830 nearly tripled the previous record, and during 1831-1840, the export of Indian opium in ten years could compare to what had been exported earlier in a whole century. In 1821, opium overtook tea to become the first commodity of the triangular trade (the import of opium to China was worth 9 million Spanish dollars against 8.4 million of Chinese tea for Britain).[10] It remained the number one staple in China's foreign trade until the late 19th century.

When the British imposed themselves as the rulers of India, they were eager to explain to the whole world that they had brought civilization and enlightenment to the sub-continent. There could not but be moral constraint against this close association between an "enlightened" government and an infamous commerce. The explanation went round that the Company's interest in opium rose from the expediency of balancing Britain's China trade. Henry Dundas even told the British Parliament in 1796 that Bengal would be impoverished of silver if opium was not sent to China.[11] Either Dundas deliberately lied, or he had not consulted the trade figures of the previous four years *i.e.,*1792-1895.

During 1817-1833, Indian cotton realized £2.2 million in China. The Company's total China investment being £3.1 million, it needed to absorb only £1.1 million proceeds of Indian goods, as the import of British goods had fetched £1.9 million. Even a half of the cotton proceeds could make up the deficiency, let alone the availability of proceeds from Indian imports other than opium and cotton valued at £4.5 million.[12] So there was no need to import opium to China to balance the British trade during this period. Earlier, in the seven years between 1802 and 1809 (excluding 1806), the total Indian cotton exported from Calcutta and Bombay to China was valued at Rs. 5,20,28,904, showing an average of Rs. 74,32,701 (equivalent to more than 0.9 million pound sterling, if we calculate at the rate of Re. 1 = s 2/6).[13] The average annual British deficiency in her trade exchanges with China in the decade 1801-1810 stood at about 0.6 million pounds, which could have been easily made up by the proceeds of Indian cotton which exceeded a million pounds a year on an average. In short, if opium were to play such a limited role of balancing Britain's China trade, not many chests of it would have been traded in the 18th century and it would have been totally given up in the 19th century.

The dichotomy between the moral constraints on one hand and the calculations of political and economic advantages on the other in British commercial interests' association with opium was reflected in the Company's opium policies. Rhetoric was continuously broadcast, like the statement by the Court of Directors in 1817 that "Were it possible to prevent the use of the drug altogether except for the purpose of medicine, we would gladly do it in compassion to mankind."[14] Not only were the Company's ships forbidden to carry opium to China, but even the licences issued by the Indian authorities to the opium clippers were camouflaged. In the licences issued in 1828 to the *Hercules* of Mackintosh and Co. the *Louisa* of William Clifton, and the *Jane Eliza* of Crattenden Mackillop and Co., it was specified that these ships were to sail to China to export a few thousand rupees of saltpetre and nothing else.[15] Actually, each of these ships left Calcutta with lakhs of rupees of goods, mainly opium. The *Jane Eliza* carried no saltpetre on board at all.[16]

The first advantage was the profit. No other commodity could be as profitable as opium, which needed little investment and a single pound of it in weight could fetch many tens of pound sterling in value. Secondly, the source of this profit was not India, but another country about which British public opinion was totally unconcerned. As the trade in opium not only did not impoverish India but, on the contrary, helped to strengthen the Indian economy in no small measure, there was approval from London.

Earning profit was both economically and politically important for the Company because it had to find the means to maintain its Indian regime. Opium was a most convenient instrument to enlist the riches of China in support of the British Raj. In the 1780s there was a sharp increase of about 200% ; then there was nearly another 200% increase in the next decade. In the first decade of the 19th century there was another 100% increase. Then, the revenue in the third decade doubled that of the first, and that in the fourth decade doubled that of the second. There is another angle to look at the increase of Bengal government's opium revenue. In 1792, it accounted for 5.2% of the total Bengal revenue (Rs. 2.9 million out of Rs. 55 million); its weightage rose to 7% in 1812 (£7.2 million out off £10 million, to 10% in 1822 (£1.4 million out of £14,163,277) and further to 20% in 1842 Rs. 1.2 million out of Rs. 9 million.[17]

Opium accrued revenue for British Raj, and simultaneously remitted back to England a part of this revenue which had become private fortunes. There was no better vehicle like opium which could transmit British fortunes homeward from India and simultaneously replenish the sources of these fortunes. In this regard, Indian opium had a greater strategic importance in the trade triangle than Chinese tea and British textiles. The British manufacturing interests should have strongly resented the westward commodity movement of the triangular trade. But the double utility of opium as both the generator and transmitter of the Indian revenue harmonized the internal contradiction of Britain's China trade between its import-orientation and its urge of expanding British exports. For, what might have been the loss of Britain's China market was compensated by the gain of her Indian market. The vital link between opium trade and the export of British manufactures is best illustrated by the panic among Manchester industrialists in 1839 that the stoppage of opium trade in China might seriously affect the Indian purchasing power for British cotton goods.[18] This was why the British manufacturing interests firmly supported British military action against the Chinese government's persecution of the native and foreign opium traders.

There is a theory that the Opium War was not due to opium which "provided the occasion rather than the sole cause of war."[19] The meaning of this observation is that there were other tensions between Britain and China which were more fundamental than the conflict over opium. But these "fundamental" conflicts (over equal diplomatic status, free trade and judicial proceedings as it is alleged) had existed for more than a hundred years before 1838. No shadow of war ever existed. It was only when the Manchu government launched a war against the opium trade (not against Britain) that Sino-British tension began to break the limit of the tensile strength (which had helped maintain harmony until then). William Jardine, the foremost British opium trader, lamented on December 16, 1838, in China that "Not an opium pipe to be seen, not a retail vendor...not a single enquiry after the drug". On January 1, 1839, he instructed his Bombay agents to let opium remain "in the hands of the Company." By April the unsold Indian opium lying with the British and other traders in China amounted to 20,000 chests, with another 32,000 chests waiting for shipment at Bombay and Calcutta.[20] Jardine had a long session with Palmerston, the British foreign secretary, on September 27, and provided the latter with maps, charts and perhaps, the determination to attend the cabinet meeting held a few days later.[21] The war subsequently waged by Britain was to cancel the earlier Chinese war. The name Opium War is not a misnomer, as it stands for an *anti*-anti-opium war (the two negatives of which cancel out each other).

Another theory asserts that the main conflict was between British commercial expansion and Chinese containment of it. Opium was merely a vehicle of this expansion. "Had there been an effective alternative to opium, say molasses or rice, the conflict might have been called the Molasses War or the Rice War."[22] Here the significance of opium is reduced to an algebraic X which stands for an "indispensable vehicle" of British commercial expansion. This theory assumes: (1) British commercial expansion vis-a-vis China could have only a fixed pattern; (2) this expansion inevitably led to war whether opium was involved or not. But we have seen that the British commercial expansion in question was an abnormal type which had the Indian opium enterprise as its locomotive and was not the corollary of the Industrial Revolution. It was this locomotive which led the two nations to a collision course. Without resorting to opium the entire pattern of the triangular trade (or British commercial expansion) would change. Thus it is illogical to describe the Opium War as an X-war.

III

The classical view that commerce achieves an equilibrium between demand and supply is not valid in our discussion of the trade triangle which was a peculiar phenomenon of imbalances. The detailed distribution of commodities in the Sino-British commercial exchange in 1817-1833 was as follows:

> out of a total of £12,847,494 of British imports to China, 85.2% (£10,926,379) being wollens, 8.1% (£1,031,343) being metals, and 3.6% (£465,388), cotton textiles; out of a total of £33,934,106 of Chinese exports to Britain, 92.5% (£31,363,087) being tea, 5% (£1,700,636) being silver, and 1.5% (£508,546), silks.[23]

The second dimension, trade between India and China, was originally meant to be a one-way India-to-China-wealth movement using China as a relay station and finally transmitting the wealth to Britain. That an opposite China-to-India movement also emerged was due to two factors. First, since the introduction of opium to the triangular trade was meant to play a double function of transmission of wealth and simultaneously replenishing the Indian treasury, the private opium exporters had to remit a part of their gains back to India to sustain their opium adventure (as there was quite an exaction on their gains by the Company's Calcutta opium sales). Secondly, as the China-bound Indian ships always sailed back without specific assignments and with plenty of accommodation, a return cargo from China was inevitable for additional profit and also for taking ballast to stand the storms of the Pacific. Thirdly, the British-Indian Opium traders often bartered their opium with Chinese smugglers for goods without paying customs duty, and shipped them back to Calcutta for re-export. Many Americans and Portuguese found it convenient and cheap to buy Chinese tea and nankeens at Calcutta.[24]

The third dimension, trade between Britain and India, is generally regarded as a topic outside the scope of the Britain-China-India trade triangle. This may be briefly dealt with by way of concluding this essay.

The salient features of the trade between Britain and India were : (1) it followed the classical pattern of trade between the colony and the metropolis; (2) a substantial part of the exchange concerned cotton and its products; (3) a good portion of the British imports catered to the needs of Europeans rather than Indians.

The Indian exports were essentially raw materials, while her imports were mostly finished products, the majority of which could be manufactured in India. The exchanges of cotton and its goods show a process of transforming India (which had been a renowned cotton textile producer of the world) into a massive consumer of British cotton textiles some of which were woven from the Indian-grown cotton.

In ten years (1821-1830) Calcutta and Bombay exported in excess £9,322,415 of wealth to Britain, and £10,774,655 to

China (which, too, was ultimately transmitted to Britain). In other words, two million pound sterling were the annual Indian tribute to Britain. But even the articles from Britain which formed a part of the British payment for Indian exports, those military and naval stores, books and stationery, liquors, carriages, hats and boots, were all for the consumption of those who were devoting their time and energy in India to the cause of transforming Indian revenue into private fortunes, then into Indian exports to China, and then into Chinese exports to Britain. This was the strange manner in which the trade triangle was complete. At last we see the equilibrium in the trade triangle under review, namely: Indian opium for the Chinese, Chinese tea for the Britons, and British Raj for the Indians !

References

1. William Foster, *England's Quest of Eastern Trade* (London, reprint, 1966), pp. 5-6.
2. M.E. Wibur, *The East India Company and the British Empire in the Far East* (California, 1945), pp. 302-314.
3. H.B. Morse, *The Chronicles of the East India Company Trading to China* (Oxford, 1926), I. 162.
4. J.A. Williamson, *A Short History of British Expansion* (London, 1958), p. 38.
5. *First Report from the Select Committee* House of Commons, 1830 Appendix, p. 84: *Yapian zhanzheng,* II, 655.
6. A.H. Imlah, *Economic Elements in the Pax Britania* (Harvard, 1958), p. 160.
7. *First Report,* Commons, 1830, T.G. Lloyd's witness, Q4181.
8. *Bengal Commercial Reports,* Vol. 31.
9. *Bombay Commercial Proceedings,* Vols. 57-76.
10. Morse, *Chronicles,* IV, 20, 22.
11. F.S. Turner, *British Opium Policy and Its Results to Indian and China* (London, 1876), p. 135.
12. Morse, *Chronicles,* II, IV, *passim.*
13. *Bengal Commercial Reports,* Vols. 14-21; *Bombay Commercial Proceedings,* Vols. 40-46.
14. Turner, *op. cit.,* p. 44.
15. *Home Miscellaneous* 1828-1840 (National Archieves of India), S. No. 440.

16. *Bengal Commercial Reports,* Vol. 40.
17. Data for 1792 from Furber, *Governor-Generalship,* p. 30; J., MacGregor: *History of Oriental Commerce* (House of Commons, 1847-48, c. 974), p. 235: for 1812 from Yan Zhongping, (ed), *Zhogguo jindvi jingjishi tongji ziliao xuanji* (Shanghai, 1955), p. 25.
18. Chang, *op. cit.,* p. 193.
19. J.K. Fairbank, *Trade and Diplomacy on the China Coast* (Harvard, 1964), p. 74.
20. Michael Greenberg, *British Trade and the Opening of China* (Cambridge, 1951), pp. 201-203; Turner, *op. cit.,* p. 279.
21. Maurice Collis, *Foreign Mud* (London, 1947), p. 274.
22. Chang, *op. cit.,* p. 15.
23. Morse, *Chronicles,* III, IV, *passim.*
24. *Bengal Commercial Reports,* Vol. 19.

5

The Opium War (1840-42) and Sino-British Contradictions*

*The Opium War*** is a booklet written by faceless authors without much pretension for research. We choose it for review not only because it is the first Communist Chinese study on the Opium War available to the English readership, but also because we get a glimpse of Chinese research findings on the Opium War by reviewing this book. Here is a small but well-shaped and forcefully presented national consensus which is at once Marxist, Maoist, patriotic and revolutionary, but not infallible.

I

The Opium War has packed in the short space of 124 pages, ten substantial chapters driving home the following viewpoints: First, the British capitalist interests cast a covetous eye on, and worked out aggressive designs against China. Secondly, the British imported Indian opium into China in ever increasing quantities according to their aggressive designs. Thirdly, opium as an external factor intensified China's internal contradictions and divided the Chinese ruling group into soft-liners and hard-liners *vis-a-vis* the enforcement of the opium ban. With the triumph of the latter over the former, Lin Zexu was sent to Canton in 1839 to stop the opium import. Fourthly, the British who had already been using three weapons—merchandise, opium and cannon—"to force open the door of China" (p. 35) answered the Chinese anti-opium moves by launching a war against China in 1840. Fifth, "the Chinese people took a stand of resolute resistance to foreign capitalist aggression" (p. 52) but were betrayed by their politically corrupt and militarily impotent

---

* This is the summary of the article written in 1977 and published in the *China Report*, Vol. XIV, No. 2 (March-April, 1978)

**Foreign Language Press, *The Opium War* (Peking, 1976).

government which was more afraid of the people than of the external aggressors. Sixthly, the Americans played the accomplice in the British aggression against China. And lasly, the Opium War turned China from a sovereign country into a semi-colony.

On the British designs on China, the Communist Chinese historians have no new evidence to offer. Nor have they made any elaborate study of all the published and unpublished British records open to any research. What distinguishes Chinese historiography from other studies is its courage and bluntness in calling spade a spade. The Chinese historians have cited Michael Greenberg[1] who would have little difficulty in agreeing with their conclusions. But Greenberg has only covertly, never overtly, condemned the British aggressiveness. Hsin-pao Chang (who may be better treated as a part of the Western scholarship in spite of his Chinese origin) has demonstrated so clearly in his book that it was Britain's commercial expansion which had brought the gunboats to China, yet the strongest words he has used to describe the British aggressiveness are : "The roaring guns of the Opium War awakened the [Chinese] empire from centuries of lethargy."[2] Everyone knows that the "roaring guns" were British, but scholarly sophistication and maturity (or aloofness from "moral scholasticism") demand that Britain be not named. Throughout his book, he has not hinted at any British desire to awaken China "from centuries of lethargy". Then, why this meaningless sentence? Obviously, the scholar has used it to fill a void caused by the withdrawal of what he had in mind but would not put it in black and white about Britain's intentions in waging the war against China. To the Communist Chinese historians the Opium War was categorically an act of aggression by British imperialism. What was even worse was the British resorting to poisoning the people of China in the interest of the British bourgeoisie. One Chinese book says: "Britain waging a war for the sake of selling a poisonous drug constitutes the most shameful leaf of human history."[3]

The basic analysis of the British aggressiveness in *The Opium War* springs from the following observation of Lenin :

"[T]he capitalist system cannot exist and develop without constantly extending its sphere of domination without colonizing new countries and without drawing ancient, non-capitalist countries into the whirlpool of world economy." (p. 7)[4] To spell out Lenin's hindsight, *The Opium War* holds that it was the textile-opium interests in league with the East India Company and the British government which had harboured aggressive designs.

In *The Opium War,* however, there is only one single mention of British economic crisis : "In 1825 the first crisis of over-production in the history of capitalism occurred in Britain." (p.3) The authors, who cite this fact directly from Yan Zhongping[5] and indirectly from Marx's *Capital,* should have carefully examined Marx's contentions. Discussing the evils of capitalist mechanised industries, Marx made a brief survey of the performance of the British cotton textile industry from 1770 to 1863. The survey demonstrated that, in the first instance, the industry was in a state of flux, chequered with prosperity, depression and crisis. It also demonstrated the industry's great resilience during the entire century. British colonies and her China trade contributed to this resilience. But Marx did not establish a direct link between the chequered career of the industry and the 1840 war (which finds no mention in this survey). If the Communist Chinese historians wish to substantiate the crisis of British-cotton-textile-industries-leading-to-the-Opium-War theory, they have to discard Marx's survey, in which he stated that the year 1836 was marked by "great prosperity" of the British cotton-textile industry, which was followed by two years of "depression and crisis" (1837-38), one year of "revival" (1839), another year of "great depression" (1840), another two years of "frightful suffering among the factory operatives" (1841-42), and yet another year of "great misery" (1843).[6] If the Opium War were the direct result and a solution to the crisis of the British cotton-textile industry, the picture of the latter's performance would have been one of deepening depression and crisis from 1836 to 1839, and prosperity from 1842 onwards.

It is pertinent to link the British expansion of her cotton textile market in India with the expansion of Indian exports of opium to China, as *The Opium War* has done. The book reminds us of the famous observation of Marx : '[T]he English cotton machinery produced an acute effect in India. The Governor General reported in 1834-35 : "The misery hardly finds a parallel in the history of commerce. The bones of the cotton-weavers are bleaching the plains of India.'"[7] It then says : "The mounting sales of British textiles in India were largely due to the fact that the Indian peasants bought them with the income obtained from the opium they were forced to grow." "So it is clear that this evil traffic was closely linked with the interests of the British government and the British bourgeoisie as a whole, and this is the reason why they were prepared to go to such great lengths to continue it." (p. 12)

The book has in another place reckoned that the British authorities in India spent only a paltry sum of Rs. 237 as the cost of a chest of "top-graded opium" (which is on the high side as compared to other reports,[8] while they got ten times that sum, *i.e.* 2,428 rupees in the Culcutta auction (which is much lower than the highest prices sold) (p. 9).[9] Even when we ignore the inaccuracies of the statistics cited in the book, we clearly see that the benefit of the opium traffic to the Indian peasants was miserably small. The increase in the Indian purchasing power for British cotton textiles resulting from the opium trade obviously came from an Indian strata other than the opium-growing peasants.

About the opium revenue to the colonial government, the book has this to say: "The colonial government of British India benefited because opium tax became a major item in its revenue, the rate being over 300 per cent *ad valorem.* Such tax collected in 1829-30, for example, surpassed one million pounds sterling, about one-tenth of its total annual revenue." (p. 10)

The effect of this observation is diluted by another observation in the book : "The British capitalists tried every possible means to change their unfavourable balance of trade with China. In the latter half of the 18th century, they found opium was a highly profitable commodity, with a good sale in China... They decided to use it to 'get a foot in the door'." (p. 8).

The triple role attributed to the opium trade in the book (*i.e.* to enhance the Indian peasants' purchasing power for British cotton textiles, to accrue a huge revenue for the British Raj, and to change the adverse balance of Britain's China trade) has obscured the historical mission of this unprecedented state-sponsored international narcotic traffic for strengthening the existence and stability of the East India Company's British Raj in India. This Raj was founded for the specific purpose of manipulating India's resources, but it also specialized in manipulating the mechanics of trade. The central task of this Raj was first to claim ownership of the Indian revenue and then remit it back to England. The relevance of China to this game of revenue-appropriation lay in the cunning scheme of the East India Company of utilising China as the midway station of revenue-transmission, in buying the prized Chinese goods with the unwanted Indian goods. The British shipping of Indian cotton to China to exchange for Chinese silk and tea can be traced way back to the pre-Raj days. And as soon as Clive claimed the revenue of Bengal and Bihar in 1757, the East India Company's gentlemen claimed monopoly of the Patna opium. That opium was called for to balance Britain's unfavourable trade *vis-a-vis* China was a myth created by the East India Company. But many modern historians and, ironically, even the Communist Chinese historians have fallen into this trap.

Like cotton, opium was instrumental in transmitting the Indian revenue to Britain. But there was a difference. The East India Company auctioned opium in Calcutta generally on credit. The opium traders bought it first and paid later to the East India Company's Canton treasury by obligation. The case here was that the Bengal government had only registered but never seen the opium revenue. The moment it was created it was on its way to Britain via China. From 1820s onwards British shipment of opium from India to China outstripped her shipment of tea from China to Britain. The entire triangular affair has been described as an exchange of Indian opium for the Chinese, Chinese tea for the Britons, and British Raj for the Indians.[10] The opium trade was no ordinary trade : it was a trade offensive against China—forcing China to contribute to British empire-building.

II

A clear understanding of the nature of the opium trade helps to analyse the main contradiction(s) which ignited the first Sino-British conflict. The scholarly moods within and outside China towards the investigation of the origins of the war are, indeed, a world apart. Outside China scholars have been following the century-old debate initiated by the sixth US President, John Quincy Adams, in 1841. Latest research works still vehemently debate the pros and cons of the cultural war, the trade war and the opium war theories. But the Chinese scholars have only marginally involved themselves in this debate.

A much more important period in the history of the opium trade was 1820-21. These two years saw the British consolidation of control over the Malwa opium production area, the East India Company claiming monopoly over the Malwa opium, Bombay opening its gates to the Malwa opium to facilitate its export to China, and the Bengal opium agencies' new policy of fast expanding opium production and export to China. These new developments in India resulted in a multiple increase of export of Indian opium to China. This invigorated opium offensive assumed a new mode of armed traffic along the China coast from 1821 onwards. It was the inauguration of the "Lintin Era" (Lingding Era).

The characteristics of the "Lingding Era" may be described thus: (1) British opium ships occupied Chinese territory and territorial waters around the Inner Lingding Island, and the Jinxingmen (Camsungmoon) and Jishuimen (Kapsui Moon) anchorages; (2) open opium deliveries were conducted right under the nose of the Chinese anti-smuggling naval forces; (3) sailors of Anglo-American opium ships clashed with Chinese navy to rescue Chinese opium smugglers; (4) British opium ships sent out schooners to deliver opium to the Chinese smugglers when the latter were restrained by the intensification of China's coastal anti-smuggling operations; (5) British naval fleet under Rear-Admiral Frederick Maitland demonstrated along the China coast in 1837 to intimidate the Chinese anti-opium activities.

All this created a pre-war tension area between Britain and China. The contradition of the opium traffic focused itself on the British efforts in fighting the Chinese prohibition. Behind this dichotomy of Chinese prohibition versus British anti-prohibition was the basic contradiction of the British quest for China's contribution to the British Raj and the Chinese resistance against this imposition.

The Opium War has more or less grasped this contradiction. "The Chinese people", it says, "had long been deeply concerned about the spread of opium and firmly demanded its prohibition." (p. 19) It was this fundamental demand, as the book sees, that created a strong anti-opium lobby in the Manchu government in opposition to the lobby for the legalization of opium. Again, it was the firm opposition of the masses "to the absurd idea of lifting the opium ban" (p. 21) that enabled the anti-opium faction of the government to win the day. The Chinese determination to intensify their fight against the opium traffic, the book suggests, brought Commissioner Lin into direct confrontation with Captain Charles Elliot, the British Chief Superintendent of Trade in China.

When Lin's measures "hit the foreign smugglers hard", Elliot determined "to undermine them". "He protested at the installation of defence at Canton, gave orders for the opium receiving ships off the Pearl River estuary to flee and prepare for battle and began to compel the British merchants at Canton to leave." (p. 28) After Lin's destruction of the surrendered opium "Elliot was pushing ahead with preparations for an aggressive war." (p. 30)

That opium was the one factor which had pushed the two countries onto a collision course is a conclusion any one can draw after reading *The Opium War.*

The non-opium war arguments consider that the British waged war against China in 1840 not with the limited aim of expanding the opium trade, but with the larger aim to settle the commercial and diplomatic relations with China on Britain's terms. The scholars cite the Sino-British settlement in the Treaty of Nanjing to substantiate their argument.

Fairbank's distinction between the occasion and the sole

cause of the war betrays an attempt to twist the point. To say that opium was the "occasion" of the war amounts to an admission of the seriousness of the opium element which created the war crisis. If no other element had created the crisis, then opium was the "sole occasion" and had a special place among the likely causes of the war.

There are several loopholes in the premise 'peace treaty decides the cause of war'. First, the Treaty of Nanjing was an event different from the outbreak of the Opium War. The motivations and strategic considerations regarding the former could be different from those of the latter. For instance, the causes which led the USA to involve itself in the war against Japan during the Second World War were not faithfully reflected in the terms and provisions in which the US concluded peace with Japan after 1945. Secondly, it was not true that Britain did not intend to write the opium issue into the Nanjing settlement. Only the stubborn resistance of the Manchu government prevented them from doing so. Thirdly, the first and foremost victory of Britain in the Opium War was to kill the Manchu government's desire to suppress the opium traffic once for all. We cannot, therefore, say that the long list which the British government put forward for settlement with China necessarily excluded the opium issue as the main cause of the war.

Fairbank's occasion-is-not-the-sole-cause argument does not lend conviction to his settlement-is-the-cause-of-war premise. The causes of the war are to be found in the developments which led to the fighting, not in the developments which followed it. Fairbank's proposition amounts to putting the cart before the horse.

Britain's pre-Opium War behaviour in China had these highlights. First, the British authorities were extraordinarily tolerant, prudent and cautious in dealing with the Chinese government of which, though, London had never had a very high opinion. Secondly, Britain was more busy with buying goods from China than with converting her into a market for British manufactures. Thirdly, Britain sent three pseudo-tributary missions to China without invitation and without being disturbed by the failure of these missions. Fourthly, Britain treated the China trade as an extension of her Indian affairs, and remained so after the abolition of the East India Company's China trade monopoly in 1833. Fifth, as *The Opium War* unwittingly admits, the British government first made up its mind to fight China only in September-October of 1839, not earlier. All this shows that Britain had all along pursued a policy of peaceful co-existence with China. If China had not disturbed the status quo of the opium trade in 1839, this peaceful policy would have lasted much longer. China's middle-kingdom arrogance, her closed-door-ness, her outmoded "tribute-system" and her refusal to admit a permanent British embassy in Beijing, had never really created any crisis in Sino-British relations. The only war-like crisis that was created was due to the opium issue.

The pre-Opium War British strategy was two fold. She used her maritime and economic power derived from her Indian boots to progressively squeeze out her European rivals from China, By the end of the 18th century, British control over China's foreign trade reached 70 per cent of the total and could have increased further if the U.S. traders had not cut into it. Even then the British maintained roughly a share of two-thirds of China's foreign trade before the Opium War. It was not a coincidence that this two-thirds monopoly in China's foreign trade had been maintained right from the signing of the Treaty of Nanjing down to the end of the 19th century. Such extraordinary continuity and stability could not have been achieved without a superior long-term strategy.

Underlying Britain's China policy was the primary quest for economic gains. *The Opium War* takes some cognizance ot this. It has itemized some of the gains. First, as we have cited earlier, there was the Indian government's opium revenue of more than £1 million per annum. Second, the opium trade was "fabulously profitable" for the British opium traders. The book cites the leading British opium trader, William Jardine, that the gross profit of opium sale in China was sometimes "as high as $1,000 a chest", (p.10) Third, opium financed the tea trade, which in turn fetched £3.3 million to the British government in 1833. (p.11) Fourth, Indian earnings from the opium trade helped promote the sale of British cotton textiles in India from less than 1 million yards in 1814 to 51 million yards in 1835. (p.11) These are penetrating insights into the British calculations *vis-a-vis* China.

The great pity about the studies of the Opium War both inside and outside China is the absence in them of a comprehensive quantitative survey of Britain's economic gains accruing from her contacts with China. There is no dearth of source materials of this work. One great merit of the British nation is that they preserve old records and accounts. Even when she loses her status of an imperial power she maintains the best library and museum in the world for the study of international imperialism. If Marx could produce his *Capital* out of the printed materials of the British Museum in London, it should not be too difficult now to produce an equally impressive work on Britain's "free-trade imperialism" or "opium imperialism" by delving into the printed and manuscript materials housed in the British Museum, the Public Records Office, and the India Office Library in London, the records of private companies deposited in the Cambridge University Library and other British and US libraries. The Indian archives in New Delhi, Kolkata, Mumbai and Chennai also provide a good complementary source of information.

As we know, the annual revenue of the British Raj was in the neighbourhood of £20 millions in the decades before the Opium War. This Indian booty Britain had acquired by paying a price. There was an administrative cost of the Indian colony. Apart from material expenses, hundreds or even thousands of British officials and soldiers died in India every year. But the gains from China were equivalent to half of the Indian colony, and without any cost. Why would Britain want to go to war with China when the plastic policy worked so well ?

Britain's China trade was no ordinary international trade. It was colonial exploitation, remittance and smuggling. That the opium trade was an imperialist device of international exploitation was pointed out long ago by India's renowned anti-colonial scholar, Dadabhai Naoroji (1825-1917): "Because India cannot fill up the remorseless drain, so China must be dragged in to make it up, even though it be 'poisoned'... All the profits of opium go the same way of the drain to England."[11]

In a colonial situation interference by foreigners assumed the form of political and legal prerogative under which a new socio-economic infrastructure was created to fashion a new pattern of production and consumption in favour of foreign economic interest. In a semi-colonial situation the foreigners' prerogatives remained invisible, but the new socio-economic infrastructure did take shape and the pattern of production and consumption did change in favour of the foreign economic interests. The mechanics of the opium trade was instrumental in such a socio-economic transformation.

Since the opium trade was forced on China at the gun-point, it gave Britain a kind of prerogative over the Chinese society. The Chinese as a nation were opposed to the trade, but could not stop its expansion. As *The Opium War* rightly points out, the British opium trade offensive created a new ruling group in China. "They opposed both the thorough suppression of the drug and its legalization, for they depended not only on the opium trade but also on the smuggling itself which, once the trade was legalized, would cease to be a source of bribes for them." (pp. 23-24) Thus, a new socio-economic infrastructure gradually took shape leading to "political decline, military impotence and financial insolvency", (p. 2) The pattern of Chinese consumption became increasingly opium-oriented, while the pattern of Chinese production developed abnormally according to the shopping orders (for tea and raw silk, etc.) of British and other foreign (especially US) traders. Foreign trade began to assume a dominant position in China's economic life. Silver, a component of China's bi-metal currency, rapidly changed its exchange ratio with copper, the other component, from the standard of 1:1,000 (1 tael of silver equivalent to 1,000 copper cash) to 1:2,000 and above, because silver was the currency used in the opium trade. This change in the exchange rate was tantamount to devaluation of the masses' currency, the copper cash, which in turn adversely affected the economic life of the common people.

We have now demonstrated that Britain's opium-oriented China trade not only exacted optimum economic gains for Britain but was actually a device of imperialist exploitation of and interference in China. It had already set a pattern of socio-economic aggression against China. What happened after the Opium War was but a follow-up of the pre-Opium War aggression. The semi-colonial infrastructure of the post-war period noticed by Lenin, Mao and other Marxist thinkers had already laid its foundation during the Canton Trade period (1760-1840) through the British strategy. In short, the opium trade was pure and simple opium trade imperialism.

III

However, Fairbank harps on cultural conflict. He thinks all troubles began with the Chinese cultural superiority complex. The Chinese could never respect foreign intruders. They regarded the carriers of the white man's burden as "uncouth and smelling of mutton fat". They described them with contempt as foreign devils, "big noses", or "hairy ones". The Ming Dynasty history book described the Portuguese as cannibals boiling and eating little Chinese children. In short, it was China's white peril xenophobia that set her on the collision course with the West.[12]

Fairbank and many other Western scholars have emphasized on the West's civilizing and benevolent influence on China. They consciously overlook and underplay the uncivilized and exploiting behaviour of the Westerners both before and after the Opium War. The Communist Chinese historians go to the other extreme. But if we compare the two opposite perspectives, we should be inclined to acknowledge the depth of the Chinese analysis rather than appreciate the Fairbankian superficiality. One often wonders why modern Western scholars should be so apologetic about what their ancestors did in China. This guilt complex and desire to white wash the historical stains have conditioned Western China scholarship to a rigidity comparable to the Communist Chinese refusal to acknowledge any positive element in the Westorn intercourse with China during the 19th century.

It seems paradoxical that while Hsin-pao Chang has broken away from the tradition of Western scholarly denunciation of Commissioner Lin, he has still to an extent inherited the Western prejudices against Lin. The anti-opium Commissioner has earned three minus points from Western scholars' commentaries : (*i*) his letter to Queen Victoria of Britain was ridiculous, ignorant and inappropriate, smacking of sinocentric chauvinism; (*ii*) his treatment of foreigners of China was high-handed and ruthless; and (*iii*) by first making the British traders surrender their opium and then destroying the drug, he helped the British traders out from the opium traffic crisis which he had himself created for them, and helped Britain find an excuse for war. Maurice Collis, a British writer, observes: "He [Commissioner Lin] had been naive enough in his headlong way to proceed against the whole foreign community in Canton, innocent and guilty, interning them, starving, constraining, insulting them, driving them on to their ships, sparing neither women nor children... The Chinese in their long years of intercourse with the West had never had so tactless an official as Lin, who had made the British Cabinet the present of a perfect case."[13]

The Opium War provides the students of the subject with a counterweight to balance the overdose of cultural conflict theory in Western writing on Chinese history. As the book carries with it the entire spectrum of Communist Chinese perspective cannot be treated lightly, and this review essay may not have done justice to all the research effort which it represents. Due to shortage of space, we have not discussed the implicity of USA in the Opium war and in the post-Opium War Western aggression against China which has been emphasized in Communist Chinese historiography.

From our discussion we can identify certain areas where fresh thinking and elaborate research efforts are called for. First, regarding the nature of the Opium War conflict, we need more research work on (*i*) the alignment and contradictions of various British interests *vis-a-vis* China, (*ii*) the place of opium trade in the long-term overall strategy of Britain in expanding her influence to China, and (*iii*) the merits and shortcomings of the Marxian theory of over-production-leading-to-colonial-expansion, and the relevance of this theory to the Opium War events. We may achieve a breakthrough in these inquiries, if we pursue the line that there existed in the British colonial scheme in Asia two distinct models—the Indian and the Chinese. Both deserve a comprehensive benefit-cost accounting. If quantitative evidence can either prove or disprove that the pre-

Opium War China model was equally attractive or more profitable than the Indian model, we would be in a much better position to determine whether Britain would have waged war on China or prolonged the pre-Opium War co-existence *status quo*, had the Chinese not launched the anti-Opium War in 1839.

Second, regarding the contraditions solved and created by the Opium War, precious little has been offered by Western scholars. On the other hand, there is much discussion and even more raw material in Chinese historiography. This does not mean that there is any dearth of historical data in the British records. A dig into the rich Sino-British mine of information is very necessary, which can particularly help us to determine: (*a*) the main Sino-British contradiction before and after the Opium War, (*b*) the weightage of economic conflict *vis-a-vis* cultural conflict in the overall Sino-British conflict, and (*c*) the validity and meaning of the Maoist postulation of Opium-War-leading-to-semi-colony in China. As war is the highest and most violent form of contradiction and conflict, and a treaty is the mechanics of solution and compromise of contradictions, we must strive for a deeper understanding of the interactions of China's internal and external contradictions (not necessarily along the Maoist line of thinking) in studying the Opium war.

References

1. His book *British Trade and the Opening of China (Cambridge, 1951)* is an important study of the Opium War in Western literature.
2. Hsin-pao Chang, *Commissioner Lin and the Opium War* (paperback, New York, 1970), p. 217.
3. Hubei University, *Zhongguo jindaiguominjingji shi* (Economic History of Modern China), (1958), p. 81.
4. Citing V.I. Lenin, "The Development of Capitalism in Russia" *Selected Works of Lenin* (Lawrence and Wishart, 1944), Vol. I, p. 379.
5. *Ibid.,* p. 406.
6. Karl Marx, *Capital* (Moscow, 1974), Vol. 1, p. 428.
7. *Ibid.,* p. 406.
8. The mention of "top-graded opium" leads to confusion. All opium produced from the Patna and Banaras factories were of the same grade. The difference in the quality of the Indian opium arose from the skill of packing which was a special subject of research in the

East India Company's opium agencies. The grading of opium actually began in China when the opium cakes were converted into pills by extraction About the opium cost, the East India Company's claim in 1819-20 was Rs. 180 per chest, while actually it was £14 or Rs. 112. See John Phipps, *A Guide to the Commerce of Bengal* (Calcutta, 1823), p. 283.

9. The highest prices of the Calcutta auction were Rs. 4,405 (December 1821) and Rs. 4,545 (March 1822) for a chest of Patna, and Rs. 4,250 (March 1822) for a chest of Banaras. *Ibid.*, p. 257.
10. Tan Chung, "The Britain-China-India Trade Triangle (1771-1840)", *Indian Economic and Social History Review,* Vol. XI, No. 4, December 1974, See *antea,* p.
11. See B.N. Ganguli, "Dadabhai Naoroji and the Mechanism of External Drain", *The Indian Economic and Social History Review,* Vol. II, No. 2, April 1965, p. 101.
12. Fairbank, *The United States and China,* pp. 141-142.
13. Chang, *op. cit.,* p. 214, 216, 217.

6

The Unequal Treaty System : Infrastructure of Irresponsible Imperialism*

I

The term Treaty System or Treaty-Port System is an invention of Prof John King Fairbank, whose other equally famous invention is the term "Tribute System". These two systems summarize the Fairbankain perspective of the entire history of China's foreign relations, with the Opium War (1840-42) as the dividing line and with the Treaty System as the Tribute System's successor or replacement. There is hardly any other specialist on this subject.

The starting point of the Fairbankian perspective is the "cultural conflict" between China and the West, which transformed into the contradiction between "trade" and "tribute" in the Chinese scene in recent centuries. "The rub came when the foreign trade expanded and finally ... eclipsed tribute entirely." *(Trade and Diplomacy,* p. 33) This is how Fairbank conceives the earth-shaking changes in China's destiny during mid-19th-century. What many others might see as the swallowing of an age-old independent empire by the international monster of imperialism is softly defined as a Sino-western rub between the Chinese obsession of tribute and the western obsession of open-door free trade. What follows logically "should make it plain", says Fairbank, "that the treaty system gradually became a basic component of the power structure of the Chinese state. The westerner in this period was a partner in a Sino-western rule over China, which by degrees came to supplant the Manchu-Chinese synarchy of the Ch'ing [Qing] period." (*Ibid.*, p. 467).

*This is a shortened version of the article that was written in 1981 and published in *China Report,* Vol. XVII, No. 5, (November-December, 1981).

Fairbank further characterises the new Chinese order, *i.e.* "the Treaty System" as a "new rickshaw-culture", with the bicycle wheel of the rickshaw symbolizing the progressive western civilization, and the coolie power of the rickshaw puller symbolizing the resilient Chinese tradition. (*Ibid*, p. 466) The treaty system is described as a joint invention of Chinese tradition and western expansion which were mutually complementary. Evidence: western gunboats which exacted concessions from the Chinese government also helped it to suppress piracy. The westerners who enjoyed the material value of China trade much more than their ancient tributetrade predecessors from Arabia, Persia and other foreign lands, were also driven by their own self-interest to save the moral values of the Manchu rulers in order to maintain the shrunken prestige of the regime. (*Ibid.*, p. 465).

A vivid analogy, indeed. Its only weakness lies in the fact that the rickshaw puller was not his own inventor. And who is the rickshaw rider? Here the missing link is too important to ignore as both the rickshaw wheel and the rickshaw puller exist for the rickshaw rider.

Fairbank seems to think of 19th-century China as cut out for western domination. The intrusion of the westerners not only fell in line with China's historical development, but the new Sino-barbarian ruling system wrought by China's European conquerers was also harmoniously wedded with the Chinese socio-political reality. "The agrarian-bureaucratic state could be headed by Manchus, and the latter could even be assisted by Anglo-Saxons so long as the Chinese landlord-scholar-official class retained its customary position." *(Ibid.,* p. 468)

While the Fairbankian perspective hardly threatens to chasten the Prince of Imperialism, it has unmistakably taken Chinese culture as the whipping-boy. This can be detected from Fairbanks confusion over the spirit of equality, or the want of it, in the conclusion of treaties between China and the western powers. Here is a typical observation: "Although the [post-Opium War] new treaties were signed as between equal sovereign powers, they were actually quite unequal in that China was placed against her will in a weaker position..." *(U.S.*

and China, 3rd ed., p. 143) If so, how could China be regarded as an "equal sovereign power" before the victorious western aggressors at the time when she was forced to sign the treaties by the latter at gun point? But, Fairbank seems to have anticipated this question, and wanted to convince his readers that even though the western powers had an edge over China militarily, they were not quite China's equal in diplomatic manoeuvring in concluding the post-war treaties, so much so that the British "were less certain how to capitalize" their victories, and "they found themselves in a diplomatic contest which was more evenly balanced." *(Trade and Diplomacy,* p. 83) How easily said than done that the Chinese could surface themselves as equals in the diplomatic contest every time after they had gone under in the military combat! Later in this essay we shall illustrate how the British diplomats prevailed over their Chinese counterparts at negotiation tables with the same ease as British fighters did in the battlefields.

The fact that Fairbank has used the terms Treaty System and unequal treaty system alternately betrays his lack of clarity in mind, which can be further illustrated by comparing two of his observations about the subject: "The unequal treaty system in China lasted a full century from 1842 to 1943 as a semi-permanent form of Western intervention in Chinese life. It was also an East Asian wing of Europe's worldwide hegemony, specially an arm of British informal empire..." *(China Perceived,* p. 86) "The British were able after the Opium War to set forth a new structure of ideas including such elements as free trade and the equality of states, which were all expressed in the words of the treaties...they were far from dominant in the day-to-day situation and could not dictate Chinese action. In fact, the path of progress for the British often lay in a judicious accommodation of Western ways to those of the Middle Kingdom." ("Synarchy", pp. 216-217).

If the treaty system was a semi-permanent form of Western intervention in Chinese life, how was it that the intervening forces "were far from dominant in the day-to-day situation"? If there was British hegemony in China, how could there be judicious accommodation on the British part to the Chinese ways?

Fairbank's Treaty System theory is a comment on the nature of imperialist aggression on China. Even more it is an exposition of China's absorption of imperialist aggression. The latter aspect is embodied in his well-known theory of Synarchy. He coined this term partly to draw a parallel and partly to distinguish between the intricate institution of joint Sino-foreign administration of the Government of China and the dyarchy of British Indian history.

There is a third eye in the Fairbankian vision to detect the presence of a foreign force in China's internal governance. "Alien rule is one of the commonplaces of the Chinese political tradition", comments Fairbank. "Throughout East Asian history runs this motif of the marriage of the steppe and the sown... Inner Asian barbarians...always participated in one way or another in the government of the Chinese empire." ("Synarchy", p. 204) This over-generalization has been extended to the point of absurdity by equating the dominant Soviet influence in China in the early 1950s with the "steppe barbarians". When he was penning the conclusion of *Trade and Diplomacy,* he saw the "vestiges of the past" "even in the midst of the continuing [communist] revolution." "Once more, a foreign element, again from the north, plays a leading part in China." *(Trade and Diplomacy,* p. 468).

What Fairbank wants to drive home is that "the Chinese state, from its rich experience with the barbarians of Inner Asia, had no lack of institutional devices by which to accommodate foreign intruders in the domestic power structure." *(Ibid)* "The role played by non-Chinese in the Chinese state during the Northern Wei Liao, Chin [Tin], Yuan [Mongol] and Ch'ing [Qing, *i.e.* Manchu] periods had some sort of historical relationship to the role played... by the British and other Western powers under the unequal treaty system, by the Japanese invaders in their "co-prosperity sphere" subsequently, and perhaps by the Russians under communism most recently." (Synarchy, p. 205) Under Synarchy, says Fairbank, "both the Manchus and the British sought to make their new order work and foster its economic prosperity. Where the Manchu emperors became the patrons of agricultural development...the British...sought to foster international and local free trade." *(Ibid,* p. 221)

Here the cat comes out of the bag. To Fairbank who thinks "the theory of imperialism is not the only avenue of approach" to the study of Chinese history, Britain and other western powers were no imperialist intruders, but only partners of the Chinese rulers in the sino-barbarian institutions of Synarchy to work jointly for the economic prosperity of China!

With this theory of Synarchy at the back of our mind, we are able to understand the true meaning of his condemnation of imperialism which is a recent development of Fairbankian scholarship. In his latest essay on treaty system in the *Cambridge History,* Fairbank seems to move away from the earlier beat-the-whipping-boy attitude. He comments that from the western point of view, the treaty system was "an institutional structure" which gradually grew into the Chinese state and society. From the Chinese point of view, "the treaties were vehicles of imperialist invasion." (p. 214)

This "treaty system interlude", observes Fairbank, existed throughout a century of "dynastic interregnum". He adds: "the treaty century saw the onset and then the height of imperialist penetration of China as well as the phase of the Chinese people's increasingly revolutionary response to it. Under the treaties, China's sovereignty was increasingly impaired; with the rise of nationalism and revolution, it was by degree reasserted." (p. 214)

All these quotations from Fairbank contradict his theory of "Synarchy" and his apology for western, particularly British, imperialism in China. It would be interesting to hear the latest comments of Fairbank, who is bitten by the bug of the perspective of imperialism, on all he had written earlier about the treaty system. Not a single word of this in the *Cambridge History* article. Has he abandoned his earlier position?

Stray observations do seem to indicate a departure from the classical Fairbankian perspective. For instance, he now thinks that the treaty system had been set up by gunfire and had to be maintained by gunboat diplomacy. Again, "gunboat diplomacy betrayed the unsolved struggle as to who should call the tune in Sino-Western contact." (p. 232) But the thrust of the new article is still the reiteration of the "Synarchy" theory, albeit in a new garb. The statement below in the latest essay removes any doubt: "One secret of the British success in China was the tacit community of interest between the British and Ch'ing [Qing] administrators. Each side represented a conquering power that had learned to rule its conquests by qualities of moral commitment and administrative skill...The treaty settlement was thus a *modus vivendi* worked out between the representatives of two aristocratic, British and Manchu, empires." (p. 217)

To get to the bottom of Fairbankian analysis about the nature of the imperialist domination in 19th-century China, the latest article, in keeping with Fairbank's consistent stand, says that Britain wanted the Treaty System partly "to foster the established interests" and partly to express "Britain's worldwide commercial expansion". He adds: "Specially, the British aim was to give stability and opportunity to the triangular trade between British, India, and the British Isles. This meant safeguarding the China market for Indian opium exports and the Chinese supply of teas and silks for London." He adds further that "the British treaty makers" were meant to "find security for *trade* in the rule of law", offering a "charter of rights primarily for merchants." (pp. 216-217) By now we get tired of pointing out Fairbank's self-contradiction. If British imperialism had any respect for the rule of law in China, it would not have pushed the "Indian opium exports" to the point of madness. But Fairbank paints 19th-century Britain as a champion of both the rule of law and also the most notorious international narcotic traffic in modern civilization! In any case, Fairbank's stand *vis-a-vis* the British aggression on China is fairly clear. It is summarized in these words in the *Cambridge History:* "Britain wanted, not to rule the Chinese empire as a colony, but to get it to follow British ways of international contact and free trade under the rule of law, which open the door to British commercial profit." (p. 232)

Even while using terms like imperialism, domination, hegemony, gunboat diplomacy, the Fairbankian perspective essentially negates the theory of imperialism which is generally understood as a system of colonial oppression and capitalist exploitation of foreign peoples. But the Treaty System conceived by Fairbank was a kind of international alliance, or an international community in which the native (Chinese) and foreign partners drew mutual benefit from each other. Such a perspective cannot provide any basis of understanding imperialism in 19th-century China.

II

As the Chinese intellectuals carried out a relentless struggle against the imperialist Treaty System right from the end of the 19th century, there is a near-unanimous viewpoint which is anti-treaty oriented and considers the Treaty System an imperialist yoke. Chiang Kai-shek and Mao Zedong were united on this point. Mao and his comrades conceived the 19th-century imperialist domination over China as one of the two mountains which had crushed the Chinese people underneath (the other being "feudalism"). Mao's anti-imperialist patriotism was also wedded with his belief in Marxism-Leninism, which subscribes to the theory of imperialism.

In the case of China, as long as she was her own master in her economic intercourse with Britain and other western powers she was not under the impact of western imperialism. A qualitative change first took place in 1821 with British opium traders embarking upon armed delivery of the drug under the protection of the Union Jack, and with British men of war standing by. So the political process of British imperialism had already been initiated two decades before the outbreak of the Opium War, symbolizing the beginning of British opium imperialism. Though no Chinese territory was ceded, there was illegal occupation of small off-shore islands and also China's territorial waters by British warships and armed opium carriers.

With the launching of the Opium War on China and binding her by the Treaty of Nanjing, Britain certainly went a step further in integrating China into her expansive economic order. The inauguration of British imperialism in China was three-pronged: (*a*) the threat of use of force, (*b*) the war, and (*c*) the treaty. Britain followed this pattern in almost all the areas which ultimately fell victims to *Pax Britannica.* What was peculiar to the Chinese scene was that whereas in other areas, like India, Britain had escalated the political process until complete take-over of the colonial administration, in China the process was never escalated but only repeated. This peculiarity had led many scholars to exclude China from the history of imperialist domination, or to assign non-imperialist patterns to modern Chinese history, as Fairbank does.

That Britain never intended to make China a second India is a historical fact recognized by historians of varying perspectives. In other words, Britain's ultimate goal was not to conquer China and subject her to direct British rule. This was the consistent British strategy *vis-a-vis* China from the early treaty days to the end of the 19th century. Yet this does not exonerate Britain from imperialist aggression against China, as China was very much a target of the imperialist process of absorbing her into the fold of *Pax Britannica.*

III

In tracing the genesis of the treaty system, let us first ascertain whether the evolution of the treaties was the outcome of Chinese efforts to neutralize British military victory, as the Fairbankian perspective wants us to believe or otherwise. Gallagher and Robinson have indicated the contrary by enumerating the British-imposed treaties "of free trade and friendship" on "weaker" countries: "The treaties with Persia of 1836 and 1845, the Turkish treaties of 1838 and 1861, the Japanese treaty of 1858, the favours extracted from Zanzibar, Siam and Morocco, the hundreds of anti-slavery treaties signed with crosses by African chiefs..." (*EcHR*, p. 11) While signing treaties with other countries was a global strategy of Britain, the Chinese government had very little experience in treaty diplomacy, and could not comprehend the implications of the documents on the dotted lines of which they were forced by Britain to sign.

Let us begin by briefly recounting the events that led to the conclusion of the Treaty of Nanjing which inaugurated the treaty era in China. We know that it was out of a sense of despair and disgust that the Chinese government agreed to sign the Treaty of Nanjing at the end of two years of stubborn resistance. This sense of disgust was reflected in an edict issued by Emperor Daoguang during the Opium War: "The English are like whales and crocodiles of the sea...But seven of our provinces have to be alerted to face the menace. All the counties and prefectures adjacent to the coast have to make defence preparations. Yet our might and power cannot be employed in storming the enemy forts and conquering the enemy grounds. Can there be any justification for our wasting the energy of the military and the civilians as well as the resources of the nation in this manner?... Is it not far better to use a word and a sheet of paper than to deploy millions of troops?"[1] This edict clearly proves that the Treaty of Nanjing was forced on China by Britain's gunboat diplomacy, a fact even Fairbank has conceded in his *Cambridge History* article. It is but fair to say that the first Sino-British Treaty was a British design to expand her economic order in China. As for the Chinese government, far from gaining an upper hand in the game of diplomacy, they were lured by the illusion created by the British aggressors that with the conclusion of the treaty and the grant of political, economic and territorial concessions to the invaders they could live in peace with Britain for ever.

It did not take them long to realize their miscalculations. In ten years Britain began to pick up the dust of dissatisfaction over the implementation of the treaty and of the necessity for its revision. A provision for revision of the trade agreement was written in Article 34 of the Sino-American Treaty of Wangxia (Wanghsia) in 1844. But the Treaty of Nanjing was a political treaty. It was a peace treaty intended to stabilize and perpetuate a peaceful and friendly atmosphere between Britain and China. Neither was the treaty meant for future revision, nor was there any provision for revision in it. Yet, British diplomacy in those years of might is right was unscrupulous, having little regard for propriety and fairness. British diplomats in China raised the question of revision of the Treaty of Nanjing on the pretext that the most favoured nation clause of the treaty granted the right of revising the Treaty of Nanjing to equalise the U.S. privilege of revising the trade agreement under the Treaty of Wangxia.

S.G. Bonham, British ambassador to China (1848-54), was instructed by London in May 1853 to take up the matter with Beijing, demanding: (*i*) all Chinese cities and ports be open to British traders without reservation, and (*iii*) British citizens be allowed to travel throughout China without restriction.

The second settlement—with the conclusion of two Sino-British treaties at Tianjin (1858) and Beijing (1860), the brief Anglo-French occupation of Beijing in October 1860, the barbarous destruction of Yuanmingyuan, the luxurious imperial summer palace, and the captivity of the Viceroy of the Two Guang provinces, Ye Mingchen, who was subsequently sent to India and imprisoned in Fort William, Calcutta, as a precious piece of war booty by Britain—was apparently a much more cruel version of the "first settlement". In content, the Treaty System which was fortified by the Treaty of Beijing was a substantial escalation of the System founded by the Treaty of Nanjing. The legalization of the opium trade, the British access to the Valley of Yangtze the additional treaty ports both along the sea coast north of Yangtze and along its banks, lighter taxation for imported British goods, permission for Chinese workers to settle down in British colonies, and the mortgage of tariff control to a foreign cadre under the leadership of a British national—all these marked greater integration of China into *Pax Britannica* than ever before.

A great leap forward was achieved by Britain's colonial economic expansion in China by a moderate use of force and a tightening of treaty control in lieu of direct involvement in China's internal governance by the British crown. The treaty, thus, played a central role in the advancement of British imperialism in China making, a special brand of imperialist domination of the world which we may call "Treaty Imperialism" "informal imperialism". Treaty imperialism or informal imperialism was no inferior to its classical form exemplified by the British Raj in India.

The history after the conclusion of the Treaty of Beijing demonstrates the fact that the treaty system was the best guarantee for the expansion of British economic interests in China. The treaty system was such a magic ring which Britain had put round China's neck. Whenever the Chinese government did not concede British demands, Britain tightened the Treaty ring and Beijing had to be obedient.

Just as the *Arrow* incident in 1856 provided the pretext for Britain to pressurize the Chinese government for the second settlement, the murder of a British interpreter, A.K. Margary, in Yunnan in February 1875 was another godsend opportunity. The British Ambassador, Thomas F. Wade, used all the cold war tactics. He half closed the British legation in Beijing, furled the Union Jack and retreated to the sea coast, in addition the British fleet menacingly manoeuvred. The Manchu government got frightened. It sent senior courtier Li Hongzhang to chase Thomas Wade, and finally, the two sides signed a new treaty at Yantai. The Chefoo Convention virtually transformed the Yangtze into the Thames by opening new treaty ports, and allowing anchoring facilities at other havens. The treaty ports, old and new, were given exemption of the Lijin levies, and new regulations were provided for the levy of duties on opium in China. Beijing agreed to send an ambassador to London, whose first protocol obligation was to tender an apology on behalf of the Chinese emperor for the murder of Margary.

The Treaty of Nanjing in 1842, the chain-treaties of Tianjin (1858) and Beijing (1860) and the Chefoo Convention (1876) stand out as the three landmarks of the Treaty Era. In a way they also mark the three different stages of integration of China into the economic order of *Pax Britannica.* In the first settlement, Britain consolidated her victory of the Opium War by establishing in the Chinese government the dignity and the touch-me-not-ness of the opium trade on the one hand, and on the other by commencing a new economic order in China with Hong Kong and Shanghai and other treaty ports controlling the lion's share of China's external trade. In the second settlement, this new economic order was further consolidated with British outposts (the treaty ports) forming a network to control the Chinese economy according to the needs of British industrial and commercial expansion. A British national's taking over administration of Chinese maritime customs amounted to a British control over the Chinese tariff, demolishing any protection to indigenous industry. Meanwhile, opium trade was legalized, and China officially converted into a nation of opium smokers. The Chefoo Convention which represented the third settlement enabled Britain to further penetrate into the Yangtze valley, the richest region in China.

From the political angle, the evolution of the Treaty System in China moved along a cycloid periodically passing through the three directions of (i) threat, (ii) fight, and (iii) agreement. The Chefoo Convention can be regarded as the apogee of the cycloid at which the distance between threat and agreement got substantially shortened, escaping fighting. Britain stabilized the Treaty System at a moderate cost of two Opium Wars. If there had not been the Boxer Movement at the end of the 19th century, China and Britain would not have become belligerents once more. A durable peace was wrought by the Treaty System, albeit a very different kind of peace from the dream of the Manchu rulers. The Manchu rulers found that they had bought peace only by obeying the orders of the British diplomats. The arrogance of the British officers in China was comparable to the British Nabobs in India, which indicates that the Treaty System in China was only a variation of British Raj in India. Treaty Imperialism or Informal Imperialism was a fact beyond dispute.

IV

Let us now examine the components of the treaty system. It combined the following political devices to facilitate imperialist interests to fasten their tentacles on the Chinese economy: *(a)* treaty diplomacy, *(b)* treaty ports, *(c)* tariff control, *(d)* interference in Chinese jurisprudence, and *(e)* interference in China's foreign affairs.

The Fairbankian perspective would think this a necessity as the Chinese diplomatic tradition was as unmanageable according to modern norms of international intercourse as the monkey's indisciplined behaviour. Superficially this has a point. But when we cross-examine the international behaviour of Britain and other western powers, we can see that the only norm in international relations was might is right. The most unequal aspect of the unequal treaties was the absence of reciprocity.

There was only one-way traffic, although on paper it did not look so. The treaties were in no way binding prodigal China to international behaviour. They rather wrought the tradition of direct interference in a sovereign country's affairs.

Contrary to Fairbank's observation, the Chinese government was utterly unprepared for the western treaty diplomatic offensive. There was no foreign ministry in Beijing, and foreign affairs had always been entrusted to the viceroy of the two Guang provinces, because Guangzhou, where the viceroy's office was based, was the only Chinese port where European traders (except the Russians) were admitted during the "Canton (Guangzhou) Trade Period". One of the results of the second settlement was the establishment of *Zongli yamen* in the imperial court which was China's first modern foreign office.

The treaty ports constituted an important part of the Treaty System. The abnormality of such ports violated all norms of international behaviour. Naming specific Chinese ports to be opened to British shipping in Sino-British treaties on the pretext that China should open to the free trade of Britain was already imperialist aggression. But this was not all.

Politically, the centre of gravity in each treaty port lay in the administrative apparatus which the foreign powers (mainly Britain) had established around the personality of the foreign consul(s). These consuls of young age and low ranking (according to their home hierarchical structure) wielded no less political influence than their colleagues in other countries, say India. By political influence we exclude direct participation in routine domestic Chinese affairs which is what Fairbank means by Britain being "far away from dominant in the day-to-day situation". But the day-to-day situation in the political field was gradually being altered through imperialist influence resulting in a centrifugal tendency which culminated in the famous declaration of neutrality by six southern Chinese provinces at a time when the allied army of eight foreign countries attacked Chinese capital in 1900. The day-to-day situation of those crucial years was vitiated by the political dominance radiated from the treaty ports. If in times of hostility, Britain and other imperialist powers could divide the loyalty of Chinese top ranking politicians, the former's political influence during peace time would be much greater. The treaty ports had played an important role in forming an undeclared British sphere of influence in the Yangtze valley much before the notorious scramble for "cutting the Chinese melon" took place at the end of the 19th century.

Moreover, any politician of vision could see that the Manchu rulers were like the setting sun, while the pro-western forces were like the rising stars in China. The treaty ports symbolized the superiority of the economic, political, and military power of western imperialism and also a daily reminder of the disastrous wars and humiliating defeats to Li Hongzhang and others, who seemed to be warned by the intruders with the ancient Chinese maxim; "If you obey me, you prosper; if you defy me, you die." They were coerced and coaxed to do the imperialist bidding.

Before we take up the economic aspects of the treaty ports, let us discuss an ugly spot allegedly associated with China's treaty ports, viz. there were prohibited areas with open notification that Chinese and dogs were denied admission.

Economically, the treaty ports first and foremost role was to integrate the Chinese economy into the imperialist world order. In this aspect, the difference between "formal" and "informal" empires was even thinner than in the political aspect. In the formal empire, say India, metropolitan became her landlord and collected land revenue from Indian soil. This was not done in China, and here was a major difference. However, as I have dealt with elsewhere, the Indian goose was kept alive and fat to lay golden eggs for Britain permanently by diverting the relentless drain into China through "opium imperialism". The result was that the informal British empire in China shared the burden with the formal Indian colony to ensure periodical remittances of surplus revenue from India to Britain. Opium imperialism had, thus equalized the disparity between the "informal" China and "formal" India, both of which became "equal" partners in paying annual tribute to the Exchequer in London. Only the nature of the tribute remained different—Indians paying land revenue, Chinese paying opium revenue.

Coming to exploitation through commercial and financial avenues, there was no inherent disparity between the formal and informal situations. Britain, for instance, could exploit informal China and formal India with equal ease if she could neutralize interference from the Chinese political authorities which were not under the direct control of Britain. Here comes the relevance of the treaty system. Every treaty concluded between Britain and China bore a central theme, *i.e.,* to neutralize Chinese political interference in British trade to the maximum possible extent. The meaning of "free trade" lies in her freedom from Chinese political interference. Having achieved this, the disparity between the formal and informal situations became non-existent. For, we know that Adam Smith (1723-90) and his disciples had already gifted to mankind a global exploitation system through the manipulation of money and goods. This system can effectively employ the talents of the whole world to earn super-profits for a handful of people who only exercise remote control. On-the-spot presence is not required for financial, industrial and commercial monopolists to exploit a far-flung area. The Jardine-Matheson Company could achieve optimum operation both in British India and "informal" British-China.

The treaty ports played a dual role in facilitating the above mentioned universal exploitation in China. First, they acted as protectors of the freedom of such an exploitation, warding off local political interference. Secondly, they provided bases of operation for international enterprises. The treaty ports facilitated the establishment of commercial and financial networks which linked individual Chinese small-scale producers and consumers with economic headquarters in the Atlantic. For instance, the Jardine Company could get direct supply of raw silk from silk-worm farmers in the Yangtze valley, and British and Indian cotton yarn was delivered directly to Chinese handloom weavers in the vicinity of treaty concessions. In this way, the economic integration of China into international finance and commercial capitalism was complete as that of India. By providing bases for international economic forces, the treaty ports themselves emerged as new economic centres in China. The Chinese economy became an export-import-oriented treaty-port economy, while the treaty ports became economically, even more than politically, China's centres of gravity.

Similarly, Hart and his Maritime Customs Services were like a double-edged sword of imperialism. One edge protected the competitive advantages of western partcularly British, imports, including opium, and the other pushed China deeper and deeper into indebtedness to western, particularly. British, financial, oligarchy. China's maritime customs revenue was not only used as mortgage against foreign loans, but was also made to pay war indemnities which the imperialist powers had imposed on China through the treaties. Thus by allowing foreigners to control the tariff, the Chinese government had not only mortgaged China's tariff autonomy, but mortgaged the maritime customs revenue itself.

Imperialist interference in China's jurisprudence was effected through the treaty provision of extra-territorial rights to foreigners in China. The genesis of extraterritoriality can only be traced to the arrogance of the imperialist culture and social Darwinism. Those Europeans who were law-abiding at home had the propensity to defy all laws abroad under the influence of imperialist culture. Social Darwinism made them disrespect non-Christian and non-white authorities. Even during the Canton Trade period, British traders had developed the touch-me-not attitude before Chinese justice. The idea of extra-territorial jurisdiction in China originated from a proposal to the British government by the East India Company's Canton Council headed by W.H. Pigou in 1784 after a European (perhaps British) had been executed by the Chinese government in the well-known *Lady Hughes* incident.[2] Although it took sixty long years for Britain to put the proposal into practice in China, the *Lady Hughes* incident was the fountain-head of British defiance of Chinese justice, which grew stronger with the expansion of British commercial and military power.

That extra-territoriality was an expression of imperialist touch-me-not-ism can be proved by Article IX of the Sino-British Treaty of Tianjin (1858), which says that Chinese government officials can arrest unlawful Britons on Chinese soil but should not subject them "to any *ill-usage* in excess of necessary restraint" (italics added). This was deterrent enough for Chinese officials. As the Chinese officials had no power to punish a foreign offender, but had to hand him over to the nearest foreign consul of the offender's nationality, they were not too sure what the foreigner might report. If he complained about ill-usage (a very ambiguous term) to the British Consul, and the latter in turn accused the Chinese officials of violation of treaty provisions, the result would be disastrous for the concerned Chinese officials. This explains why during the Treaty Era, few Chinese officials dared apprehend foreign offenders. Even if they did, few offenders got punished by the authorities of their own nationality. China under the Treaty System was a paradise for foreign criminals.

Treaty of extraterritoriality was not only exemption of foreign offenders from lawful punishment of the land, it also constituted a foreign interference in China's internal affairs because of the invocation of extraterritorial rights to protect the "protégés". Foreigners could name naturalised persons and even Chinese as their proteges, who could then enjoy the same judicial immunity as the foreigners did. This protege clause of the Treaty System gave green signal to the missionaries to meddle with legal disputes between Christian converts and their non-Christian compatriots. Such interventions were mainly responsible for the rise of anti-Christian riots which were widespread in China at the end of the 19th century.

China maintained her sovereignty in foreign affairs only in name. The treaty powers not only dictated terms to the Chinese government when they dealt with it in bilateral matters, they also did not remain indifferent while watching China's transactions with others. The treaty ports in China were all controlled by British consuls, who only tolerated parallel control by the French in Shanghai but nowhere else.

There was a peculiar British relationship with Beijing which other powers could not emulate. The Treaty System was a British strategy to integrate China into *Pax Britannica* according to the dynamics of British economic expansion, while her European counterparts came to China only to claim a share of the spoils. Treaty diplomacy, treaty ports, treaty tariff control, and treaty extraterritoriality were all British political mechanics of, by and for British interests. Others who came to share the spoils only obtained fringe benefits.

Treaty diplomacy, treaty ports, treaty tariff, treaty extra-territoriality and the treaty system's overall interference in China's internal and external affairs are the indisputable evidence of the existence of a well-conceived and comprehensive infrastructure of governance which the imperialist powers, particularly Britain, had imposed on China. Whether one calls it treaty imperialism or integration imperialism, or informal imperialism, or "free trade" imperialism, or even Synarchy, makes little difference.

V

British irresponsible imperialism over China represented the magic power of universal management of capitalist economy, in addition to Britain's ability to stabilize the existing socio-political order in China. Accumulated experience in the Far East had made Britons experts in dealing with various segments of China's ruling elite, how to deter them, coax them, divide them, deceive them and disarm them. British imperialism was not face to face with the Chinese masses in the "indirect" treaty rule, with the Chinese ruling elite forming a barrier. When the masses showed hostility to the new governance, British arms were ready to deal with them without mercy. But the Chinese casualties under irresponsible imperialism were caused mainly by British bullets, not so much by British killing—bullets were fired on Britain's behalf by Chinese and Indian soldiers. In this aspect, Liang Qichao's conception of ten thousand Britons versus four hundred million Chinese is misconceived. For, during the 19th century not even one hundred thousand among the four hundred million Chinese had united to fight the ten thousand. Before they could confront the British, they had first to overthrow the national ruling machine, which was a gigantic task. British irresponsible imperialism had, in fact, integrated itself with China's national ruling machine in dealing with the masses. Such an integration had given British irresponsible imperialism vitality to survive until the overthrow of the national ruling machine.

Irresponsible imperialism, in this sense, is a sophisticated alliance of native and foreign rulers. By alliance I do not mean

Synarchy, which is a culture-oriented perspective, while the alliance between imperialism and national ruling elite in China had a deep socio-economic root-exploiting the masses for their parasitical but indulgent existence. Of course, the alliance was no real commonwealth of co-prosperity. It was a combination of collusion and collision, charged by hot-and-cold struggle-compromise and love-hate relationships. But there was give-and-take, mutual sharing of economic gains and mutual reinforcement of political security. The superiority of irresponsible imperialism over the responsible one lies in the fact that the indigenous power structure is by and large preserved intact.

The treaty system in 19th-century China had only added an aspect of remote control to the existing ruling system of the land. The strength and weakness of this system thus centred round over-dependence on China's *ancien regime.* The British irresponsible governance in China virtually died the day the Manchu government was overthrown. Thereafter Japan and United States made attempts to revitalize irresponsible imperialism in China under their aegis without much success, simply because China's internal political situation was undergoing a convulsion. Finally, it was the American guns captured by the communist army which boomed the death knell of both the *ancien regime* and irresponsible imperialism in China.

Let us now examine the inter-relationship between the imperialist power's responsible and irresponsible overseas governance. Although we have conceived irresponsible governance as a superior and more sophisticated form of imperialist domination as compared with responsible government presided over by the metropolitan power, we should not forget that the latter is the foundation of the former. The Treaty System in China would have been unthinkable if there had not been British Raj in India. We have often compared India and China as a pair of colonial twins which was a fact. However, in the international order of *Pax Britannica,* the two countries were placed in different roles by the London rulers. This may be briefly spelled out.

In many ways, British conquest of China was a corollary of her conquest of India. First, there was the triangular trade and opium. Suffice it to say that if there had been no Indian opium the pattern of British aggression against China would have taken a totally different turn. Second, the two Sino-British war nicked opium which had laid the foundation of the Treaty System could never have been fought had India not been a British colony. For, the British expeditionary forces were assembled in India and mostly manned by Indian sailors and soldiers. Third, the security forces in the British concessions of the treaty ports were dominantly Indian, thousands of turbaned Sikhs being employed as security police, traffic constables and gatemen, earning the nickname Redheaded (because of the red turban) among local Chinese. Fourth, India was British Empire's military, political and economic headquarters in the East; the British officers in China, including the Governor of Hong Kong, had to take orders from India. In a way, India was a step closer to the metropolis than China. Fifth, there was a difference between "responsible" and "irresponsible" imperialism in Britain's economic strategy. As I have discussed in my last article, in the scheme of British policy-makers Indians were to be the major consumers of British cotton textiles, while Chinese were to be the major consumers of Indian opium. One of the aims of selling Indian opium in China was to augment the Indian purchasing power for British textiles.

Irresponsible imperialism was made more irresponsible by the linkage between the treaty system and opium imperialism. This is illustrated by an observation of Fairbank: "In the cases of the consular service and opium trade there is some verisimilitude, for the superintendent of British trade, who was concurrently H.M.'s minister plenipotentiary of China and governor of Hong Kong, was the administrative head to whom the consuls looked for instructions, while the beautiful harbour of Hong Kong and its city of Victoria were the entrepot where opium cargoes from India were stored to await shipment to the receiving stations [in China]" (*Trade and Diplomacy,* p. 156)

To prove this verisimilitude, let us cite "The Hong Kong Government Ordinance No. 2 of 1858" enacted by 'His Excellency Sir John Bowring, Knight, LL.D., Governor and Commander in Chief of the Colony of Hong Kong and its dependencies, and Vice Admiral of the same, Her Majesty's plenipotentiary and chief superintendent of the trade of British Subjects in China." The title of the Ordinance reads: "An Ordinance for Licensing and Regulating the Sale of prepared Opium." Explaining the purpose of issuing the Ordinance in his letter addressed to his superior authority in London, Bowring regarded opium as "an article pre-eminently suited for taxation" by the Hong Kong government. He also enunciated a new policy of freeing the trade in "raw opium" (meaning the opium imported from India) from fiscal interference and subjecting "prepared opium" (meaning the opium extract prepared by Chinese for the pipes of the opium-smokers) to strict Hong Kong government monopoly. The Ordinance (approved by the Crown) armed Bowring with an additional authority—licensing the trading enterprises "to boil and prepare opium, and to sell and retail opium so boiled and prepared."[3] Bowring thus became a six-headed prince of darkness with the sixth head as the licensing chief for preparing and selling opium extracts in China in addition to the five heads already listed in his Ordinance.

Responsible and irresponsible imperialism are mutually complementary, just as India and China were in 19th century within the *Pax Britannica.* As the British enterprises in China were unthinkable without the foundation of British Raj in India, the latter's survival and prosperity were equally unthinkable without the opium trade and treaty system in China. Money and goods flowed from the domain of Britain's responsible government in India into the domain of Britain's irresponsible governance in China and vice versa. Both flows formed a confluence of super-profits for the metropolis.

If imperialism is the highest stage of development of capitalism irresponsible imperialism is the highest stage of imperialist development. The treaty system in China was the highest stage of British imperialism. However, by resorting to irresponsible imperialism in China, Britain was expanding her economic power and political influence to the extent of imbalance—much beyond what the narrow base of the British Isles could sustain. When the Treaty System in China collapsed at the onslaught of Chinese nationalist movement and with the exhaustion of the First World War, it was the beginning of a downward trend for *Pax Britannica.* The British lion was truly the jungle king of the predatory international order when the treaty system in China yielded the best results for her in the last three decades of the 19th century. With the loss of both China and India by 1947, the British lion shrank to the size of a cat. After Britain no imperialist power has had any success with irresponsible imperialism, which now virtually vanishes. The Treaty System in China was, thus, the only success story of irresponsible imperialism. Its rise and fall deserves a more careful and exhaustive study than is possible in the present essay.

References

1. Tan Chung, *China and the Brave New World: A Study of the Origins of the Opium War 1840-42* (Allied Publishers, New Delhi, 1978), p. 220.
2. H.B. Morse, *The Chronicles of the East India Company Trading to China, 1735-1834* (Oxford, 1926), Vol. 2, p. 107.
3. *Irish University Parliamentary Papers: Area Studies, China* (1972). Vo1. 31, pp. 364-374.

7

European Harpies Sucking Chinese Juice : A Case of Commercial and Finance Imperialism*

There is a general feeling of difficulties among the students of nineteenth-century China to concretize the Hobsonian economic imperialism. The difficulty, first of all, arises from the interdisciplinary nature of the concern—involving history, political science and economics which requires the student to have an integral approach of the three disciplines. But, there is difficulty at another level. Whenever a historical phenomenon is traced to its economic root it immediately acquires a tinge of determinism which is shun by non-Marxist scholarship. As a result, whereas on other topics of 19th century Chinese history non-Marxist scholars have made a great contribution to enrich their studies, no one has made a systematic study of the economic aspect of imperialism in China throughout the 19th century. On the other hand, the Marxist scholars in the English languages world may seem to have been more pre-occupied with other academic concerns than caring to look at the history of 19th century China in any depth. All this, perhaps, explains why there is no single book (in English language at least) specially dedicated to the study of commercial and finance imperialism in China. However, we study the dimensions of history according to historical facts, but not to the availability of books. The fact that there is no good book of reference on such an important issue is all the more challenge for the students of Chinese history to apply their minds on the topic.

*It is an abbreviated version of the article that was published in Tan Chung, *Triton and Dragon* (Delhi, 1986).

I

Imperialism is a concept which "assumes a consistent, calculated master-plan guided by an evil spirit of acquisitiveness and expansion", as two well-known European experts on imperialism, Richard Koebner and Helmut Dan Schmidt have put it.[1]. This shows that even as a general conception, the phenomenon of imperialism must have its economic content, *i.e.* the acquisitiveness of wealth for one nation at the cost of another. However, the discussion of economic imperialism has to go deeper. We know that although the nineteenth century had already seen the birth of imperialism, the theory of imperialism was only born along with the birth of the twentieth century. The father of this theory was the celebrated English economist, John Atkinson Hobson (1858-1940), whose literary output on imperialism appeared in 1900-1, culminating in the publication of his famous book *Imperialism* in 1902, Hobson says :

> There is not a war, a revolution, an anarchist assassination, or any other public shock, which is not gainful to these men; they are *harpies who suck** their gains from every new forced expenditure and every sudden disturbance of public credit.[2]

The men described by Hobson as 'harpies' were the 'financial dealers', *i.e.* the 'investors' and the holders of "business capital", whom Hobson regarded as "the gravest single factor in the economics of imperialism."[3] Although Hobson was regarded in his times as an economic heretic, no one can say that he was no economist. In fact, he was one of the greatest economists on the development of capitalism, which, to Hobson, was the "taproot" of imperialism".[4] So, imperialism as a theory (as different from an ordinary concept) was first conceived by an economist, not historian, and should be treated as an important subject of economic history. If before Hobson imperialism was just a general concept and sentiment, the *post-Imperialism* (1902) academic studies have turned them into a theoretical framework which has its primary concern on economic

---

*Italics added.

imperialism. If we bear this in mind, we have opened up new vistas for the study of imperialism in nineteenth century China.

Even the Marxist scholars should not contest the idea that it was Karl Marx who had anticipated Hobson's theory of economic imperialism. Although Marx did not use the specific word of "imperialism"—a term made fashionable by Hobson and Lenin in the twentieth century—he had already laid the foundation of the theory of imperialism in his various writings.

There are three aspects in Marx's thinking which have a close affinity to our discussion. In the first place, Marx saw the interlinkage between the birth of the capitalist economic system and colonialism which is the same thing as imperialism.

In the second place, Marx, in his article "The British Rule in India" (1853), already made a statement which was comparable to what we have quoted from Hobson earlier. Said Marx :

> All the civil wars, invasions, revolutions, conquests, famines, strangely complex, rapid and destructive as the successive [British] action in Hindustan may appear, did not go deeper than its surface. England has broken down the entire framework of Indian society, without any symptoms of reconstitution yet appearing.[5]

In the third place, he had already conceived the idea of what we may call "commercial imperialism". Marx used the expression of "corrosive influence of commerce" which was a "revolutionized" force of the capitalist industrial production.

While we have traced Hobson's theory on imperialism to the writing of Marx, we should also see how Hobson has developed Marx's ideas. One important contribution of Hobson lies in his highlighting the key role played by the "financiers" in generating the force of imperialism. Hobson listed the financial interest as the economic nucleus of imperialism, and it was to this nucleus that other economic interests like iron, shipbuilding, armament industry, military services etc. were attached. "These strong definite economic interests are the principal propellers of aggressive imperialism", observed Hobson.[6]

Taking a cue from Marx, Hobson described imperialism as "the combination of economic and political forces" the sources of which lay "in the selfish interests of certain industrial, financial, and professional classes, seeking private advantages out of a policy of imperial expansion and using this same policy to protect them in their economic, political and social privileges against the pressure of democracy."[7] Here, we have the sociological starting point of the concept of imperialism. If we are permitted to dot the i's and cross the t's of Hobson's basic framework for an extension of it to the scene of nineteenth-century China, we can safely assert that all the British and other European 'military aggrandizement' from the Opium War down to the eight-nation armed expedition to the Chinese capital in 1900 arose from the avarice of certain European gentlemen (or social classes according to Hobson,) who were obsessed with their capital. This, indeed, is what we mean by "commercial and finance imperialism" as a contrast to ordinary, non-militant and non-aggressive activities of trade and commerce and capital investment, if indeed such harmless trade and investment exist in international intercourse.

No serious historian, whether Marxist or non-Marxist, can ignore Lenin's work on *Imperialism, The Highest Stage of Capitalism* which has, on the one hand, so much improved upon Marx and Engels in the understanding of a capitalist society, and, on the other, driven the apologists of imperialism to a tight corner. Lenin did not talk of Marx's 'capitalism', which entered a new phase in Lenin's time: "the new capitalism definitely superseded the old" in his words.[8] Lenin's starting point was that from the 1860s there began the 'modern monopoly' in European economies. "The first important period of development of monopoly commenced with the international industrial depression of the seventies and lasted until the beginning of the '90s.'[9] The boom at the end of nineteenth century saw the firm establishment of monopolist capitalism and the transformation of capitalism into imperialism, added Lenin.[10]

Lying at the taproot of this transformation was the changed role played by the banks, *i.e.* the financiers, from that of 'humble middlemen [in the making of payment] into a handful of monopolists' and completed the 'fundamental processes in the growth of capitalism into capitalist imperialism.'[11] This transformation coincided with what Lenin termed as the 'personal union' of the banks with the 'biggest industrial and commercial enterprises' followed by another 'personal union' of the banking-industrial combine with the policy-making government, thus creating the 'financial oligarchy' and making the "finance capital" the uncrowned king of the capitalist society.[12]

In this article, I have an occasion to examine P.T. Moon's China chapter in totality primarily to build up our case of finance imperialism than offering a critical appraisal to Moon's scholarship. Moon has divided the West's invasion of China into two phases :

First phase (1840-80)—'not true imperialism',

Second phase (1880 onwards)—'genuine imperialism'.[13]

Moon characterizes the nature of Sino-British conflict during the First Opium war as a dispute over the "real issue" of the 'commercial open door'. To him, Britain was generous enough only to exact "an indemnity" and also the extra-territoriality which was very necessary for British traders to live in China, "for Chinese law and Chinese punishments were incomprehensible and seemed *barbarous* to foreigners."[14] And the Chinese should thank their stars that British troops had refrained from taking "a large slice of [Chinese] territory" which they "could have" done, but, instead, were only "content with the tiny island of Hong Kong".[15] Interestingly, Moon should think this manner of "open door" "almost the opposite of imperialism"[16], betraying his own generosity for imperialist behaviours that seizing a small island by force from a big country like China was regarded by him as no impairment of the noble character of Britain. Thus, all the concessions which the Western powers exacted from China in all the treaties which the former forced upon the latter from the 1840s down to the 1880s, not excluding the cessions of quite a bit of Chinese territories to Britain, France and Russia, are described by Moon as the "first-fruits of the opening of the Far East". Only "later came imperialism."[17]

However, there is a saving grace in Moon's open-door generosity which says : "But the opening of the Far East led inevitably to a desire for monopoly of markets, mines, and railway-building, hence for monopolistic 'spheres of influence,' and also for naval bases, and in some cases territory. This was genuine imperialism, and it has been the dominant factor in the Far East since the 1880's."[18] Here, we notice that Moon is at variance with his own paradigm. In one place, he seems to have given the impression that there were first the opposite-of-imperialism open-door first-fruits (territorial conquests notwithstanding) to be followed by genuine imperialist aggressions. In another place, he has actually regarded the open-door as the opening to genuine imperialism culminating in the post-1880 period which was dominantly imperialistic in character.

There was first the initiatives of the European powers to build railways in China from 1876 onwards which invariably tagged with the seeking of rights for mining. This kind of railway building, as Moon sees, "led naturally to the marking out of 'spheres of interest' ".[19]

Moon illustrates his point by recounting how Britain threw all her diplomatic weight in addition to the employment of the gunboat threat to make the Manchu government yield to Britain the right of railway construction between Beijing and Hankou (Hankow) at the end of nineteenth country:

Finally, Moon takes stock of 'imperialism in the Far East', and criticises European and Japanese imperialists for looking "primarily to immediate profits" and concerning with "their own generation". "The stakes in which they have been interested are the Chinese railways, and mines, and commerce, and loans, and naturally, the strategic and territorial accompaniments of such economic affairs."[20]

We see in these discussions Moons paradigm of 'genuine imperialism': (1) the selfish interest of the financiers, (2) the close collusion between the imperialist financiers and their governments, and (3) the "strategic and territorial accompaniments" (meaning political, diplomatic and military aggressions) of 'economic affairs' (meaning commercial and financial aggrandizement).

Moon's last-minute inclusion of "commerce" along with

railway concessions, loans and territorial conquests, etc., in the Chinese scene at the end of the nineteenth century is not only interesting, but also significant. It is but an admission of the existence of commercial imperialism in nineteenth-century China. We all know that British and other European commercial activities in China did not suddenly spring out at the end of the nineteenth century. The commercial activities were the starting point of Europe's head-on collision with China. The way in which the British navy was called upon to gain railway right concessions at the turn of the century repeated its earlier role to push forward the interest of the British opium traders half a century ago. The manner in which the British diplomats served the interest of British financiers at the end of the nineteenth century had many preceding examples in the 1840s and 1850s which resulted in the legalization of opium trade in China.

When Lenin propounded his theory of imperialism, his focus was on the internal development of capitalism. He would not have denied that the external behaviour-pattern of imperialist powers remained quite consistent throughout the nineteenth century as Hobson saw it. Lenin's capitalism-transforming-into-imperialism is anologous to a chick's transforming into a hen. The chick does not lay eggs while the hen does. There is a qualitative change. Yet, the food and other habits of a hen remains the same since the day she becomes a chick. Lenin's highest stage of capitalism, *i.e.,* imperialism, was qualitative different from the earlier stage of capitalism while its aggressive policies towards China and other colonies or semi-colonies were inherent from its chick days. Hence, tracing imperialism backwards to its formative period does not contradict Lenin's theory of imperialism in spirit. As finance imperialism was still in its mother's womb during the three decades between the Opium War and the birth of financial oligarchy, it was commercial imperialism which was the chick of the hen of finance imperialism.

Our above discussion has attempted to pursue the line of imperialism theory to its logical end by the method of transposition of the categories propounded by Marx, Hobson and Lenin. This exercise has helped us to grasp the dynamic force of imperialism in 19th century China, viz. it began with commercial imperialism from even the pre-Treaty days, while this commercial imperialism generated finance imperialism from 1880 onwards. The capitalist mode of production was the root of both commercial and finance imperialism.

II

We may be allowed to paraphrase Lenin's famous adage to that finance imperialism was the highest stage of commercial imperialism in nineteenth-century China. If this can stand, then we can say that commercial imperialism was the lower or preparatory stage of finance imperialism. Although 1880 can be regarded as the watershed, there could actually be no dividing line between commercial imperialism and finance imperialism. The development was from quantitative to qualitative changes. Finance imperialism had its embryonic manifestations before 1880, while commercial imperialism continued to exist and prosper after 1880 in the semi-colonial situation in China.

There is almost no need of any theory to establish a case of commercial and finance imperialism in nineteenth-century China. China herself is the most eloquent witness. Before the East India Company sent opium to China, the country had been one of the richest of the world. Opium and other forms of imperialism brought her down slope and slided into the company of one of the poorest among nations. Nineteenth-century China was a typical case of the development of underdevelopment under the capitalist-colonialist-imperialist system to borrow the words of Andre Gunder Frank.

Frank thinks that imperialism must be understood not as the empire of some particular country but essentially as a certain kind of relation between the metropolis or its members and the periphery. Hobson, Bukharin and Lenin, says Frank, have used the concept of imperialism 'to refer to certain worldwide relations of the end of the 19th and beginning of the 20th century, a time of colonial expansion by the industrialized or industrializing metropole".[21] He conceives of the existence of a "single worldwide capitalist-colonialist-imperialist system which came to dominate most of the globe. "Only the development of socialism has permitted any people already suffering from metropolitan produced peripheral underdevelopment to escape from the structure of the world capitalist system and from its consequent underdevelopment."[22]

First, the world embracing system of imperialism had already come into existence in the 19th century which can hardly be refuted. Moreover, there cannot be any doubt that nineteenth-century China was penetrated and transformed by, integrated into the world imperialist system. The only modification we wish to make vis-a-vis Frank's observations is to push the inauspicious date of this imperialism-China marriage from Frank's starting point...the end of the nineteenth century...backwards by several decades, dating back at least to the beginning of the treaty system, if not earlier. Let us dot Frank's i's and cross his t's to transpose this point of his to the nineteenth-century Chinese scene.

From the end of the nineteenth century onwards there developed the 'political incorporation of China' and the penetration of Western missionaries, and the cut off of Chinese control over her 'dependencies', after the establishment of a large and interrelated body" of foreign investments in shipping, manufacturing, mining, railways and banking which also formed a part of China's economic incorporation into the imperialist world order.[23]

Apart from nineteenth-century China's integration into the economic system of international imperialism, the second point to take off from the base of Frank's framework is the effectiveness of trade being used as an integral part of the process for foreign imperialism to achieve the miracle of taking away from China "with both hands", viz. first introducing some capital in China's economic development, and then, taking away the gains from China which was more than the initial investment, and using the remaining capital to secure China's dependence on the world capitalist development.

Let us understand the nature of the development of under-development in Chinese economy.

The first and foremost damage was the rampant import of narcotics into China from British India which, as we have so repeatedly stressed, became a reality only courtesy of British imperialism. The name of British Raj goes down in human history as the only shameless government which has openly established a ministry for the large-scale of production and sale of narcotics in international trade. And the sale was virtually exclusively meant for China. It was no coincidence, that out of the three wars Britain has ever waged against China, two of them have been nicknamed as "Opium Wars". It was because of these Opium Wars and their intimidating effect and various treaty provisions which have helped the British narcotic trading interests create the following world records.

The first record created in 1867 was that narcotics amounted to 46 per cent of the total imports of China which was 31,994,576 taels of silver in value. If this import cost was to be borne by every Chinese at that time, it would mean that every two Chinese families (assuming the average size of a Chinese family having six members) were impoverished in that year by one tael of silver, which was no small damage, judging from the fact that the majority of the Chinese population in that year could not earn as much as ten taels of silver for their livelihood. Yet, the nation had to bear still higher import costs of opium in the years to come.

In 1879, the total value of opium import into China reached the dazzling height of 36,536,615 taels of silver which was the highest record of not only the import of China, but, perhaps the trade in any single item of commodity in any bilateral trade among nations in the nineteenth century. Soon after the turn of the century, the narcotic import into China increased further to cross the limit of 40 million taels of silver in a single year, and the British commercial imperialism celebrated the year of Chinese revolution (1911) by importing 48,256,745 taels worth of narcotics into China which is the highest record of narcotic trade in human history. Before such startling statistics, could any scholar was able to maintain that there was no commercial imperialism in Chinese history, but everything was legitimate, justifiable, equitable and mutually beneficial to international trade and commerce between China and the European powers according to the norms of the free world.

The second economic damage which China suffered in the nineteenth century under commercial imperialism was caused by the ruinous pattern of import and export trade pertaining to raw cotton and cotton goods. For the first time in Chinese history, China which had never been able to supply enough raw material to her cotton textile handicrafts industry turned to be a major exporter of raw cotton from 1860 onwards. In 1879, the total value of Chinese export of raw cotton leaped three times of that of the previous year, and reached 13,161,051 taels of silver. And the highest export of raw cotton by China in the nineteenth century was registered in 1882, amounting to 24,811,595 taels of silver in value. We know that one of the largest Chinese industries before 1840 was the cotton textile industry which used to provide employment and livelihood to millions of Chinese. The new emerging enthusiasm in exporting raw cotton from China (which was surely the master stroke of British imperialism as it had done in India) would inevitably ruin the traditional Chinese economy and make innumerable Chinese suffer in livelihood.

Coupling with this large scale of export of the much needed raw cotton from China was the unprecedented heavy imports of cotton fabrics and yarn from Britain and British India. The annual value of import of British cotton textiles (*i.e.* cloths) crossed 20 million taels of silver in the 1880s, 30 million taels in the first half of the 1890s, and 40 million taels in the last five years of the nineteenth century. The annual import of cotton cloths of various descriptions into China touched the highest point in 1899, registering a total value of 48,857,835 taels. This sudden flooding of the Chinese markets with British cotton cloths was accompanied by the introduction of a new item into China's foreign trade, *i.e.* the cotton yarn produced from both Britain and British India. This import crossed the two million bar in annual value in the 1970s, the three million bar in 1879, the four million bar in 1881, the five million bar in 1883, the seven million bar in 1884, the 12 million bar in 1887, and reached 13,427,150 taels in 1888.

The pincer movement of British commercial imperialism by exporting large quantities of raw cotton from China and importing even larger quantities of cotton textile goods into her was a severe blow to the traditional Chinese economy. In the first place, China was exporting her raw materials cheaply and was made to pay for foreign finished products at a premium.

Secondly, China was suddenly transformed from a famed textile exporter in historical times into a heavy importer of cotton textiles which meant total displacement of the traditional cotton textile handicrafts industry of China. Cotton textile industry has been a vital economic sector for all countries. Restrictions to foreign imports have been a practice since many centuries earlier down to the present day. Even the United States time and again resists foreign demands in enhancing import quotas of cotton fabrics and garments. China would have done the same if she had been an independent sovereign country in the second half of the nineteenth century. Because of commercial imperialism she became helpless in protecting her domestic cotton textile industry.

One may argue that China's being transformed from a traditional exporter into a major importer of cotton textiles in the nineteenth and twentieth centuries was mainly due to the backwardness of Chinese technology vis-a-vis the advanced technology of Britain, which had nothing to do with imperialism. This is sheer oversimplification. The modern Indian experience shows that given certain protection and facilities, the *khadi* (handspun yarn) and handloom (handloom weaving mill-spun yarn) products can compete with mill-produced fabrics both in the domestic and international markets. This is because the cotton fabrics are a highly sensitive ecological and sociological commodity, the charm of which is created by complex factors involving both mechanic efficacy and human skill in addition to such cultural elements like artistic sensitivity, responses to colour etc. Modern technology can enjoy certain advantages, but not absolute advantage. This largely explains why in the present-day international market cotton textiles from developing countries like India and China have an edge over the same produced by highly developed industrial countries. The large-scale imports of textiles and exports of cotton by China during the last few decades of the nineteenth and first few decades of the twentieth centuries represented a highly abnormal development typical of that of a colony under the assault of commercial imperialism.

The statistics of the extraordinary trade in cottons we have just now seen are symptomic of the twin-damage to Chinese economy. On the one hand, the traditional Chinese cotton textile industry received neither protection nor facility to compete with its modern British counterpart, hence, for nearly a century the name of China virtually disappeared from the front-line cotton textile exporters. (But, with China's gaining liberation from the imperialist yoke in the last three and half decades, the Chinese cotton textiles have once again become many a splendid thing in international market.) On the other hand, for the larger part of a century from the Opium War onwards the entire Chinese population had been exposed to direct exploitation of' British cotton textile monopolist interests until the founding of the People's Republic of China. We see clearly the shadow of Andre Frank's metropole-exploiting-periphery scenario. This reminds us what the British hero of Opium War and Treaty of Nanjing, Sir Henry Pottinger, said to the Manchester industrialists in 1844 that he had opened up the oyster of China and it was for the British merchants and industrialists to gather the pearl, that "all the mills in Lancashire could not make stocking stuff sufficient for one of its [China's] provinces."[24] The irony implicit in Pottinger's braggadocio was that British cotton textile industry had to depend on imperialism to conquer the markets of China.

The importance of large scale imports of British cotton textiles into China deserves to be further examined both from the British angle and from the Chinese angle. We know that both Marx and Engels have evinced great interest in analysing the British cotton textile expansion into India and China, and the Marxists have always regarded it as a classical example of modern colonialist and imperialist exploitation of the colonies and semi-colonies. We must also point out the fact that from the end of the nineteenth century cotton textile imports surpassed opium as the largest category of imports into China. Whereas opium was the crowned king of British commodity expansion into China for a whole century from the 1770s to the 1870s, this position was overthrown by cotton textiles from the 1870s down to the eve of the China's communist take-over. If we divide British commercial imperialism into two phases and use the dominant commodity to characterize each phase, it was clearly British opium imperialism followed suit by British cotton-textile imperialism. This transition was itself significant in two ways. First, opium was not an industrial product while cotton-textiles were. Thus, the transition signified China's being ultimately brought under the impact of Industrial Revolution. Secondly, while opium imperialism was barbarous, inhuman and illegal (according to present day standards), the same cannot be said about the cotton-textile imperialism.

III

In discussing the damage of modern imperialism to traditional Chinese economy we have to keep a longer time span in view. Here, we have a serious limitation in this book as our period terminates in 1900 while commercial and finance imperialism, developed further into the 20th century. Finance imperialism, in particular, had just raised its ugly head at the turn of the century. This makes it necessary for us to exceed the limit of the book a little bit, particularly to facilitate our discussion on finance imperialism.

At the outset of this essay we have seen that the institution of banking forms the core of the theory on imperialism. We can only superficially attribute the following imperialist roles to the foreign banks in nineteenth-century China :

1. Absorbing Chinese savings to invest in exploitative ventures to harm Chinese national interest.
2. Issuing and circulating bank notes in China which amounts to minting money of Chinese soil which should have been an exclusive right of the sovereign government of China which was non-existent.
3. Meddling in Chinese government affairs.

About the first role of the foreign banks they had taken full advantage of the fact that there was no Chinese bank on her own soil before 1897. Even after the establishment of Chinese banks the rich Chinese still preferred the foreign banks for better security. For instance, the important courtier Prince Qing (Prince Ch'ing) had deposited 1.2 million taels in the British Hong Kong and Shanghai Banking Corporation at the interest rate of 2%.[25] Chi-ming Hou repeats his contention that foreign investments in China were not substantial, which has been refuted by Dernberger.[26] Granting that Hou's contention is correct, we have here an important factor of foreign banks absorbing local Chinese investment.

About the second imperialist role of foreign banks in China, foreign bank notes functioned as an additional Chinese currency. We know that in the nineteenth century, the Chinese official currency was in the form of copper coins and silver ingots. Even before the Opium War, foreign silver dollars had become popular among Chinese merchants for their convenience and preference by the opium traders. After the opening of China such foreign silver dollars became more popular and had an edge over the twin currency of China. The circulation of foreign bank notes in China as legal tender further strengthened the foreign monetary supremacy. We know that notes can be printed at will, and many modern governments resort to it as deficit financing. But in the Chinese situation such a weapon was controlled in the hands of foreign financial oligarchy while the Chinese government itself did not avail of it. Even Chi-ming Hou concedes that : "The bank notes, whether issued in or brought to China, were tantamount to an export of capital from China,"[27] which is tantamount to recognizing the foreign banks as the instrument of economic drain.

Regarding the third imperialist role of foreign banks, Parker Moon has already told us how the British financiers had commanded the British gunboats to wrest the railway building right from the Chinese government.[28] One of the dominant organizations of British financiers was the Hong Kong and Shanghai Banking Corporation, which still exists and issues Hong Kong dollar-notes today. It was first incorporated in 1864. By 1886, it possessed a deposit of 5 million dollars mainly from the Chinese source. The Bank had two eminent accounts : (1) the Treasury Chest of British government, and (2) the Inspector General of the Chinese Maritime Customs, Sir Robert Hart. The Bank became the medium chosen by Hart and the Chinese government "for raising loans on the European market." "No other bank could have been so useful to Jardine, Matheson in its business of building Chinese railways.[29] Out of the 27 Chinese government loans, 16 or 69.4% of the amount was borrowed from this British bank, thanks to the services of Hart.[30] We have here a vivid example of the financial oligarchy and the two types of personal unions as conceived by Lenin.

References

1. R. Koebner and H.D. Schmidt, *Imperialism: The Story and Significance of a Political World, 1840-1960* (Cambridge University 1964), p. xxiv.
2. J.A. Hobson, *Imperialism: A Study* (An Arbor paperback, 1965) p. 58.
3. *Ibid.*, p. 57.
4. Hobson's *Imperialism* has a whole chapter under the caption of "The Economic Taproot of Imperialism", see *ibid*, pp. 71-93.
5. Karl Marx and Frederick Engels, *On colonism : Articles fr te Newton York Tribute and other writings* (New York, 1972). pp. 37-37, citing "The British Rule in India", *New York Daily Tribune*, No, 3804, June 25, 1853.
6. Koebner and Schmidt, *op. cit.*, p. 252, citing Hobson's *Capitalism and Imperialism in South Africa.*
7. Hobson, *op.cit.*, p. 196.
8. Lenin, *op. cit.*, p. 8.
9. *Ibid.*
10. *Ibid.*, p. 20.
11. *Ibid.*, p. 31.
12. *Ibid.*, p. 45-46.
13. Parker T. Moon, *Imperialism and World Politics,* (New York, 1926), p. 321.
14. *Ibid.*, p. 322.
15. *Ibid.*, p. 323.
16. *Ibid.*, p. 321.
17. *Ibid.*, p. 330.
18. *Ibid.*, p. 321.
19. *Ibid.*, p. 337.
20. *Ibid.*, p. 358.
21. Andre Gunder Frank, *On Capitalist Underdevelopment* (Bombay, 1975). p. 56.
22. *Ibid*, p. 96.
23. *Ibid*, pp. 110, 126.
24. Pelcovits, *op.cit.*, p. 16.
25. Yu Suyun et al, *op. cit.*, p. 71.

26. Dernberger, *loc. cit.,* p. 28.
27. Hou, *Foreign Investments,* p. 57.
28. Moon, *op.cit.,* p. 338.
29. Maurice Colis, *Wayfong, The Hong Kong and Shanghai Banking Corporation* (London, 1965), pp. 60-61.
30. Xu Yisheng, "Jiawu Zhong-Ri Zhanzheng qian Qing zhengfude waizhai" (Foreign debts of the Manchu government before the Sino-Japanese War in 1894), *Jinji Yanjiu* (Economic Studies), No. 5, 1956, pp. 110-107.

8

God Shied from Celestial Kingdom : Christian Missionaries in 19th Century China*

Before discussing the challenge and response between the Christian missionaries and the native people in nineteenth-century China, let us first gain a little insight into the historical background. Christianity has an elder-brother in Buddhism. The three noble aspirations of the modern European Christian culture, *i.e.* liberty, equality and fraternity, can be traced to the teachings of the Buddha, who was called by the ancient Chinese as "King of Equality" If we are allowed to use the modern parlance, China had long been a "developed" country in religious teachings (thanks to her proximity with India) as compared to the "underdevelopment" of religion in ancient Europe.

The Chinese used to have a lot of enthusiasm in religion when Buddhism was refreshing. Lots of temples and pagodas were erected with government and private money. Emperors proclaimed themselves as the disciples of the Bodhisattvas. National festivals were organized with the Chinese of Heaven (the emperor) taking the lead in paying homage to Buddha relics and innocent people cutting off their own arms in front of the relics expecting the miracle.

As time passed, such religious fervour diminished. When the English, French and Americans were seized by their newly found evangelic enthusiasm typical of the mood of a young priest in the nineteenth century, China was already an old saint

*This is a condensed version of the article 'God Shied from Celestrial Kingdom. Christian Missionaries in Nineteenth Century China' that was written in 1986 and published in Tan Chung, *Triton and Dragon*, (Delhi 1986).

ready to renounce her deities. This Chinese religious mood was incomprehensible to the Western Christians.

I

The metaphor of honeymoon may not be appropriate as we know that the young Europe-American Christianity was coming to China on board the gunboats, and wishing to stay as a conqueror. One eternal regret of the modern Western Christian culture is that it has conquered everything except the heart of China. Of all the nooks and corners of the world never has there been any people who have so stubbornly resisted Christian evangelism as the Chinese did in the nineteenth century. Nor have so many Christian missionaries been killed by non-Christians in peace time as they were killed in nineteenth-century China. Besides, practically all the westerners in China after the 1842 Treaty of Nanjing, be they admirals, sailors, diplomats, traders, investors, and adventurers, had their way excepting the Christian missionaries. Why was it so?

There is an *a priori* perspective among Western scholars in which they view historical even modern problems concerning Sino-foreign relations. This perspective sees the Chinese cultural tradition as ethnocentric, self-righteous, and unreasonably proud vis-a-vis foreigners. And the cause for this was China's existing as a cultural island, far away from other advanced cultural centres, compounded by a close-door policy.

If the Chinese in the nineteenth century were really so incurably self-righteous and anti-foreign, it would be indeed in vain for anybody to try to convert them into Christians. But, I think, such a perspective cannot help us to gain any insight into the reason why China was not destined to become a Christian state much as the hardest efforts had been made on the part of the Christian missions. This is because there is some basic defect in this perspective.

First of all, the perspective is not founded on sound evidence. It is too sweeping to say that because of the Chinese name of their country, Zhongguo (Chung-kuo), having the connotation of "middle kingdom" hence the Chinese culture is ethnocentric, and because of the ancient Chinese calling foreigners "barbarians" hence they always feel superior to the foreigners.

It is rather strange that so many foreigners had visited China and written about their visits before the advent of the modern Europeans. Never had any one of them felt that the Chinese had the air of superiority, nor testified that they had been stigmatized as barbarians.

Of course, the Chinese have said many harsh things about the modern westerners, calling them names during the late nineteenth century. Almost all the examples which the scholars have cited to prove China's xenophobic tradition belong to this category. But, it is clear that this xenophobia was merely a reply to the Western powers' anti-Chinese activities, which should not be treated as a constant tradition of China. In that way, the Chinese was the most maligned foreigner in the entire Western media during the nineteenth century. But, the Chinese had not forced the Europeans to buy opium, nor waged wars on Europe and demanded European payment of indemnity after storming their cities and looting their treasures, nor taken away European territories and established Chinese concessions in Manchester or Venice. Even if the Chinese had done all this they would not have been more xenophobic than the Western powers who had trampled under their feet the Chinese sovereignty, dignity and sensitivity. What is topsyturvy in the contemporary China scholarship in the West is the scholars' singing praises for the culture of the aggressors while condemning the cultural tradition of the vourquished.

The second theory about the failure of the Christian evangelic movement in China is propounded by Paul A. Cohen. He thinks that there is an "anti-Christian tradition in Chinese thought". This tradition arose from what he terms as "heterodoxy-orthodoxy antithesis" in the Chinese cultural tradition.

In a culture with the long and rich experience like China's, there have been developments and trends of various directions. Whatever Cohen might say, he cannot deny the fact that China was one of the major Buddhist countries in history. If this is so, he cannot build up a theory of China's anti-Christian tradition with a non-existent Chinese anti-Buddhist tradition. China had no anti-Buddhist tradition. Her anti-Christian demonstrations have to be studied *de novo*—delinking with her historical Buddhist experiences.

Christianity became a substantial cultural force in China. The Christian influence on the all-powerful Manchu Emperor Kangxi (K'ang-hsi) (1662-1722) was almost as great as that of Buddhism on the great Tang ruler, Taizong's. However it was the international interference from the European community of Catholicism which ultimately averted the repetition of history—another round of China's passionate embrace of a foreign religion which would be Christianity this time. The cause of this interference was partly due to the intra-Catholic controversies in the name of safeguarding the Christian purity (known as the "Rites Controversy") and partly due to the rivalries of the vested interests within the Catholic world. Apparently, it was the rivalry between the Jesuits on the one hand and the Dominicans and Franciscans on the other which ignited the religious controversy. Actually, the rivalries between the European nations, like France, Italy and Portugal, were also at work, because most of the Jesuit missionaries in China came from Italy and Portugal.

The central issue of the intra-Catholic controversy rested on the basic approach of evangelization whether Christianity should develop in a non-Christian culture with due respect for the sensitivity of the native culture or demanding a total severance of cultural ties of the native country on the part of the converts. The Jesuits are known to have been pursuing the former approach which was the secret of their success in China and other countries, including India.

The controversy started with a vigorous anti-Jesuit campaign by a Spanish missionary of the Dominican sect, Juan Baptista de Morales onwards. The controversy lasted many decades resulting in several major resolutions passed by the Vatican court.

These resolutions were followed by two Papal edicts, the first, the Bull *Ex illa die* of March 1715 issued by Pope Clement XI, and the second, the Bull *Ex quo singular!* of July, 1742, issued by Pope Benedict XIV. Before the issue of the Bull *Ex illa die,* Charles Maillard de Tournon was sent to China as the Legate of Roman Holy See to uphold the papal decrees. The Legate arrived in China in 1705, and was received by Emperor Kangxi in his summer resort at Chengde with courtesy and hospitality. But the talks ensued between the Chinese monarch and the Papal envoy were not too pleasant. he emperor who had been a pupil of a Jesuit missionary, Schall, in his boyhood, and who had been in a mood to help solve the controversies among the Catholic missionaries, finally realized the rigidity of the Holy See and its lack of respect for his authority in China over his subjects. Thus, Christianity missed the golden chance of developing a cordial relationship with the Chinese ruler who was the all powerful Emperor Kangxi, which would have become a great advantage for the spread of Christianity in China.

Can we blame the Chinese ethnocentrism or the Chinese obsession for orthodoxy for it? Quite contrary it was the Christian orthodox which had ruined the chance. After all, it was a European Christian tradition that the heretic is more dangerous than the infidel. That the Roman Papacy would prefer risking the ruining of the Christian cause in China to tolerating the impurity of the Jesuits' Christian practice somewhat sealed the destiny of evangelization of Christianity in China. The second point to note is that the Chinese emperor was a more independent political and moral authority than the kings of Europe in the eighteenth century. Not only were the kings of Catholics Europe, but owing to the historical tradition the Roman Holy See could arrogate itself a superiority vis-a-vis the Catholic kings. But, the papacy had no authority whatever over the domain of an independent country like China. Imagine if the Chinese Confucian missionaries going round in Europe with the Beijing government issuing edicts ordering the European Confucian converts to show disrespect to their own cultural traditions and even to their national heroes and rulers how would the European kings react to it ?

II

Why Christianity did not make headway and why was there a popular anti-Christian current in nineteenth-century China have to be understood from the particular challenge and response between the Christian and Chinese cultures during the century. Our attention on such particular situations should not be diverted by over-generalizations about the Sinocentrism and anti-heterodoxy syndromes.

It may be noted that despite the great East-West controversy over the Christian rites and the anti-Christian attitude of the Chinese government in its wake, China still had 1.5 lac Catholic converts in 1800, The 19th century started with a promise for Christian evangelism in China.

There was saving grace also of the "Rites Controversy" in Europe out of the debates over the Jesuit proceedings in China the enlightened section of European intelligentsia began to admire the Chinese culture, particularly her philosophy and art. Voltaire, the renowned eighteenth-century French writer and philosopher, even regarded China as a model for Europe. A by-product of this new-rising European interest in Chinese culture was the emergence of the rococo art style in the beginning of the eighteenth century. It is a fact that different cultures do not clash with each other if there is no vested interests involved. The paradigm that East is East, West is West, and East and West will never meet is a deliberate distortion of international development by certain sections of the Christian world with aggressive designs towards the East.

One more historical phenomenon which was disadvantageous to the late coming of Christianity to China was the development of subversive activities of Chinese peasant masses under the umbrella of religion. The unique feature of religion in Chinese history was the natural marriage between religions and power struggles. There was the famous Buddhist monk who became the founder-emperor of the Ming Dynasty in the fourteenth century. From that time onwards, the potential of subversion in any religion became a recognized fact in Chinese polity. When religious activities became potentially subversive in China, no foreign religion could escape the suspicion of the watchful eyes of Chinese authorities who jealously guarded their sovereignty. This was not the case when Buddhism first arrived in China.

The sensitive issue of religious subversion was brought alive by the famous White Lotus rebellion sporting the well-known Indian religious symbol - lotus - which seriously challenged the reign of the first Chinese emperor in the nineteenth century, Emperor Jiaqing (Chia-ch'ing) (1796-1820), from its inception. The reign of Jiaqing which had put down the rebellious White Lotus by mobilizing a great amount of money and man-power became particularly nervous about religious preaching. In 1805 he issued an edict asking the official to be vigilant against foreigners and Chinese preaching Christianity in any part of China. The edict ordered the arrest of any foreigner who would engage in non-commercial activities and preaching religion at Guangzhou-Macau or other places where the foreigners had sneaked in. In 1814, another imperial edict was issued describing Christianity as a "potential worry for the state" *(guojia zhi yinyou)* which was "even more menacing than the White Lotus". The ghost of Bull *Ex illa die* was haunting the Jiaqing government as Christianity wanted to remove all the traditional authorities in China. This edict was issued a few months after a surprised raid of the imperial palace by some White Lotus assassins who had come very close to attacking the emperor.[1] One thing to notice in the second edict is that Christianity was described as "yiduan" (i-tuan), the word which Paul Cohen has translated as "heterodoxy". It is abundantly clear that it was not the heterodox aspect of the White Lotus or Christianity which really bothered the Jiaqing government, but the danger of subversion in religious activities in China.

Unfortunately for Christianity, the Christian Westerners in nineteenth-century China not only did nothing to help erase the Chinese suspicion of Christianity, but even deliberately exhibited their potential subversive power in every sphere of their activities, defying Chinese prohibitions, challenging Chinese laws, citing Confucian sayings to argue with Chinese officials. This created a vicious circle of more Chinese suspicion leading to more Chinese restrictions on Christian Western activities, and more defiance on the part of the latter. It was in this vicious circle that the Western Christian gained the taste of Chinese arrogance and unreasonableness while the Chinese ruling clique viewed Christianity as the most serious threat to Chinese sovereign authorities—a threat so enthusiastically kept alive by the behaviour of Western Christians.

To put it bluntly, the Western Christian world knew only one method in its expansion into China, viz. the method of conquest. The method, of course, worked beautifully in the political, economic and diplomatic fields. The Christian West could by sheer force convert China into a nation of opium smokers, to convert Chinese cities and towns into "treaty ports" to convert the traditional Chinese mode of international contacts into the unequal treaty system etc. But, nobody could convert the heart of China into that of a Christian. As a matter of fact, the method of conquest is counter-productive in any religious expansion. The Christian West sowed only seeds of hatred against Christianity in China every moment when it fired guns to kill Chinese lives, when it dumped narcotics to the Chinese coast, when it concluded an unequal treaty with the Chinese government, when it shipped away treasures from the Chinese ports. God says that men are born in sin. Christian activities in nineteenth-century China were born in so great a sin which deserved much greater punishment by God than the stealing of the forbidden fruit by adam and eve. The 19th century Christian missionaries were dreaming in vain the conversion of China into Christianity—a miracle which God would never have granted.

III

The evangelic approach of the Jesuits in China from the sixteenth to the 18th century was that of give and take. They were courteous and generous to the Chinese culture, and the Chinese culture became courteous and generous to the exotic value system which the Jesuits wanted it to appreciate. The critics of this approach at that time were opposed to such a trade. They wanted only one way traffic, viz. the Chinese culture should embrace Christian culture, but not vice versa. The spirit of crusade seems to be inherent in the Christian evangelization. In a crusader's mental dictionary there is no word like "compromise" or telerance or coexistence. His mind's track is so narrow that he can only think of "conquest" and ask for the pagan's surrender. This is not a sign of strength, but rather a syndrome of weakness and immaturity. In comparison with the spiritual old men of Asia (particularly India and China), Christianity was a mere innocent and big-headed child in the eighteenth century. It was a pity that when this young Christianity revisited China after 100 years, it had hardly grown up in maturity and tolerance. Varg observes that "the missionaries demanded that the Chinese provided evidence of having made a sincere and complete surrender."[2] So, the crusader's spiritual heritage was very much alive in the veins of the 19th century missionaries.

Indeed, the Christians who came to nineteenth-century China were, almost without exception, messengers of another god. This new god, was the reincarnation of force. So, this was the new Christian spirit even before the Opium War. In the eyes of this spirit, China was unfit to be regarded as a sovereign nation, but was as bad as a bunch of bandits and pirates (which reminds us the Guangzhou preaching scene). The Chinese character was marked by debauchery. And the best way to deal with the imbecile Chinese was force.

In 1870, there occurred the first Chinese mass demonstration against Christian missionaries. The demonstration was preceded by the circulation of reports that many children among the residents of Tianjin (Tientsin) had been kidnapped, and the confession of an arrested kidnapper that he had sold children to an orphanage at Tianjin run by a French mission, the Sisters of St. Vincent de Paul. As mass resentment grew stronger and stronger, the Imperial Commissioner stationed at Tianjin, Chonghou (Ch'ung-hou), was trying to investigate into the matter and pacify the Chinese anger. However, the French Consul at Tianjin, Henri Victor Fontanier, behaved like a mad dog in the face of a huge Chinese mass demonstration. He first fired at the Chinese Commissioner who had come to the spot to control the crowd. Chonghou was not provoked by Fontanier's hostility and tried to persuade the latter to stay at the Commissioner's office until the mob disappeared. The pig-headed French Consul said he had nothing to fear the coward Chinese and charged into the crowd. On encountering the Tianjin magistrate who was there to control the crowd, Fontanier fired his pistol at the magistrate, wounding fatally the magistrate's attendant. This ignifed the mass fury who beat him to death on the spot, and in its wake destroyed the French Consulate, the French church and the orphanage, and killed every

Frenchman that could be found. The French Catholic sisters were stripped naked and cut into pieces. At the end of the massacre twenty-one foreigners (fourteen of them French) and between thirty and forty Chinese converts lost their lives, and the properties destroyed included four English and American chapels in addition to the French loss. The Tianjin authorities arrested many leaders of the mob and executed sixteen of them immediately to pacify the Western anger.[3]

This was probably the first ever incident of a colonial people refusing to swallow insult of colonialist behaviour and venting their mass fury on imperialist officials and Christian missionaries in such a daring manner and large scale. Force was a game which everyone could play. For once, the advocates of brutal force had the table turned against themselves. I have read many Chinese accounts of the incident and found none of them blaming the behaviour of the Tianjin masses. Some even treat those being executed by the Tianjin government after the incident as martyrs *(yishi)*. Any people with self respect and national dignity would behave likewise in similar situations.

From 1870 onwards the dormant anti-Christian (in fact, anti-imperialist) volcanoes began to erupt one after another much as Chinese government had tried to suppress them. Paradoxically, at this point the former advocacy of the employment of brutal force against China - the voice of the U.S. missionaries began to show signs of confusion and uncertainty. Some missionaries became worried that God might be using the Chinese anti-Christian riots to punish the Christians on account of the sins committed by the latter earlier. There was, of course, no lack of those who remained as militant as ever. Many wanted to teach China with another bloody lesson to demonstrate that "British and American blood" was "sacred".

In the Sino-Japanese War (1894-95), many Christian missionaries were ready to accept Japan's invasion of China as an act of Providence. Their supporting the aggressor against the aggressed was the sure sign of total moral imbalance.

Finally, it was expected that when the Boxers' anti-Christian rage exploded at the end of the nineteenth century, there should be another round of outburst of anti-China tirade from Christian missionary quarters.

The Christian missionary in nineteenth-century China had assumed a dual role as the pollen-carrier of modern civilization as well as the *agent provocateur* of Western imperialism. The Christian was the overall identity of all the Western imperialist activities in China. The Westerner who brought opium to China in huge armed-to-teeth ships was a Christian. The Westerner who strafed bullets into the chests of Chinese military and civilians was a Christian. The Western diplomat who yelled at the Chinese mandarins was a Christian. The Westerner who shipped materials and treasures away from China was a Christian. The Westerner who burnt the Beijing Summer Palace, Yuanmingyuan, and looted its invaluable jewels and decor was a Christian. The Westerner who lived in luxurious foreign concessions in big Chinese cities where ordinary Chinese and stray dogs were barred from entrance was a Christian. The Westerner who built imposing churches in which activities were shared only by a few selected Chinese was a Christian. The Westerner whose behaviour in China was above the regulation of Chinese law, and who moved in the Chinese interior with either the Western or Chinese armed protection was a Christian. There was no mistaken identity of this Western Christian—an imperialist aggressor whose presence in China was the root cause of miseries of millions of Chinese. Any Chinese anti-Christian sentiment was first and primarily the reaction to this Christian totality in nineteenth-century China. In other words, a large percentage of this anti-Christianism was anti-imperialism.

IV

No study of the Christian missionary question in nineteenth-century China is complete without examining the interrelationship between the missionary activities and the rise of anti-Christian riots towards the last decades of the century culminating in the outbreak of the Boxer Rebellion (the Yihetuan Movement) and its ultimate clash with the Western (plus Japanese) powers in the last two years of the century. I wish to briefly discuss three issues which concern both the subjects - missionaries and the Boxers. First how far were the missionaries to be blamed for the outbreak of the boxers?

Second, how really anti-Christian were the Boxers and other anti-Christian riots? Third, what was the impact of the Boxer Movement on Sino-Western intercourse in general and Christian missionary activities in China in particular?

The causes beyond the missionary control were: (1) Chinese anger at the seizure of territory by the powers, (2) mass displacement of means of livelihood due to the building of railways, the introduction of steamboat services, and the establishment of post offices, (3) the dominance of "reactionary elements".

We can discern from these issues the inter-linkage between the Christian missionaries and the rise of the Boxers. First of all the Boxer Movement was a manifestation of the Chinese mass tolerance of the accumulation of foreign insult and injury that had reached its breaking point. The sudden eruption of rebellious spirit and energy was the result of the amalgamation of grievances of the entire country from top to bottom, ranging from the Empress Dowager's hatred against the foreign powers moral support for the 1898 "Hundred Days' Reform" down to the anti-foreign sentiments among the refugees at Tianjin city who thought their being displaced in livelihood had some thing to do with the arrival of the foreigners in China. Of course, there was the Chinese gentry's grievance against the missionaries. It is a proper historical prespective to view the Boxers' anti-foreignism in totality, *i.e.* as the revolt of the entire nation against the Western imperialist oppression which had assumed the dimension beyond human tolerance. Imperialism was a multinational package being clamped down on the head of China. Christian missionaries formed a part of this package. This is what Purcell meant by saying that the Boxers were anti-foreign therefore anti-Christian as the anti-Christian element was an in-built part in the anti-foreignism. We should not discuss the Boxers' anti-Christian sentiments in isolation.

The missionaries could have done something to integrate themselves with the Chinese masses (like taking a firm stand to protest against the imperialist aggression on China, and working for the improvement of the living conditions of the Chinese) and freed themselves from this unfortunate role of the reminder of Western imperialist aggression in the minds of Chinese masses. But, they did exactly the opposite to segregate themselves from the Chinese society, and conducted their affairs in closed-door conditions. This was the main reason of their becoming the targets of the mass outrage against the "ocean devils". Of course, it was rather tragic that they should bear the brunt of the Chinese anti-imperialist rage while the real culprits stayed in their luxurious houses either in the foreign concessions of Chinese cities or in their home countries unharmed. The missionaries were sacrificed as the scapegoats of Western imperialism.

However, we shall be untrue to history if we forget that, as a whole, the nineteenth-century missionaries represented a progressive, dynamic and superior cultural force of the world. When such a force interacted with the Chinese people, there was bound to be some impact on the Chinese society. One positive feature was the arrival of many serious scholars among the missionaries who dedicated themselves to the enterprise of translating Western literature of various subjects (including the Bible, of course) into Chinese, and introducing the Western development to Chinese intellectuals through the diligent printing press of the church. In this enterprise, they had the help of a large number of faceless Chinese intellectuals. This progressive cultural influence represented by the missionaries accentuated the conflict between the old and new orders—what Marx described as the dissolution of the mummy of the *ancien regime* of China which had been "carefully preserved in a hermetically sealed coffin" after contacting the fresh air from the Western world.[4] The missionaries were instrumental in bringing in this fresh air which caused the deterioration of the sick cells of the Chinese culture.

Obviously, Fairbank's two paradoxical images of the missionaries as a part of imperialism on the one hand, and a revolutionary outsider within the Chinese society on the other, appear to be very ambivalent. One vital link is missing in the observations of Fairbank, viz. what was the missionaries attitude towards the main source of Chinese people's misery at that time? We know that the force of imperialism not only worked hard to bleed China white, it also did its utmost to perpetuate the decadent *ancien regime* in China. As Fairbank rightly says, the missionaries had automatically become a part of the ruling force which was the guardian angel of China's *ancien regime.* If they were genuine revolutionaries, they would surely move away and even rebel against this status which history had imposed on them, and stood firm on the side of the suffering Chinese masses. The greatest missionary ambivalence lies in their hobnobbing with the *ancien regime*. We need only mention the example of the Taiping Rebellion to see how the Western powers had helped to suppress the historical chance of China's emerging as a more civilized nation according to the West's own yardstick. At that time, few, if any, missionary had voiced a protest against the unholy alliance between the Christian powers and the anti-Taiping-Christian forces in China.

The readers may draw a parallel between Fairbank's ambivalence and my highlighting the progressive character of the missionaries in nineteenth-century China after criticizing them as the *agents provocateur* of imperialism. I think these two aspects are not contradictory, and are, in any case, a historical phenomenon. But I differ fundamentally with Fairbank in regarding the missionaries as the predecessors of the great revolution of China, *i.e.* the Communist Movement. I think Fairbank has over-emphasized the importance of the external factor in the working of China's internal contradictions. Fairbank is wrong when he thinks that because the missionaries were outsiders therefore their contributions to the Chinese revolutionary process have not been recognized. Many foreigners have worked and even died for the Chinese revolution. Just mention two well-known names: the Canadian, Henry Norman Bethune, and the Indian, Dwarkanath Shantaram Kotnis. How much has China been beholden to them! I cannot think any foreign missionary who had really contributed to the Chinese revolution but was ungratefully branded by the Chinese as "imperialist". Of course, Fairbank is not referring to any individual but to the missionaries as a whole, which was all the more difficult to qualify as a revolutionary force in Chinese history after we have learnt their anti-China sentiments from Miller, Varg and others. This is the first substantial difference between Fairbank's premise and mine. I think the Chinese revolution would have given the missionaries their due if they had contributed to it as asserted by Fairbank. The motto of serving the people being a Chinese emulation of the foreign missionaries? No ! There were ample such examples in ancient Chinese history. The Indian Buddhists had set far better examples a thousand years before the arrival of the Western missionaries. The *Bodhisattva* tradition of Mahayana Buddhism had made popular in China the noble spirit of postponing one's own *nirvana* (liberation) to obtain the salvation of the people long before such an idea dawned on the Western civilisation.

Secondly, the main contention of this essay has already manifested another difference between Fairbank's perspective and mine. Fairbank, perhaps too much overwhelmed by his grandfather's noble example, has a fixed assumption that all those who had clad themselves in the clerical garb and gone to China in the last two centuries were dedicated messengers of salvation. I don't deny that there might be such individual example. But, from the examples which we have come across in this essay, we have noticed that most of the missionaries who had gone to China in the nineteenth century started very young and rather immature. There was a great element of adventurism in their choice of the China career. Not only adventurism and careerism were the order of the day, but their social background was in the grip of the Darwinist spirit. Such a social milieu could not have thrown up a category of Westerners who would fit Fairbank's description of the pioneers of revolution in China.

However, I would certainly agree with Fairbank that the kind of limited roles played by the missionaries (such as treating the subjects, women and youth as respectful human-beings etc.) had created problems for the *ancien regime* of China. And a part of the anti-Christian sentiments exhibited by the Boxer and other riots in the nineteenth century could be the result of this struggle between the old ideas and new. This is why I have highligted the progressive aspect of Christian evangelism in nineteenth-century China. The missionaries had carried a certain amount of the progressive cultural pollen into the pistil of Chinese culture, although many of them might have done so unconsciously.

Purcell has made an important point that there was a success syndrome created by the Western powers for the popularisation of Christianity. "Association with success" says Purcell, "was always a powerful inducement to the shrewd Chinese, and the rise in the number of converts after the failure of the Boxer uprising can as fairly be ascribed to this factor as can its decline after Communist Revolution of 1949."[5] Imperialism itself was a powerful force of social change if we take a cue from Andre Gunder Frank's Metropole-Periphery development. In the newsocial order of the imperialist era, both metropolis and periphery developed in China parallel to the existing Chinese social order. Naturally, many clever Chinese flocked the Christian missions to get a share in the new-rising metropole much to the dislike of many others who found their life deteriorating with the development of the periphery. The cultural struggle between the old and new coincided with this social change of redistribution of fortune and success which only intensified the conflict between the old and new. Fairbank, Paul Cohen and others have emphasized the involvement of the gentry in the growth of anti-Christian sentiments. It was true that many among the adversely affected in the new equations of prosperity-versus-poverty under the impact of the Western imperialism were those who could be described as the gentry stratum in an over-generalised way. But, their opposition to the Christian missions was more due to the socio-economic factor than due to cultural reaction.

In the discussion the second major issue concerning Christianity and the Boxers, viz. how far were the Boxers really anti-Christian, I am more inclined to accept Purcell's premise that the Boxers were anti-foreign therefore anti-Christian rather than his other observation that the Boxers were both anti-foreign and anti-Christian. The Chinese anti-foreignism was largely due to her anti-imperialism. Was it also due to Chinese anti-Christianism? We have seen very little evidence to this.

The conditioned reflex syndrome which shows that it was the presence of the foreign missionaries before the eyes of the Chinese masses which had visualized the anti-imperialism targets. But, missionaries were not the only targets. Angry mobs also attacked foreign diplomats who also can be brought into the conditioned reflex syndrome. Even Japanese, who were not Christians at all, got killed in this so-called "anti-Christian" fury. We can say that the Boxers and other anti-Christian mobs did not mean to single out missionaries for attack. They actually wanted to attack all foreigners. It just so happened that the majority of the foreigners available for attack who were the least protected by the imperialist fire power were the missionaries. It was merely a coincidence that the targets of the anti-foreign fury happened to be missionaries.

We see very clearly that in the manifestoes of the Boxers there is no element of religious conflict between Christianity on the one hand and the Chinese beliefs on the other. If there was any gentry intellectual involved in the Boxers, such manifestoes must have been his brain children. Yet, there is no scholarly content in them. We can conclude that neither the illiterate masses, nor the intellectuals of the Boxers knew anything about Christianity. They even did not know the essence of Confucianism or Buddhism. Their main concern was to drive away the foreign devils from China.

To put in proper historical perspective, religious fundamentalism has never been a dominant trend in China at any point of time. The occasional religious conflicts taken place in Chinese history were the clashes between vested interests using religion as a cover. The Boxers were like other Chinese who had inherited a strong secular tradition. They were least interested in religious controversies. They themselves represented no religious interest. But, they hated all foreign aggressors including their missionaries. To them the presence of Christianity was no different from that of the railway lines. They were the eyesore to the Boxers because they symbolized the dominance of Wstern imperialism. At the moment when they plucked the rails they had hardly given any thought whether such materials would be good for them in a changed atmosphere. They were not anti-railway *per se*. The same is true about their so-called "anti-Christian" sentiments. They had not thought of what Christianity was at the moment when they were burning the churches and killing the missionaries. They did it for the sake of destroying foreign imperialism.

There was apparently, as the Boxers were accused in the Western world, an element of cowardice on the part of the Boxers. When they had declared the Western powers as enemies, they should have from the very beginning directed their struggle against the troops of the powers instead of turning their wrath on the unarmed missionaries, and even their women and childern. There was barbarism in their behaviour, but no more barbarous than the armed Westerners in China who had killed far more Chinese civilians, including women and children, than the Boxers had killed the Western Christians. Yet, if we look at the issue from a different angle, we cannot lay the blame squarely on the Boxers for their choosing wrong identities in their struggle. The transposition of identities had first started by the Christian missionaries themselves. The idealism in all religions, as also in Christianity, lies in treating all the God's creatures with empathy and kindness. From the bellicose pronouncements of the Western missionaries, we can say that this noble idealism had been abandoned by the Christian missions even before their clergymen arrived in China. It is obvious from those pronouncements that the real God (the one who would treat the Chinese as much His children as the Westerners) had been transposed. The Prince of Peace had been transposed to the Prince of War. The Society for the Diffusion of Gospel had been transposed to the Society for the Diffusion of Bullets etc. In a word, Christianity had transposed itself in nineteenth China to imperialism, while the real Christianity of peace, humanism, universal love, and international equality had never arrived in China. The Boxers had correctly identified this falsehood of the Christian god, and attacked this transposed Christianity. In this way, the conditioned reflex syndrome was also a syndrome of transposition of identities.

The Western culture has been known for its dualistic character—being a binary existence of good and evil. Among the eight armies which raided China in 1900 to quell the Boxers, only the Asian army, *i.e.* the Japanese, did not join others to loot, rape and indulge in other acts of carnage after the Boxer resistance being over. It is a well known fact that a worst Western colonialist abroad has always been a good Christian at home. Here again, it is the technique of the transposition of identities of the Western culture which has kept alive the hymns for the colonial heroes who would have been condemned as the worst villains had they been non-Christians, and had they committed their crimes in life at home.

This brings into focus the effect of moral decadence of Western imperialism in all times, and, of course, in the nineteenth century. Culturally speaking, imperialism is a moral disease. Although many historians have still not been able to diagnose this disease (some even go to the extent to attribute revolutionariness to it), it would be recognized so in future, sooner or later. If, in this essay, we have proved the implicity of the Christian missionaries in imperialism, we cannot but arrive at the conclusion that it was this moral decadence of Christianity which was the cause of its undoing in China.

What was the impact of the Boxers on the Christian world? There is no gainsaying that the whole world was shocked beyond description. The first people who were shocked were those who had merrily planned to cut the sweet Chinese melon into the so-called "Spheres of Influence"—a disguised term of "Polandization". The integrity of China was saved. Paradoxically, it seems that only the Christian powers learnt the lesson, but not their non-Christian Asian counterpart—Japan. It was, as it were, that the Boxers had dictated to the Christian powers a "thus far, and no further" upper-limit. And the latter accepted the message. How was it that the Christian powers could get the Boxer message, while Japan failed to do it? This was because that the Boxers/attack was on the transposed Christian God of Might-Is-Right, the idol of which was severely damaged by the Boxers' heroism. Instead of the Christian missionaries, it was their enemy—the Boxer - who was the real harbinger of the Communist revolution in China. The Boxer and Communist movements in China, joined by the national movements of India and other countries, have ultimately destroyed the old imperialism and colonialism of the world. Being one of the decisive anti-imperialist, anti-colonial shots, the Boxer Uprising has made a significant contribution to human civilisation in this historical evolution.

The Boxers and other anti-Christian riots in nineteenth-century China also shocked the Christian societies in Europe and America. Christian activities in China were subjected to severe censure in the mass media at home. Even famous writers, like Mark Twain, joined the fray against the missionaries. As a result of such public criticism, the missionaries began to become susceptible to Chinese sensitivities in the 19th century. The sacrifice of the Boxers' blood resulted in the purification of Christianity. It looks like that the displaced God began to return. By that time, the Celestial Kingdom was already preoccupied by another God, *i.e.* Revolution. The romance of China with this God Revolution lasted until the death of Chairman Mao, and the termination of the Great Proletarian Cultural Revolution, during which period, all the other gods were under attack, and a number of religious monuments which had survived the vicissitudes of history were destroyed. The post-Mao government is now spending large sums of money to repair and take other measures to restore historical premises of various religions, including Christianity. Religious activities are being revived. Christian hymns are again heard in China. May be not in the distant future, the Pope of Rome would land in Beijing, and beam at the largest television audience of mankind, and say: "love your culture, God bless you!"

References

1. *Qing Renzong Junhuangdi shilu* (Veritable records of Emperor Jiaqing), (reprint, Taipei, 1964), *Juan* 152, p. 12; *juan* 274, p. 23 (*juan* 290, p. 9.
2. Varg, *op. cit.,* p. 19.
3. An account of the event is given in Paul Cohen, *op. cit.,* pp. 229-233.
4. Karl Marx, "Revolution in China and in Europe". *New York Daily Tribune,* No. 3794 (June 14, 1853).
5. Purcell, *op. cit.,* p. 127.

9

American Policy of "Open Door" and China*

China's defeat in the first encounter with Japan (1894-95) laid bare the decadence and helplessness of the Manchu dynasty and invited the imperialist powers to engage themselves in a scramble for concessions. The treaty of Shimonoseki which was signed on April 17, 1895, between China and Japan ceded, among other concessions, the Liaodong (Liaotung) peninsula and Taiwan to Japan. Cession of the Liaodong peninsula to Japan led to the triple intervention by Russia, Germany and France, who forced Japan to return the peninsula to China at a price of 50 million taels. Immediately after the triple intervention, Germany asked for a naval base as a reward. Despite China's initial resistance to the demand, Germany got Jiaozhou in 1897, and similarly Russia was given Port Arthur in 1898. Not to lag behind the Russians and the Germans, the British leased Weihaiwei and Kowloon and claimed the entire Yangtse Valley, the French established a "sphere of influence" in Guangdong, Guangxi, Yunnan, and Japan obtained Fujian. All these areas were claimed to be "spheres of influence" of the treaty powers which meant :

---

*This short piece was written in 1986 and was included in Tan Chung, *Triton and Dragon,* (Delhi, 1986) in order to cover all major aspects of nineteenth century China.

I am indebted to Prof Bipan Chandra whose constant encouragement and generous help made it possible for me to write this essay. My thanks are also due to Prof R.L. Shukla and Mr P.C. Verma who read and corrected the earlier draft of the article. Suchitra has edited the article and also helped me in sundry ways. I also express my sense of gratitude to Professor Tan Chung who had included my piece in his collection. **Triton and Dragon** Responsibility for any error in facts or interpretation is, of course, mine.

—D.N.G.

(*a*) That the area assigned to a particular power would not be alienated to any other power,

(*b*) That the power concerned would enjoy exclusive or monopoly position in respect of economic privileges in its "sphere of influence."

The partition of China into "spheres of influence" alarmed American merchants and financiers who feared that the European powers would restrict outside investment and trade within the areas under their control. The situation called for action because owing to its preoccupation with the Spanish War and the Cuban rebellion, the United States had had no opportunity to press for such a "sphere" for its commercial and financial interests. To offset this unfavourable position the U.S. Government announced in 1899 the doctrine of equal commercial opportunity in China for all foreign powers. This is popularly known as the Open Door because its pronouncement meant that the United States would get a free passage through the door the western powers had already hewed in the Chinese empire.

I

Though the policy of Open Door was finally and officially enunciated by the United States, the British played an important part in its conception. Why did Britain which had carved out a "sphere of influence" for her merchants, financiers and industrialists, play such an important role in the conception of the Open Door?

Since 1840 Britain had played the leading role in the exploitation of China. She held the strongest position even at the time of the outbreak of the Sino-Japanese War and was able to get the lion's share of Chinese trade and investments. Her trade with China amounted to 65 per cent of China's foreign trade, and 85 per cent of all exports and imports of China was carried in British vessels.[1] Partition of China was a grave menace to British trade at a time when she found it difficult to devote enough energy to the Far East because of her disastrous embroilment in the Boer War in South Africa. In particular, she was seriously concerned about the Russian threat to north China and the French advances in the south. Both Russia and France by threatening the territorial integrity of China were putting into jeopardy the trading interests of Britain. Her policy of opposition to any further economic or territorial concessions to France and her support to China's suzerainty over Korea to counter the increasing influence of Russia in the Far East completely failed. The Sino-Japanese War removed the last barrier to Russia's penetration from the north and, as has earlier been pointed out, led to the partition of China into "spheres of influence." The British government was not only interested in maintaining its advantageous position in the Yangtse Valley, but also in guarding its interests against exclusion from other parts of China. There is no doubt that after 1895 Britain had got the opportunity to give two of the three big foreign loans taken by China and had secured two leased territories (Weihaiwei and Kowloon) and by far the greatest mileage of railroad concessions, but as Fairbank has opined, "No amount of success in a partition of China could benefit British interests when they already dominated the trade of the whole country. Concessions and spheres could only reduce her area of trade."[2] Of course, no more concessions would mean no more to herself but this was not an equal sacrifice, because Britain had already had more than she could absorb or manage. She would benefit the maximum from the removal of the discriminatory tariffs in all the spheres and concessions. As George Marion has pointed out, "Her unique position as moneylender and exporter to the world, would enable her to get more from her rivals' spheres than they would get from hers."[3] Under these circumstances the British Cabinet, on the one hand, secretly discussed about partaking in the dismemberment of China, while on the other hand proclaimed its faith in the Open Door, and even on January 17, sent their first feeler for an alliance with Russia. When this failed to produce results, they turned to the United States.

Rebuffed by the Russians, the British Government approached the U.S. government with the suggestion that the two governments should take joint action to ensure equal commercial opportunity for all the treaty powers. But, Secretary of State John Sherman and William McKinley, the President of the United States, rejected the proposals by saying that though they were not "unmindful of the situation in China and its possible effect upon American trade interests," but all their "advices up to the present time indicate no foreign occupation which interferes with that trade or aims at exclusive commercial privileges."[4] The British Government renewed the proposal in January 1899 but without any positive response from the United States.

The important role that Britain played in the conception of the Open Door, is also clear from the fact that the first Hay notes were actually suggested and drafted by an Englishman, Alfred E. Hippisley, a member of the Chinese Maritime Customs Service. It is very well known that John Hay, the American Secretary of State, depended on his de facto adviser, William W. Rockhill, on affairs in the Far East. Rockhill in turn was guided by Hippisley. When in 1899 Hay asked Rockhill to draw up a draft of the Open Door, Rockhill did so by putting up a revised version of a memorandum drawn up by Hippisley on the subject on August 7, 1899. Rockhill's memoradum formed the substance of the Hay note. As the American scholar, Foster Rhea Dulles, has remarked :

> The influence of Great Britain in the evolution of our policy is clearly apparent. It is highly revealing to realise how the notes to the powers, so generally credited to John Hay himself, were inspired, if not actually written, by a British subject visiting Baltimore.[5]

However this interpretation of the timing of the Open Door has been challenged by Thomas J. McCormick:

> "It grossly overestimates the influence of quite a peripheral figure whose ideas were wholly unoriginal... and whose efforts in no way affected the timing of the Open Door Notes."[6]

What McCormick fails to appreciate is that it is not merely the question of the timing but that of the overall commercial and financial interest of the British. It was this interest that had motivated them to take the initiative in the direction of keeping the status quo in China.

II

The question lies in why did the U.S. Government that had rejected the British proposals twice, change its attitude and advocate the Open Door in the middle of 1899? Despite the

American Government's rejection of the British proposals, the fact remains that the American financiers, industrialists and businessmen had been mounting pressure on their Government for a change in its China policy. It was largely due to this pressure that John Hay declared the policy of the Open Door in September-October 1899. It is well-known that the foreign policy of a sovereign state is guided by its self-interest and that the American policy in China was no exception to this rule. Therefore, the change in the American policy from that of non-intervention to that of active intervention in the Chinese affairs can be understood only when we examine the changes, both economic and political, that had taken place in the United States by the end of the last century.

While the European powers were actively pushing their interests in China and were busy carving out "spheres of influence", the American Government was pre-occupied with the problem of its expanding frontier. The post-Civil War period witnessed a rapid industrialization. Not only the products of agriculture trebled during 1850-1900 (from $1,600,000,000 to $4,417,070,000), but, what is more important, between 1860 and 1900 the total railroad mileage increased from 30 thousand to 193 thousand; capital invested in manufacturing industry from $1 billion to $10 billion and the number of workers from 1.3 million to 5.3 million. The annual products in terms of value had gone up from $2 million to $13 million. The tremendous economic changes that took place in the post-Civil War period transformed the very nature of the American Society. The United States which had ranked fifth in the value of manufactured products in 1840, and fourth in 1860, took the first place in 1894. At that time she produced twice as much as Britain and half as much as all Europe put together. But the rapidly growing American industry found an immense and growing market at home and, therefore, felt no immediate and strong urge for foreign outlets for its products. Imperialist predilections of the American bourgeoisie found adequate outlet in Latin America. It does not, however, mean that American officials and merchants were altogether indifferent to the future expansionist interest of the United States. In fact, the Secretary of State, William H. Seward, had in the 1860s tried to secure the future American interests, if not hegemony, in the Orient. He had purchased Alaska from Russia as a halting stop to the Far East. He had fully cooperated with other powers in forcing China and Japan to open their doors to Western commerce. However, as yet there was not much pressure from the industrial, financial and commercial interests for expansion in the Orient and, therefore, there was no noticeable change in the American policy in China. Consequently, the United States lagged behind other powers in the race for markets and "spheres of influence" in China. A comparison of the two following tables would make it amply clear that whereas America's exports to China had increased over 200 per cent in the decade after 1890, they formed only two percent of her total exports.

Table 1. Exports from the United States to China

Year ending June 30	*U.S. Dollars*	*Year ending June 30*	*U.S. Dollars*
1890	7,385,362	1896	11,613,134
1891	13,469,687	1897	17,984,472
1892	10,557,546	1898	16,258,094
1893	8,117,059	1899	22,225,965
1894	10,072,273	1900	23,745,000
1895	7,856,880		

Source: Charles S. Campbell, *Special Business interests and the Open Door* (Yale University Press, 1851), pp. 10-11, citing F.R. Hitchcock, *Our trade with Japan, China and Hong Kong, 1889-1899* (Washington, 1900).

Table 2. Total Exports from the United States

	1890 (Calendar Year)	*1900 (Calendar Year)*
Europe	682,585,856	1,111,456,000
North America	95,517,863	202,846,000
South America	84,722,122	41,384,000
Asia	22,854,028	60,598,000
Africa	17,375,745	89,956,000
	4,446,934	22,178,000
Total	857,502,548	1,470,050,000

Source: Charles S. Campbell, *op. cit.*, p. 11, citing *Commercial Relations of the United States with Foreign Countries during the year 1900* (2 Vols., Washington, 1901), Vol. I, p. 87.

Moreover, total American investments in China were less than $25,000,000. Thus Americans were playing only a minor role in the race for investments in railways, mines and industries in China. At the crucial time when other powers were busy carving out spheres of influence and acquiring leaseholds in China, the U.S.A. could claim no share in the loot as it was engaged in war with Spain and later with the people of the Philippines.

By the 1890s the end of the American frontier was reached and the United States had become the leading industrial nation of the world. Growing surplus of manufactured goods began to appear, and "with the growing economic surplus which sustained the colourful and exuberant culture of the gilded age ran an increasing pressure for foreign markets and investment opportunities."[7] The United States Government began to be urged by the industrialists to look outwards, *i.e.,* to embark on imperialist ventures. "Let the foreign outlets for... surplus products be closed, and no protective policy can save the American manufacturer and labourer," wrote the *Journal of Commerce* on February 1, 1899.[8] "Competition in most lines of industry," declared the *United States Investor,* "has reached the point where an outlet for surplus stocks becomes an imperative necessity."[9]

Thus it was universally and sincerely believed that the future survival of American industry and business depended on foreign markets. It came to be realised that U.S.A. had stayed at home for too long and that the time had come for the country to step resolutely onto the international scene. In the political circles too it came to be felt that the U.S.A. had no option but to launch an expansionist policy. A.J. Beveridge summarised the prevalent mood as follows :

> American factories are making more than the American people can use; American soil is producing more than they can consume. Fate has written our policy for us; the trade of the world must and shall be ours. And we will get as our mother (England) had told us how. We will establish trading posts throughout the world as distributing-points for American products. We will cover the ocean with our

> merchant marine. We will build a navy to the measure of our greatness. Great colonies governing themselves, flying our flag and trading with us, will grow about our posts of trade. Our institutions will follow our flag on the wings of our commerce. And American law, American order, American civilization, and the American flag will plant themselves on shores hitherto bloody and benighted, but by those agencies of God henceforth to be made beautiful and bright.[10]

This belief dominated the thinking of industrialists, businessmen and statesmen to such an extent that the whole trend of international relations came to be interpreted in terms of a worldwide struggle for markets. "Back of every political complication of today are trade considerations, wars, treaties, colonization schemes and all intricacies of diplomacy are really in the final analysis but means...of acquiring wealth," thus asserted the *United States Investor.*[11] In the same vein the *Journal of Commerce and Commercial Bulletin* wrote in the issue of January 9, 1899, "International politics has simply become a series of questions relating to the development of trade."[12]

III

The most alluring prospect in this respect was the opening of Asia to conquest and exploitation. Problems of over-production could be solved, it was urged, if American commerce could be developed in the Orient and if, in particular, the Chinese markets could be secured for American goods. Senator A.J. Beveridge enthusiastically declared :

> Our largest trade will henceforth be with Asia. The Pacific is our Ocean... And the Pacific is the Ocean of the commerce of the future. Most future wars will be conflicts for commerce. The power that rules the Pacific, therefore, is the power that rules the world. And with the Philippines that power is and will forever be the American Republic.[13]

Charles Denby Jr., a secretary of the U.S. legation in Beijing wrote confidentially :

> The markets of the Orient are the heritage of her [U.S.A.] merchants, and time will inevitably come when the voice of

> the Republic will be heard in the Orient courts with the same accent of authority as in the commonwealth of South America.[14]

Though the American exports to China formed only 2 per cent of her total exports, the important point is that the increase in the decade after 1890 was to the tune of 200 per cent, a far larger increase than any other area except the African Continent. This convinced a major section of the American merchants, financiers, and, of course, statesmen about the future potential of the Chinese market. Worried about over-production they were attracted both by the size and the population of China. *The Banker and Tradesmen and Massachusetts Law Reporter* emphasized the point when it wrote :

> In China there are four hundred millions of people more than five times as many as exist in the United States. The wants of these fose hundred millions are increasing every year. What a market![15]

The issue was again and again highlighted by the business journals and magazines of the time. Whereas for the president of the Chicago Board of Trade the opportunities were, "such as were never presented to any other nation,"[16] to the Bradstreet's they seemed "the greatest which manufacturing nations have ever enjoyed."[17] Eager statisticians calculated that even if a bushel of flour was consumed by every Chinese a year the "entire American crop would be wanted..."[18] or if each of the Chinese bought one biscuit a day American factories would have to run day and night to meet the demand.[19] The *Journal of Commerce and Commercial Bulletin* clinched the issue when it wrote that Chinese markets could be preserved for the American exports, "the serious problem—where can we find markets for over-production surplus manufactures?—would be in no small measure solved."[20] The China issue, though only at times, overshadowed even the paramount question of war against Spain. But before the U.S.A. could think of some effective measures to protect its industrial and financial interest in China, it had to deal with the islands of Hawaii and the Philippines because the Philippines were the gateway to the Chinese empire.

IV

Many American merchants and naval officers had, of course, been advocating establishment of the U.S. naval bases in the Pacific for more than half a century, but it was not till the 1890s that the U.S. Government took concrete steps in this direction. After a great deal of controversy between the two political parties, the Republican President, McKinley, finally took action to annex the scenic islands of Hawaii in 1898. In the same year, United States went to war with Spain. As a consequence, the U.S.A. supported by the Filipino patriots, conquered the Philippines, an erstwhile Spanish colony. And when the people of Philippines showed a desire to rule themselves, American troops went into action against the nationalists led by Aguinaldo. The Filipinos could be subdued only after a prolonged guerrilla war lasting nearly four years. Controversy raged in the United States over the question of annexation. Those who were opposed to the occupation of Philippines pointed out that the United States had come into existence as a pledge to the idea that man should not be governed without consent. Conscious of the expense of overseas dominions, standing armies, and navalism, and the danger of being embroiled in imperialist wars, they were more worried about the departure from the earlier Pacific traditions. Senator Tillman exclaimed :

> Republican leaders do no longer dare call into question the justice or the necessity of limiting negro suffrage in the South... Your slogans of the past-brotherhood of man and fatherhood of God have gone glimmering through the ages![21]

> Mark Twain condemned, in vitriolic language, the use of the rifle and "the water-cure" to civilize and Christianize the people of Philippines.

Supporters of McKinley justified the action by appealing to the White Man's Burden, the struggle for existence, "racial" destiny and American traditions of expansion. They stressed the dangers of a general war if the Philippines were left open to a European scramble. They saw the almost parental responsibility for the allegedly childlike Filipinos, and the incapacity of that people for self-government. They were more than sure, that it was in the potential market of the East that the annexation of the islands had become a necessity.

By 1890 Americans had definitely discovered their imperialist interest in the Far East in general and in China in particular. The advocates of annexation proclaimed that the Philippines were a gateway to the Chinese market. Apart from the fact that the islands would themselves provide an outlet for U.S. goods, they would, in fact, provide a valuable base, both economic and naval, for the protection of the American interests in the Far East and would also help in counteracting the increasing European influence in China. As an enthusiastic Senator proclaimed in the summer of 1898 :

> The booming guns of Dewey's battleships sounded a new note on the Pacific shores, a note that has echoed and re-echoed around the world, and that note is that we are on the Pacific, that we are there to stay, and that we are there to protect our rights, promote our interests, and get our share of the trade and commerce of the opulent Orient.[22]

The American financier, and at this time Assistant Secretary to the Treasury, Frank A. Vanderlip, wrote in the *Century Magazine* (August 1898) that the Philippines were the gateway to reach the countries with one half of the humanity and, therefore, could be called the king of the Orient. Senator Mark Hanna, a leading figure of the Republican Party, a faithful adviser to the President and a prominent spokesman of the prevailing mood, declared :

> If it is commercialism to want the possession of a strategic point giving the American people an opportunity to maintain a foothold in the market of that great Eastern country; for God's sake let us have commercialism.[23]

He further wrote :

> With a strong foothold in the Philippines islands...we can and will take a large slice of the commerce of Asia that is what we want. We are bound to share in the commerce of the Far East and it is better to strike while the iron is hot.[24]

There can be no doubt that the Chinese question, illuminated by the opinion of business, government and the military and the growing crisis in China, had a progressive impact upon the shaping of America's Philippines policy.[25]

V

But just when the American bourgeoisie was discovering its Manifest Destiny and starting to look outwards it found itself threatened with exclusion from the Chinese market. American merchants were afraid that they might be crowded out by the European powers who were busy carving out China into spheres of influence and who might impose direct or indirect prohibition and erect tariff barriers within their own "spheres of influence." It was inevitable that the European imperialist powers would favour their own merchants and financiers by promoting the sale of their goods and investment of their capital within these semi-colonial possessions on the Chinese soil. They were especially and unitedly opposed to American expansion in Asia. The American Government had sufficient evidence of the fact that Germany, Russia, Austro-Hungary and, most of all, Britain would follow a discriminatory policy against the United States. American bourgeoisie, therefore, became restive and demanded immediate action from the government to save American interests in China from the impending menace of exclusion.

The most decisive pressure for a stronger China policy came in particular from the two interests: the cotton-goods industry and the American China Development Company. The cotton-goods industry manufacturers were worried because most of their exports went to north China and Manchuria which had come to be dominated by Russia. As Campbell has pointed out, "Faced by a prospective loss that would mean ruin, men connected with the cotton industry were among the most fervent and persistent advocates of governmental action in support of the Open Door in China."[26] Like the cotton-goods industry manufacturers, the China Development Company, formed for the purpose of acquiring railway concessions, was a determined advocate of a more vigorous policy in China. These two interests favoured a change because their financial involvement surpassed that of any other business interest.

In addition to these two major interests, a large number of other interests like the exporters of kerosene, wheat flour, steel and iron manufacturers and, of course, the American firms doing business in China also threw their weight behind the lobby that desired a change in the American policy in China.

All these business interests began to build their pressure on the American Government not only through the columns of many sympathetic journals and magazines, but also through their trade and commercial organisations. For example, the leading Chambers of Commerce and the Boards of Trade, including those of New York, Philadelphia, Boston, Baltimore, San Francisco and Seattle, sent memorials to President McKinley, urging immediate action. Lead was taken by the New York Chamber of Commerce, and its petition of February 3, 1898, became the model for all the other Chambers of Commerce. It contended :

> That the trade of the United States to China is now rapidly increasing, and is destined, with the further opening of that country, to assume large proportions unless arbitrarily debarred by action of foreign governments... That, in view of the changes threatening to future trade development of the United States in China, the Chamber of Commerce.. .respectfully and earnestly urge that such proper steps be taken as will commend themselves to your wisdom for the prompt and energetic defence of the existing treaty rights of our citizens in China, and for the preservation and protection of their important commercial interests in that Empire.[27]

The resolutions of other Chambers of Commerce of big cities of America talked in the same vein.[28] The U.S. Government, therefore, felt compelied to take some action.

What course of action could be followed depended on the options available to the McKinley administration. There were three viable choices and the United States government seriously considered them all. One obvious course of action could be to accept the existing situation—to recognise the "spheres of influence" and join in the partitioning of China. But this line was ruled out because of strong anti-imperialist criticism which prevailed in the U.S.A. Other factors deterring such a course was the involvement of administrative and military burdens and concentration of American sales and arteries of distribution in zones controlled by Russia and Germany. As McCormick has described, "a small slice of the pie," which was all the U.S.A. could acquire if China was partitioned, "held little attraction for such men who wanted (and thought they could get) the major share" of the China market.[29]

The second alternative was to make common cause with other Open Door supporters like England and Japan. There is sufficient evidence to the fact that serious thought was given to this line of action. But ultimately it did not find favour with the policy framers because they did not want to deprive themselves of complete freedom of action. It was feared that the American people would not favour "a policy that seemed to be taken under British pressure or would possibly be interpreted as pulling British chestnuts out of the fire."[30] Moreover, the British and Japanese ambivalence towards the Open Door made them unreliable allies. It was also felt that such an alliance might require the possible use of force which the U.S. Government was neither in a position to resort to nor willing to take in China. Compared to other European powers, the United States was weak in naval and military power.

Under these circumstances, the best possible tactical line was one of advocacy for the Open Door. McCormick has summed up the situation as follows :

> What the United States wanted was not force but coexistence and economic competition for open markets; an "eat-your cake-and-have-it-too" policy of peace and market domination... Neither partitioning nor military alliance offered practical means to realise the desired American ends; only the consensus neutralisation held any glimmer of hope... [31]

VI

Another force that played an important role in the declaration of the Open Door in 1899 was the advocacy and desire of the Christian missionaries for a change in the American policy in China. As far as the American missionaries in China were concerned, the Treaty of Tianjin (Tientsin) had accorded a privileged status to them. Article 29 of the Treaty had provided that :

> The principles of the Christian religion, as professed by the Protestant and Roman Catholic Churches, are recognised as teaching men to do good, and to do others as they would have others do to them. Hereafter those who quietly profess and teach these doctrines shall not be harassed or persecuted on account of their faith. Any person, whether citizen of the United States, or Chinese convert, who, according to these tenets, peaceably teaches and practises the principles of Christianity shall in no case be interfered with or molested.[32]

Within no time missionaries established themselves in the interior and acquired "perpetual leases" of land and demanded protection from the Chinese authorities. They were fully backed by their government in securing this protection. For example, in 1886 when anti-missionary and anti-foreign riots broke out in various parts of China, the American Government secured a direct and explicit statement from China that their missionaries were entitled to every right that had been granted to the French. As Tyler Dennet remarks, "In the course of years the missionary question as viewed by the American Government had come to be one of our national prestiges..."[33]

It was in the background of this situation that the Philippines islands were seen by the missionaries as a base for their further extension in the Far East. And when these islands were annexed in 1898, the American missionaries' dream of converting the Chinese empire into Christianity was revived. The American scholar Foster Rhea Dulles has expressed the feelings of the missionaries thus :

> They saw the further extension of our influence in the Far East as aiding them in their immense task of bringing Christianity to the Chinese people.[34]

The partition of China into "spheres of influence" also meant restrictions on the activities and freedom of the missionaries of the countries other than the domineering power. Just like the American merchants, businessmen, industrialists and financiers, they also hailed the decision of the annexation of the Philippines islands and threw their weight behind the move for a change in the American policy in China.

VII

Owing to the interplay of several factors, the most important of which was, of course, the pressure of the various economic interests, the idea of the Open Door began to find favour with the U.S. Government and in September-October 1899 the U.S. Secretary of State, John Hay, sent identical instructions to the U.S. representatives in London, Berlin, Paris, St. Petersburg, Rome and Tokyo asking them to request the powers concerned to give the following assurance :

> "1. (That it) will in no wise interfere with any treaty port or vested interest within any of the so-called 'sphere of influence' or leased territory it may have in China.

"2. That the Chinese treaty tariff of the time being shall apply to all merchandise landed or shipped to all such ports as are within said 'spheres of influence' (unless they be free ports), no matter to what nationality it may belong, and that duties so leviable shall be collected by the Chinese Government.

"3. That it will levy no higher harbour dues in such 'sphere' than shall be levied on vessels of its own nationality and no higher railroad charges over lines built, controlled or operated upon within its 'sphere' on merchandise belonging to its citizens or subjects of other nationalities transported through such 'sphere' than shall be levied on similar merchandise belonging to its own nationals transported over equal distances."

The U.S.A. Government further declared that the U.S.A. "will in no way commit itself to any recognition of the exclusive rights of any power within or control over any portion of the Chinese empire under such agreements as have recently been made" and that it apprehended that "there is danger of complications arising between the treaty powers which might imperil the right insured to the United States by its treaties with China."

The Open Door Notes not only asked each of the nations, to which they were addressed, to give its own assurances but also urged upon them to cooperate with the United States in obtaining the assurances of all other nations. In other words, they were asked to use their influence with the other powers to get the principles which were enunciated in the Hay notes, accepted by all of them.

The Hay Notes placed the powers in a most awkward position as they were reluctant to accept any restrictions on the exploitation of their "spheres of influence" and leased territories. At the same time none of them was willing to come out openly in favour of a policy of open annexation and monopolized "spheres of influence", and, therefore, none dared either openly reject the American proposals or accept them. The powers, all the same, did not find it too difficult to accept the Hay Notes in general as they were all nearly in the same position as the U.S.A. in their competitive exploitation of China and were willing to accept some systematisation of the "rules of the game" as a safeguard against any one of them trying to establish exclusive domination over China. The replies of the powers expressed their acceptance of the American declaration, but with evasions, reservations and ambiguity and making their acceptance conditional upon acceptance by other powers. England excepted Kowloon from any application of the Open Door doctrine. France objected to the term "sphere of influence". Germany recommended minor changes; and Russia replied that she was already following an open door policy. In view of her past policies, the Russian reply was an effective rebuff to the U.S. initiative. Of all the powers only Italy gave an unqualified approval which might be explained by the fact that apart from the United States she was the only other power which had no "sphere of influence" in China. Among the big powers, Japan was the only country to show enthusiasm for the American proposals. She was as yet too weak and underdeveloped economically to participate in railway and other loans through which China was being partitioned into "spheres of influence." She was, therefore, quite willing to endorse the Open Door proposals, which would prevent the partition of China till she was ready to play the role of a major power in the Far East. This would also give her enough time which could be used to immobilise Russia, her rival in north China.

Hay should have been dismayed by the replies of the powers, for they amounted, in effect, to the virtual rejection of the notes. But he refused to accept failure and resorted to the age-old device of diplomatic bluff. Hoping to win such strong public support for his policy at home and abroad that no nation could dare issue a public denial to his declaration, he announced on March 20, 1900, that the replies received to his notes were satisfactory and that assent of all the powers was "final and definitive."

The Hay notes of 1899 were followed by the dramatic event of the Yi He Tuan uprising against the foreign missionaries and the exploitation of China by the imperialist powers. The foreign powers looked upon the uprising as a threat to their position in China and took collective steps to crush it. The U.S. government, forgetting for the time being the Open Door and age-old policy of non-intervention in the internal affairs of other countries, contributed 2,500 soldiers to the joint expedition of nearly 19,000 men organised by the imperialist powers to suppress the Yi He Tuan uprising.

The joint expedition, though successful in its objective of crushing the Yi He Tuan movement, resulted in the unprecedented rivalry among the imperialist powers. The presence of the troops of various powers on Chinese soil led to widespread jockeying for positions of influence and control in different parts of China. This was especially true of the large-scale Russian troop movement in Manchuria. The U.S. Government saw that the Open Door was in danger. It was afraid that the powers might avail of the opportunity to dismember the Celestial Kingdom. To prevent such an eventuality, Hay, once again, had recourse to diplomatic pressure. In a circular note sent to the powers concerned on July 3, 1900, he declared that "the policy of the government of the United States is to seek a solution which may bring about permanent safety and peace to China, preserve Chinese territorial and administrative entity, protect all rights guaranteed to friendly powers by treaty and international law, and safeguard the principle of equal and impartial trade with all parts of the Chinese Empire.[35]

This note reiterated the original notes of September and October 1899 and supposedly amplified the earlier proposals:

But in reality it revealed many new aspects of the U.S. policy. The United States now extended the Open Door policy to cover the whole of China instead of limiting it to only the "spheres of influence" and foreign leaseholds. Moreover, the United States for the first time declared that it stood for the territorial integrity of the Chinese Empire. In spite of the fact that the circular note of July 1900, being merely a declaration of policy did not call for a reply, many of the powers found it advantageous to publicly accept the principles enunciated by Hay with their identical declarations of policy. Within the span of a few years nearly all the powers in one way or another expressed their adherence to the Open Door doctrine, that is, to the principle of equal commercial opportunity in all parts of the Chinese Empire, even though this adherence was of an entirely ephemeral character in view of the flexibility with which the doctrine was interpreted by each one of the powers to suit its interest and convenience.

VIII

The United States for many decades till 1949 continued to reiterate the Open Door and press for its acceptance by all the powers. Since the end of the First World War, the Open Door had been a much proclaimed and hallowed cornerstone of the American policy in China and consequently a great body of mythological literature has grown around it. It is, as a matter of fact, one of the most popular myths. In its popular legendary form Open Door stood for equal commercial opportunity and territorial and administrative integrity of China. The State department declared in 1940 that these were the twin principles on which the American policy in China was based. It was also believed to have saved China from partition during and after the Yi He Tuan uprising. It was said to be the basic feature that distinguished the democratic foreign policy from the imperialist policy. This popular myth has been provided with an academic garb by John K. Fairbank whose works on China are known for their pro-imperialist bias in general and pro-American imperialism in particular. Tracing the development of the two Hay notes and analysing their impact on China, he has commented :

> In this way the Open Door doctrine developed two main tenets: the integrity of China and the equal treatment of all foreigners there. Viewed cynically, the doctrine of China's integrity was a device to prevent other powers, for example, Russia, from taking over areas of China and excluding us from there. But the Independence of China has also appealed to Americans as a matter of political justice. Until recently it fitted the doctrine of self-determination and sovereignty of weaker nations, which constituted one of our major political sentiments.[36]

But many of his fellow American historians have disagreed with this viewpoint. They have firmly asserted that the Open Door was, in the main, to protect those American economic interests which were bound to be threatened by the partition of China. The leading light of the American scholars who have seen the link between the Open Door and the U.S. economic interests is Prof. Owen Lattimore. The Open Door, as he has aptly described, was a policy of hitch-hiking imperialism and me-too imperialism. He has pointed out that though the United States did not take lead in seizing territories etc., she did demand that whatever was gouged out of China by any other nation should not be monopolized by that nation alone, but shared with all comers. Open Door did not propose a cessation of imperialistic demands on China; they merely registered a claim of me-too.[37] That is to say, the United States did not question the right of other nations to make demands on China; only wanted a share in the consequent gains and a guarantee that American merchants and investors would not be denied further opportunities. "Joined not to internationalism, which the world and especially the American people have adopted, the Open Door principle is likely to turn out to be little more than the old imperialism with a new name."[38] Therefore, we can say that the theory that the Open Door stood for China's territorial and political sovereignty and integrity and that it saved China from partition is a myth and an illusion which, however brilliant, serves to hide the truth which runs counter to its claim.[39] "Our 'Open Door' was further designed to fasten chains tighter on the common victim of the powers—China,"[40] observes Marion. Many other US scholars have joined Owen and Marion to call the bluff of the Open Door.

To probe deeper into the historical events, we find that China was saved from partition not by the Open Door but by the conjuncture of certain historical forces, which may be highlighted :

(*a*) Rivalries among the imperialist powers made it difficult to arrive at an agreement on the division of the spoils, leaving each one fully satisfied. No one was powerful enough to exclude others from the pie.

(*b*) The international balance of forces prevented any single power or combination of powers from unilaterally destroying Chinese sovereignty.

(*c*) The ascendance in the last quarter of the 19th century of finance imperialism replaced the old form of domination over China, *i.e.* territorial conquest, with a new and subtle strategy.

(*d*) The Chinese people's anti-imperialist movement, the first manifestation of which was the powerful Yi He Tuan uprising, was developing from strength to strength, forcing the imperialist powers to respect China's sovereignty.

IX

The main purpose of the Open Door policy was to safeguard U.S. commercial and financial interests in China. We should remember that the U.S. Government showed such scant respect for Chinese sovereignty that while proclaiming to be its defender, it did not even consider it necessary to consult the Chinese Government before announcing the Open Door. This would not have been if the U.S. Government really had the Chinese interest in view. However, one question still remains, *i.e.* why should there be so much fuss about the Open Door? This deserves our examination.

We know that the American government is constitutionally a democratic government, depending on popular support for the success of its policies. It is at the same time a bulwark of the commercial and industrial interests. When a government or an institution has one face in theory and another in practice, it is bound to rely on myth-making. Myth-making, especially in the field of foreign affairs, is meant to be an effective means to cover up the contradiction between the democratic theory and the oligarchic practice. Public support is much needed for supporting expansive policies lest they might become unpopular. There was particular urgency for such popular support of the U.S. Far Eastern policies. The American people at the time were firmly opposed to any imperialist adventures abroad or intervention in the internal affairs of other countries. The memory of their own War of Independence and the Civil War, in which some powers had tried to intervene on the side of the southern confederacy, was very much alive in their minds.

Moreover, they had every sympathy for people still groaning under foreign domination. They had shown their great love of freedom by helping the people of Latin America achieve independence from their Spanish and Portuguese masters.

The American people would, consequently, oppose any effort to take the U.S.A. along the imperialist path. It was because of this democratic nature of the U.S. that there existed a formidable obstacle for those interests who dreamt of a vast Pacific empire with exclusive market. A myth had therefore, to be created, a myth which could take advantage of the American people's sympathy for the underdogs, *i.e.* Chinese victims of feudal backwardness and imperialist aggression and exploitation. Thus, there was born the myth of the China-saving Open Door.

It would, on the one hand, serve the economic designs of the American commercial and financial houses, and on the other, win over the popular support for these designs by appealing for the humanitarian feelings of the American people. The myth of Open Door was made to appear to the American people that the U.S. government stood for the defence of the poor, unfortunate, fast multiplying people of the ancient land of China.

It was actually the State department's creation in the face of tough competition from the European imperialist powers. The ruling classes of the U.S.A. have always made a clever use of such myths in the field of foreign policy taking advantage of the people's ignorance of the firsthand knowledge of foreign affairs.

One of the best examples of this intermingling of the sordid and ugly with the sacred and beautiful by the American ruling groups is furnished by President McKinley's justification of his decision to impose American rule over the Philippines in 1898 just after the islands' being liberated from Spanish possession. This is what he later wrote to a group of his fellow-Methodists about his decision:

> The truth is I didn't want the Philippines and when they came to us, as a gift from the gods, I did not know what to do about them. I sought counsel from all sides—Democrats as well as the Republicans—but got little help. I thought first we would take only Manila; then Luzon; then other islands, perhaps, also. I walked the floor of the White House night after night until midnight; and I am not ashamed to tell you, gentlemen, that I went down on my knees and prayed almighty God for light and guidance more than one night. And one night late it came to me this way—I don't know how it was, but it came: (1) that we could not give them back to Spain—that would be cowardly and dishonourable; (2) that we could not turn them over to France or Germany—our commercial rivals in the Orient—that would be bad business and discreditable; (3) that we could not leave them to themselves they were unfit for self-government—and they would soon have anarchy and misrule over there—worse than Spain's was; and (4) that there was nothing left for us to do but to take them all, and to educate the Filipinos, and uplift and civilize and Christianise them, and by God's grace do the very best we could by them, as our fellow-men for whom Christ also died. And then I went to sleep, and slept soundly...[41]

It should be noticed that in this short extract McKinley touched upon "almost every string in the familiar harmony of imperialism"[42] as described by the American historian of modern imperialism, Parker T. Moon. And so the U.S.A. gained its first colony in the Far East, while the American people had the satisfaction of believing that the soul of the little brown brother was being saved.

If we examine the policy of the Open Door a little more closely we will notice that the first Hay notes were limited in their scope. They did not say anything about China's territorial integrity or safeguarding her political independence. Hay raised no protest against the scramble for spheres of influence. Instead, he recognised the existing spheres and assumed that the "sphering out" of the empire would continue in future. He did not make an appeal to the nations to relinquish political gains which they had acquired at the cost of China so far. The notes made no direct or indirect reference to mining and railroad concessions and to capital investment. The U.S.A. did no even demand equality in these fields. The Open Door was sought to be applied only to the leaseholds and "spheres of influence", without affecting the tutelage of the domineering powers and the vested interests they represented. All what the Hay notes tried to accomplish was the acceptance of the principle of "equal commercial opportunity" for all nations in dealing with China. Their only stipulation was that in the powers' various "spheres of influence" and leaseholds there should be no discrimination between the powers as regards customs duties, port charges and railway rates. Guided by the apprehension that "there is danger of complication arising between the treaty powers which might imperil the rights insured to the United States by its treaties with China" (First Hay Note), the U.S. government merely sought to ensure certain specific conditions of free trade to the merchants of all nations, even in case of the actual partition of China. As Charles and Mary Beard have aptly remarked :

> Though devised with realistic and practical ends in mind, the policy of Open Door also had a lofty moral flavour, pleasing to Chinese, missionaries, anti-imperialists, and pacifists alike. At the same time it gave American economic interest in the Far East about all the guarantees that the state of popular sentiments at home warranted...with the high sanction of the Open Door policy, Secretary Hay and his successors under Roosevelt and Taft bent their energies to the work of securing for American citizens equal trading privileges in all parts of China and equal opportunities for investment in the development of railways and natural resources."[43]

The U.S. government did not fight for anything more than equality for two reasons :

(*a*) American interests arrived on the Chinese scene quite late, after the European powers had started for a long while. Their fairest chance for securing a share in Chinese market was to prevent others from monopolizing it. They, therefore, pressed for equal competition in the exploitation of China.

(*b*) As we have seen earlier the American people were not yet ready to support naked imperialism. "We do not think that the public opinion of the United States would justify this government in taking part in the great game of spoliation now going on"[44] admitted John Hay. Later when the American might abroad increased and public opinion at home became more receptive to ideas of imperialism, perhaps more direct steps could be taken. "That was the heart of the matter. President McKinley was personally willing to take a hand in the carving up of China, if it was to come about, but feared that the hinterland of America was not yet fully indoctrinated with any such view of Manifest Destiny."[45] observe Charles and Mary Beard. Similar logic later led the American Government to broaden the Open Door to include the guarantee of the political and territorial integrity of China.

The Open Door was in reality an extension and further development of the previous U.S. policy in China, *i.e.*, the "most favoured nation" doctrine. The United States had claimed the right to enjoy every privilege which Britain and France had, through two wars, forced the Manchu government to concede. The Americans had been sharing every privilege acquired by foreign enterprises in China from the treaty provisions, concessions or settlements. Since the U.S. had not acquired a territorial concession or settlement in China, she had taken full advantage of concessions acquired by other powers and of the international settlements. America had a full share in the foreign administration of the Shanghai International Settlement. Her citizens enjoyed complete extraterritoriality while residing in China. The Open Door was meant for an extension of such enjoyments to the spheres of influence. The United States desired through this doctrine to take full advantage of the newly opened economic opportunities in China without actually taking part in the scramble for "spheres of influence."

The Open Door was a policy best suited to modern imperialism. While preventing the political partition of China, it, in a way, hindered financial penetration of China which could, as surely as direct conquest, transform China into a direct dependency and even colony of the foreign end of the purse strings. By preventing other powers from using methods of non-economic character for monopolizing Chinese market for goods and investment, the Open Door attempted to create conditions which would, because of the U.S.A.'s primacy in modern finance and industry, lead to its supremacy in the long run. Thus it was an attempt to change the form, but not the substance of imperialism in China.

The Open Door also served the purpose of regulating and keeping under control the rivalries among the imperialist powers over the spoils in China. "The Open Door formula brought into being in fact, though not by specific declaration, a league of countries with maritime access to the trade of the Far East, to maintain conditions under which they could compete with each other and could enjoin Russia, which alone had easy, commercially exploitable access to China by land, to observe those conditions."[46]

One reason why the doctrine was more or less accepted in theory by the powers was that they realised that none of them was strong enough to swallow up China all alone. None of them was yet prepared to measure strength with others in war. The only alternative to the elimination of non-economic forms of struggle among the powers was an all out scramble which might result in war. With the help of the Open Door they could fight out and try to resolve intra-imperialist contradictions and conflicts without re-course to arms. On the other hand, they realised that it might be more profitable to mutually enjoy privileges wrested from the Chinese regime by any one of them than to indulge in an indecisive and unpredictable armed conflict. Consequently the powers decided to approve the Open Door in the absence of any better alternative and thus give it currency and wide acceptance which the United States was incapable of giving on its own. As a matter of fact, the Open Door became the basic policy of all the powers in their mutual relations with China. The Boxer protocol was based on the Open Door.

The Open Door did not result in the preservation of China's integrity. It merely preserved Chinese market for joint exploitation and control, instead of the previous tendency to partition it into "spheres of influence". This facilitated the development of international finance imperialism under the auspices of international consortium of banks. In the final analysis, the Open Door was of, by, and for finance imperialism. China was saved from becoming polandised or a single power controlled colony thanks to the Open Door which, nevertheless, brought no cheers to China who was made to wed the destiny of a hyper-colony in the words of Dr. Sun Yat-sen.

References

1. William L. Langer, *The Diplomacy of Imperialism* (New York, 1951), p. 167.
2. John K. Fairbank, *The United States and China* (Harvard University Press. 1971), p. 296.
3. George Marion, *Bases and Empire - A Chart of American Expansion* (New York, 1949). pp. 89-90.
4. Cited in A. Whitney Griswold, *The Far Eastern Policy in the United States* (Yale University Press, 1964), p. 42.
5. Foster Rhea Dulles, *China and America: The Study of the Relations since 1784* (Princeton University Press, 1967), p. 110.
6. Thomas J. McCormick. *China Market: America's Quest for Informal Empire* (Chicago, 1967), p. 128.
7. Charles and Mary Beard, *The Rise of the American Civilization* (New York 1934), Vol. II, p. 480.
8. Charles S. Campbell, Jr, *Special Business Interests and the Open Door* (Yale University Press, 1953), p. 2, citing *Journal of Commerce and Commercial Bulletin,* February 1, 1899.
9. *Ibid.,* p. 3, citing *United States Investor,* No. 9; 1898, p. 593.
10. *Ibid.,* p. 5, citing C.G. Bowers, *Beveridge and the Progressive Era,* (Cambridge, 1932), p. 69.
11. *Ibid.,* p. 4, citing *United States Investor,* No. 9 (1898), p. 593.
12. *Ibid.,* p. 4, citing *Journal of Commerce and Commercial Bulletin,* January 9, 1899.
13. Cited in Dulles, *op. cit.,* p. 105.
14. *Ibid.,* p. 100.

15. Campbell, *op cit.,* p. 12, citing *Banker and Tradesman and Massachusetts Law Reporter,* No. 24 *(1898),* p. 776.
16. *Ibid,* p. 12, citing *Bradstreets,* No. 97 (1899), p. 451.
17. *Ibid,* p. 12, citing *Chicago Board of Trade,* Forty Second Annual Report (1899), p. XXXVIII.
18. *Ibid,* p. 12, citing *Official Proceedings of the Ninth Session of the Trans-Mississippi Commercial Congress,* July 1897, p. 251.
19. *Ibid.,* p. 12, citing *Literary Digest,* No. 19, (1899), p. 607.
20. *Ibid.,* p. 12, citing *Journal of Commerce and Commercial Bulletin,* December 28, 1897.
21. Cited in Charles and Mary Beard, *op. cit.,* p. 484.
22. Cited in Dulles, *op. cit.,* p. 101.
23. Cited in Marion, *op. cit.,* p. 85.
24. McCormick, *op. cit.,* p. 119. Also Campbell, *op. cit.,* p. 16, citing *World* (New York), August 29, 1898.
25. McCormick. *op. cit.,* p. 122.
26. Campbell, *op. cit.,* p. 21.
27. *Ibid,* p. 35, citing *New York Chamber of Commerce,* Annual Report, 1897-1898, p. 75.
28. For details of the petitions sent by other business organisations and how the campaign was organised in favour of a change in the American policy in China by these economic interests, see Campbell, *op. cit,* pp. 25-37. Also McCormick, *op. cit.,* pp. 91-95.
29. McCormick, *op. cit.,* p. 135.
30. Dulles, *op. cit.,* p. 108.
31. McCormick, *op. cit.,* p. 137.
32. Cited in Tyler Dennet, *Americans in Eastern Asia,* (reprint, New York, 1963), p. 562.
33. *Ibid,* p. 573.
34. Dulles, *op. cit,* p. 108.
35. Daniel M. Smith, *American Diplomatic History: Documents and Readings* (Massachusetts, 1964), p. 323.
36. John K. Fairbank, *op. cit,* p. 298.
37. Owen and Eleanor Lattimore, *The Making of Modern China* (London, 1945). p. 121.
38. Tyler Dennett. "The Open Door", in Joseph Barnes (ed.), *Empirt in the East* (London. 1934). p. 204.

39. On myth-making with special reference to the capitalist societies see Barrows Dunham, *Man against Myth* (New York, 1962).
40. Marion, *op. cit.,* p. 92.
41. Cited in Daniel Smith (ed.), *op. cit.,* p. 287. For A.V. Beveridge's statement see *ibid,* pp. 287-290.
42. Parker T. Moon, *Imperialism and World Politics* (New York, 1947), p. 394.
43. Charles and Mary Beard, *op. cit.,* pp. 494-495.
44. *Ibid.,* p. 495.
45. *Ibid.*
46. Owen Lattimore, *The Situation in Asia* (Boston, 1949), pp. 28-29.

PART–III
PEASANT REBELLIONS

10

Chinese Peasant War for Taiping Dreams (1850-64)*

*The Taiping Revolution*** is one of the latest and shortest critical accounts of this historic event. It was originally written for China's vast masses of workers, peasants and soldiers for a post-Cultural Revolution refreshing of historical memory. A text of about 50,000 Chinese characters packed with facts and presented in the Maoist perspective by the history teachers of Fudan and Shanghai Normal Universities, this book is rendered into 178 pages of simple and readable English, with a few omissions here and there from the original Chinese narrative. Students of Chinese history in India and other countries will find it useful to begin with to understand the nature and significance of the Taiping Movement.

I

Like its sister volume *The Opium War,* this one too offers us a spectrum through which we get a glimpse of Communist Chinese historiography on the Taiping movement, which contrasts sharply with Western historiography on the topic.

As the Chinese perspective represents the Maoist viewpoint, it is important to know what Mao Zedong has written on Taiping. The "War of the Taiping Heavenly Kingdom", as Mao recalled, was one of the eight major events in China's 100 year history before the Communist revolution (the other seven events were: the Opium War, the Sino-Japanese War of 1894, the Reform

---

* The original article that was written in 1977 and published in *China Report,* Vol. XIV, No. 3 (May-June, 1978) has been abridged for the present book.

** Foreign Language Press, *The Taiping Revolution,* (Peking, 1976).

Movement of 1898, the "Yi He Tuan Movement" [Boxer], the 1911 Revolution, the May Fourth Movement of 1919, and the Kuomintang Northern Expedition in the 1920s).[1] Broadly all these events occurred in the formative period of "China's bourgeois-democratic revolution".[2] The bourgeois-democratic revolution is the first of a two-phase Chinese revolution in the Maoist scheme aiming at changing "the colonial, semi-colonial and semi-feudal form of society into an independent, democratic society". Mao not only treated the Taiping Movement as the second major strike of this revolution, but also regarded its leader Hong Xiuquan (Hung Hsiu-ch'uan) as the earliest "progressive" who, along with Kang Youwei (K'ang Yu-wei), Yan Fu and Sun Yat-sen, "went through untold hardships in their quest for truth from the Western countries."[3]

This perspective placed both Hong Xiuquan and Mao Zedong and both the Taiping and the Communist Movements within the same epoch—the epoch of China's struggle against the *ancien regime* propped up by the native feudal and foreign imperialist forces. The Taiping, said Mao, had launched a "war against the Ching regime, the running dog of imperialism." He thought "the Western bourgeoisie" had "created two categories of people" in China: (1) the minority of "flunkeys of imperialism", and (2) the majority of "gravediggers of imperialism."[4] Both the Taiping and the Communists were the vanguards of the latter.

The Maoist revolution has claimed as its ancestries both the Taiping revolutionary tradition and Marxist internationalism.

In his famous essay "The Chinese Revolution and the Chinese Communist Party", written in December 1939, Mao discerned in Chinese history a series of great "peasant revolutionary wars", from the uprisings on the eve of the Christian era down to the Taiping Movement: "The scale of peasant uprisings and peasant wars in Chinese history has no parallel anywhere else.

The class struggles of the peasants, the peasant uprisings and peasant wars constituted the real motive force of historical development in Chinese feudal society. For each of the major peasant uprisings and wars dealt a blow to the feudal regime of the time, and hence more or less furthered the growth of the social productive forces. However...every peasant revolution failed; and the peasantry was invariably used by the landlords and the nobility, either during or after the revolution, as a lever for bringing about dynastic change. Therefore, although some social progress was made after each great peasant revolutionary struggle, the feudal economic relations and political system remained basically unchanged."[5]

Mao thus made three points. First, the peasant uprisings and wars were a unique feature of Chinese history. Therefore, Chinese intellectuals, including historians, should distinguish the Chinese historical characteristics from those of European history, with which alone Marx was familiar and commented upon. Secondly, peasant uprisings and wars—*i.e.* class struggle between peasantry and feudal repressive forces—constituted the dynamic element in China's socio-politico-economic progress amidst the changing fortunes of dynasties. Thirdly, because of the absence of "correct leadership such as the proletariat and the Communist Party", peasant wars in the past were not able to liberate the peasantry from the feudal socio-political system which still reigned supreme till the last century, despite the repeated overthrow of feudal regimes.

One cannot but notice the inherent contradictions in this Maoist perspective. First, Mao wrote in the same essay that: "The extreme poverty and backwardness of the peasants resulting from ruthless landlord exploitation and oppression is the basic reason why Chinese society remained at the same stage of socio-economic development for several thousand years."[6] This contrasted with Mao's own assessment that "some social progress" and "the growth of the social productive forces" had resulted from peasant wars. Second, Mao unwittingly placed the Taiping War in two different categories: one, the never-liberating-themselves peasant-war category, and the other, the bourgeois democratic revolution category which progressively developed into the Communist revolution in less than a hundred years.

Undoubtedly peasant wars constituted an important part of China's historical heritage, despite the distortions and suppression of information in the rich literature left behind by China's gentry class. The scholarly debate among Chinese historians has resulted in the discovery of this heritage. The debate has helped Chinese intellectuals to view their past as a gradual process of social evolution with peasants' struggles as pace-makers.

A near consensus emerged from the debate, that the wars waged by the peasants had the element of anti-feudalism. because, the wars were born out of the contradictions between productive forces and feudal relations of production. The dissidents argued that the peasants had only directed their attacks on feudal regimes, but not on the feudal system itself. This argument was unacceptable to the majority who thought it illogical to separate the feudal system from the feudal regime. "When the peasant wars challenged feudal regimes, they, in reality, challenged the feudal system."[7]

Chinese historians derived from peasant movements a crude revolutionary ideology often cloaked in religious creed. Most historians felt that China's peasant struggles were gradually perfecting themselves and attained the highest form during the Taiping Movement.

II

The Taiping Revolution not only has a clear Maoist ideological perspective but is also based on a wealth of Chinese literary sources. The Chinese Historical Society published eight volumes of source materials on Taiping in 1952 from Shanghai (compiled by a team of veteran historians led by Xiang Da, and entitled *Taiping Tian'guo*. This was followed by a series of publications of the photographs of documents and objects left by the Taiping rebels.[8] The People's Republic set up a special Memorial Museum for Taiping Heavenly Kingdom. The Museum published in 1963 from Shanghai six volumes of source materials entitled: *Taiping tian'guo shiliao congbian jianji.* (A Brief Collection of Taiping Heavenly Kingdom Historical Materials). There are a host of publications of Taiping source materials both before and after 1949 which we shall not detail. Besides, there are several Chinese historians both inside and outside the People's Republic, famous names like Lo Erh-kang, Jen Yu-wen (Chinese name Jian Yuwen), Guo Tingyi etc. who have published many books and articles on the Taiping. Jen Yu-wen published his Taiping history in English in 1973 entitled

The Taiping Revolutionary Movement (Yale University Press), who joined Ssu-yu Teng and Vincent Y.C. Shih, both U.S. scholars of Chinese origin, are the few major authors in English on the Taiping Movement. There were also a group of Chinese scholars who helped Prof Franz Michael to bring out his three famous volumes of *The Taiping Rebellion: History and Documents* (University of Washington Press, 1966).

The Taiping Revolution views the Taiping movement both as a revolution and a peasant movement. "The Taiping Revolution was the first great high tide of the revolution in the history of modern China." (p. 168) It adds: "From the first moment of its existence, the Taiping Heavenly Kingdom directed its attack against the feudal ruling class represented by the Ching [Qing] dynasty and against the foreign capitalist aggressors. In taking on this anti-imperialist, anti-feudal role it prepared the way for the democratic revolution. Its military history has been a constant source of inspiration to the Chinese people in their revolutionary struggles." (p. 173)

The main points of the book in support of the proposition of Taiping being a peasant revolution are :

(1) "The Taiping Revolution battered the superstructure of the feudal society." Hong Xiuquan's (Hung Hsiu-ch'uan) denunciation of the Manchu emperor "was an indirect negation of monarchical dictatorship." His condemnation of the Confucian classics "struck hard at the stubbornly fortified reactionary feudal superstructure." (pp. 174-175)

(2) "The Taipings sought to transform the feudal society by building an ideal society where people were equal." The Taiping rule over the lower stream of Yangtse resulted in the down-grading of the socio-economic importance of the landowning class in the area since then, which only indicates the heavy destruction of the feudal social order by the Taiping movement. (pp. 175-177)

This perspective is very different from Western academic appraisals.

Two premises have now emerged in the study of the nature of the Taiping Movement: (*a*) Taiping was a typical traditional Chinese peasant rebellion and not a revolution in the modern sense; (*b*) Taipig deserves to be treated as a full-fledged revolution. At the outbreak of the Taiping war the Western world seemed immensely impressed. Both Karl Marx and *The Times* of London hailed the event in idential terms. Marx called it a "formidable revolution" and predicted that it would affect the fate of entire Europe.[9] *The Times* called Taiping the greatest revolution the world has yet seen and one of the most important and remarkable movements of mass protest in modern history.[10] Paradoxically, the more the Western academics have understood China the less appreciative they have become towards the revolutionary character of the Taiping Movement. The movement is commonly called Taiping rebellion, seldom Taiping revolution.

The dichotomy before us is now clear. On the one hand, we have Marx and his followers not insisting on a rigid distinction between revolution and rebellion, and more than ready to proclaim the Taiping movement a revolution. On the other hand, although both Barrington Moore and Kung-chuan Hsiao have not attempted to place the Taiping Movement in either category, they have not used the term "Taiping revolution", implying their reservation.

Whether Taiping was a revolution or rebellion is related to another question—was it a peasant movement? Chinese Communists, from Mao Zedong down to any ordinary history student, have no second opinion about the premise that Taiping was a peasant movement and a peasant war against the *ancien regime.* This seemingly indisputable conclusion has been arrived at not only by looking at the Taiping Movement itself, but also by taking a long-term historical perspective of the innumerable peasant wars which had preceded the Taiping war. In Marxist theory the basic contradiction in a feudal society is between the peasantry and the feudal ruling elite. Mao reinforced this by including the peasantry among the motive forces of Chinese revolution. Hence, all armed uprisings against feudal governments in Chinese history are regarded as peasant wars.

This Communist Chinese perspective defines peasant war on the basis of a broad historical and sociological analysis, irrespective of the fact that some leaders and a section of followers of a particular uprising might not be peasants. Of course, since the peasants have always formed the overwhelming majority of Chinese population, any large-scale mass uprising was bound to be dominated by the peasantry.

There is, however, the general feeling among Communist Chinese historians that in spite of the revolutionary spirit of the Chinese peasantry, all peasant wars in Chinese history have proved to be incapable of liberating the peasant class from the feudal yoke. This shows that before the emergence of the Communist Party, the Chinese peasantry remained a "class in itself", and was never transformed into a "class for itself." When it remained a "class in itself", the peasant war was characterized by spontaneity *(zifaxing),* not by consciousness *(zijuexing)* which only a "class for itself" is capable of.[11]

III

There is a clear contrast between the two corpuses of Taiping historiography: the Chinese Communist over-emphasis on the affinity between the peasantry and the Taiping and the disregard of the peasant connection of the Taiping movement by the U.S. or rather the Sino-U.S. scholarship. (Here I avoid the generic term Western, knowing fully the different perspective of the French China historians[12] from that of the Michael-Shih-Teng trio on this issue).

The unconcern of the U.S. scholarship with the affinity between Chinese peasantry and the Taiping movement is shown by its failure even to mention Taiping in a symposium specially devoted to the study of "Peasant Rebellion and Communist Revolution in Asia."

The insensitivity of US scholarship to the revolutionariness of Chinese peasantry is probably caused by, among other things, their obsession with the Chinese dynastic cycle. The seriousness of the peasant problems is not only lost in the stereotyped dynasty analysis of Eranz Michael, but it is obscured by his terminology of farmers, small farmers, working farmers, tenant farmers, and the common farming population which are mentioned side by side with the terms "peasants" and "landlords."

The dynastic cycle theory reduces the study of Chinese history to simple geometry. Scholars who have expounded it have never made it clear whether this dynastic cycle is an unalterable course of China's historical development, or whether it is just a historical co-incidence that the decline of every Chinese dynasty was attended by identical phenomena. Some scholars say that while the Western Christian civilization believes in unilinear development, the orientals, particularly Chinese and Indians, have always believed in cyclical development. Again, it has not been made clear whether it was the ancient Chinese belief that has predestined China's historical development to dynastic cycles, or whether it was predestined by an ethnical sinocentric magical power to develop at such variance with the historical development of other parts of the world. If there is no clear answer to these questions, then the dynastic-cycle analysis remains unsupported by logical reasoning.

The dynastic-cycle theory smacks of the long-standing Western intellectual prejudice about China's historical changelessness. The change of dynasties in China was like the change of governments in any other country. While change itself repeats, history does not. Every dynastic decline in China was characterized by the particularity of its historical circumstances, not by the generality of the dynastic cycle which exists only in the scholars' imagination. The outbreak of the Taiping war was unprecedented in Chinese history. Hence no dynastic-decline analysis can explain its causes.

Another weakness of the dynastic-cycle analysis of the causes of the Taiping movement lies in the fact that the Taiping movement was a contributory factor to the Manchu dynastic decline—a fact conceded by both Michael and Teng. One qualitative difference of the Taiping war from many other peasant uprisings is that the Taiping army challenged a dynasty which still had a powerful image and vitality. The Manchu crack troops were still intact. Their strength was not seriously tested (though some of its coastal units were mauled by the British navy during the Opium War). It is, therefore, more correct to say that the Taiping was a cause of Manchu dynastic decline rather than vice versa. The real cause of the Taiping war must, thus, be differently conceived from the theoretical framework of the dynastic cycle. It is in this respect that we appreciate the perspective of the booklet *The Taiping Revolution* which forthrightly points out in its opening pages that the background of the Taiping war was marked by an intensification of China's internal contradictions caused by the Opium War.

The booklet takes the straight and understandable stand that, as a feudal society, there was a basic contradiction between the landlord class and the peasantry. Not only did the landlords exploit the peasants but continued to annex land in an unending process, stripping the peasants of their meagre belongings, (p. 5) Then, the Opium War created pressures against this social base in three directions: (1) the newly liberated opium trade poured opium in ever-increasing quantities into every coastal port of China and drained out 20 million to 30 million taels from China every year; (2) the Manchu government ruthlessly squeezed the people to pay war indemnity to Britain and (3) with foreign capitalism setting in the native economy was impaired and rural properties devalued. Under the new pressures, rural exploitation was intensified, and land annexation increased. (pp. 2-4) A case is cited in the book: "In 120 years prior to the Opium War, a big landlord family called Meng, of Changchiu County in Shantung [Shandong] Province, bought only 46 *mu* (roughly 1/6 acre) of land in seven separate transactions. Between 1840 and 1850 this family bought land 15 times in all, totalling more than 196 *mu.*" (pp. 6-7)

Unfortunately, the book does not give examples from the two provinces of Guangdong and Guangxi which were the cradles of the Taiping revolution. Some Communist Chinese historians have already gathered such data. Liu Da'nian, now Director of the Institute of Modern History in the Academy of Social Sciences, wrote in 1959 that on the eve of the Taiping war there was a saying in Guangxi: "The boundaries are open and most of the land goes to the rich, and the majority of the people remain tillers." Some landlords in the province got even one million catty (more than half a million kilograms) of grain every year from their tenants or sharecroppers. In neighbouring Hunan, which sent a large number of leaders and fighters to the Taiping army, landlords occupied 50-60 per cent of the land, and 60 per cent of the total population were tenants who had hardly any land of their own.[13] About Guandong province where the Taiping leader, Hong Xiuquan, was born, more than 90 per cent of the paddy fields were tilled by landless tenants in early 1930s.[14] The situation would not have been much different on the eve of the Taiping war.

Sharecropping was the main mode of feudal exploitation. From the Western Han Dynasty dating back to centuries before Christ down to the present century, 50 per cent had been the standard rate of sharecropping in China's land tenancy, *i.e.* 50 per cent of the harvest of the land was taken away from the tenants by the landlords who contributed nothing to production except owning the land. The Institute of Economic Research in China's Academy of Sciences conducted in the early 1950s a sample survey of 34 cases of sharecropping during the period between 1796 and 1820 which was fairly near to the time of Taiping. The finding of the survey is :

Crops Shared by Landowners

Above the rate of 50 per cent	4 cases	12%
At the rate of 50 per cent	19 cases	56%
Below the rate of 50 per cent	11 cases	32%
Total	34 cases	100%

Landlords adopted one of the two standard methods to exact 50 per cent of the harvest from tenants. One was to require the tenants to surrender half of what the land actually yielded; another was to fix beforehand the amount to be submitted at the time of the harvest, whatever the actual yield might be.

An additional burden on the tenants was the security money to be deposited with landlords before obtaining the tenantry. In places where usury was high, landlords would enhance the security money (sometimes even lower the rate of sharecropping) to earn interest from it.

There were always far more farming herds than adequate land to employ their labour. When the demand for renting land among the landless peasants was high, they competed with each other to enlist themselves as tenants. Landlords could dismiss the tenants at will. Tenantry being a sort of coveted "privilege", tenants had little scope to bargain, and had to tolerate the landlords' increasing exploitation which included periodical offerings of presents, free labour services, etc.

The socio-political order of the land strongly protected the landlords in their exploitation of the tenants. In Shanyang county in Jiangsu province a law was enacted by the local government in 1827 which was specially designed to punish tenants who were varified as 'abominable tenants', 'treacherous tenants', 'mischievous tenants', 'unyielding tenants' and 'crafty tenants.' The landlords employed thugs—the notorious 'Dog-legs' *(goutuizi)* in Chinese peasants description—to coerce the tenants. They frequently raided tenants houses, beat them up and took away their belongings, even their wives and children to the landlords' houses.[15]

The Taiping Revolution holds that "foreign capitalist aggression added to the growing contradictions inherent in [Chinese] feudal society itself" (p. 7), and thus correlates the Opium War with the Taiping movement. It points out that the secret societies challenged the authorities more actively after the Opium War, while the two provinces most directly affected by the Opium War—Guangdong and Guangxi—were turned into revolutionary hotbeds. (pp. 7-9) All this conveys Marx's point that instead of hypnotising the Chinese people, British opium actually awakened them. The book cites on page 4 an observation from Marx's famous essay on the Taiping movement entitled "Revolution in China and in Europe", but omits his most interesting and thought-provoking comment in the same essay which reads thus: "The English cannon in 1840 broke down the authority of the [Chinese] Emperor and forced the celestial empire into contact with the terrestrial world. Complete isolation was the prime condition of the preservation of old China. That isolation having come to a violent end by the medium of England, dissolution must follow as surely as that of any mummy carefully preserved in a hermetically sealed coffin, whenever it is brought into contact with the open."[16]

IV

The Taiping Revolution depicts Hong Xiuquan and his followers as revolutionary fighters using religion only as a vehicle to disseminate revolutionary ideas. They are not regarded as religious fanatics. The book says: "Hung Hsiu-ch'uan's identification with religion enabled him to use Christian tenets to claim that he was sent by Heaven on a mission. This was his preparation for the revolutionary cause of 'killing the evil to protect the righteous and of wiping out injustice among men." (p. 16) This translation is at variance with the original Chinese text. In the Chinese text, the authors, after citing a rhyme from Hong, asserts: "It is here that the connection between Hong Xiuquan's thought and Christianity began. And by this connection, Hong merely borrowed the name of God to declare that he had received instructions from Heaven to shoulder upon a special mission..."[17]

It is not enough to trace one leader's motivations to characterise a mass movement of the magnitude of Taiping. This movement was jointly created by about a dozen top leaders who were close associates of Hong and shared his responsibilities of organization and fighting. Then there were the tens of thousands of veteran fighters who formed the backbone of the movement. Lastly, there was the mass following. All these people must share a common aspiration to put up such a valiant fight against the heavy odds of the society, whether it was for the cause of God or for their own mundane interests. Whatever Hong's own inclinations, he had to make his ideology reflect the general aspiration of his followers. We are more inclined to think that the Taiping fighters' socio-politico-economic stakes were much higher than their devotion to God.

To concede the proposition that Taiping religiosity was a practical psycho-political expediency is not to ignore the religious aspect of Taiping life.

There is an assertion in *The Taiping Revolution* which appears to be controversial: "... the Society [of God-worshippers] when stripped of its religious mantle, was actually a revolutionary organization advocating an anti-religious philosophy of struggle." (p. 18) Such a conclusion is not seen in any Chinese research work on Taiping. It is actually a distorted translation of the original text in Chinese. The original observation is: "Although the Society for the Worshippers of God had religious colour, if stripped of its mysterious cloak, it was undisputedly a revolutionary organisation. It demonstrated a philosophy of struggle which was contrary to religion."[18]

The Taiping's spectacular success in its early years has left an impression on its commentators that, after the seizure of Nanjing in 1853, the Taiping could have ridden on the tide of victory to achieve a more magnificent feat. Thus, the theory has emerged that, if the Taiping army had not halted at Nanjing but marched on northwards, it could have taken the Manchu capital, Beijing, and legitimately overthrown the Manchu dynasty. The entire course of Chinese history then would have been different. This theory was first advanced by Lindley, who observed: "The Tienwang [Heavenly King], by settling down at Nanking and commencing to defend his position, committed a vital error, and one that lost him the empire. If, instead of so doing, and affording his enemies time to rally and recover from their panic and concentrate their forces, he had aimed at the once terminal point, Peking, beyond all doubt, the very *eclat* of his victorious march would have carried him with an almost resistless triumph into possession of the capital and the consequent destruction of the Manchoo dynasty would have given him the empire."[19]

This is as good a theory as any other. When the Taiping forces could storm Nanjing they could have stormed Beijing if the internal and external situations at that time had remained unchanged. However, we have no idea about the Taiping calculations in settling down at Nanjing. One reason might be that the core of the Taiping army was from the sub-tropical south. It had in its retinue a large crowd of women, children and aged people who would have found it more difficult to continue the long march and acclimatize themselves in the north. Another likely reason for their preference for Nanjing might have been its vicinity to foreign powers. Most Taiping leaders initially had a kind of illusion about the support of the Christian world for their cause.

A more serious charge is that they were attracted by the luxuries and comforts which the Nanjing region offered. It is difficult to confirm or disprove the widely circulated charge (by Manchu propaganda media and by European accounts) that Hong Xiuquan' was a coward, opportunist and a selfish leisure-loving person, that he indulged in luxuries at Nanjing, that he engineered the civil war in the Taiping capital resulting in the murder of two of his old associates (Yang Xiuqing and Wei Changhui) and the departure of another (Shi Dakai) in addition to the loss of lives of veteran fighters and families in thousands. Worse still, Hong has been accused of establishing a family rule after the civil war, of putting his useless brothers, sons and relatives in key positions interfering with the strategies of the fighting wing in which they played no role.

In his analysis of the causes of Taiping's failure, Fan Wenlan categorised them into subjective and objective. The subjective causes were: *(a)* factionism—not only among the top leaders but also in regional divisions, *i.e.* the veterans from Guangxi had the blue-eyed-boy treatment, while the non-Guangxi fighters were discriminated against; *(b)* conservatism—slackening military expeditions and indulging in feudal etiquette after their conquering of Nanjing; *(c)* hedonism—indulging in luxuries and pleasure-seeking in Nanjing. All these were regarded by Fan as a shortcoming of the peasant class. The two objective causes were: *(i)* the combination of the anti-revolutionary forces having surpassed the Taiping revolutionary force; and *(ii)* the absence of an advanced proletarian class in Chinese society to lead the revolution to victory.[20]

The Taiping Revolution echoes Fan's opinions in these words: "Because of the historical conditions prevailing in China at that time, with the new class force still waiting to be born, the Taiping Revolution could not benefit from the leadership of the Chinese working class and its Party, so it could neither overcome its weakness, nor completely formulate the strategy and tactics with which to vanquish the enemy." (p. 173)

The premise that the absence of a proletarian class precluded the possibility of victory of any peasant revolution in China was endorsed by Mao Zedong and accepted by the historians of mainland China. To some Western scholars this is unacceptable. Vincent Shih observes: "The Communist claim that the [Taiping] movement failed because of the lack of proletarian leadership can be dismissed without a hearing. The man who led the Chinese Communists to power can hardly be described as a proletarian."[21]

Shih has not understood the proposition. There is a lot of difference between the proletariat as a class and an individual proletarian, and between a class 'for itself' and a class 'in itself.' The Marxist premise is that only with the arrival of a modern industrial proletarian class (different from the pre-industrial lumpen proletariat) is it possible to have a correct leadership of the vanguard of the proletariat, *i.e.* the Communist Party. In concrete terms, if the Taiping movement had a Communist Party within it the internal mass massacre of 1856 would not have taken place the three isms pointed out by Fan Wenlan would not have raised their ugly heads. And there would have been a superior revolutionary ideology free from religious fanaticism and a more rational programme free from absolute equalitarianism.

Another 'objective cause' of the Taiping failure, according to Fan, was the overwhelming challenge of the enemy forces. This has hardly been given the academic attention it deserves. Two points particularly merit a brief discussion here.

The first point arises from the following observation in *The Taiping Revolution:* 'The Ching government, was already a tool for aggression in the hands of Britain, France, Russia, America and other Western capitalist countries. The foreign invaders feared that should the Chinese people overthrow the Ching government, the interests they had gained through aggression would be forfeited, so no sooner had the Taipings established their political power, before they had the chance to carry out their great ideal, the invaders conspired with the Ching ruling class to strangle the Taiping Revolution. Chairman Mao, in summing up the historical lessons of China's democratic revolution, has pointed out: 'Earlier revolutions failed in China because imperialism strangled them...' (pp. 171-72) This is a blunt assertion which eminent Western specialists on Taiping can seldom endorse. In a book designed specially to discuss Taiping interactions with Western powers (cf. *The Taiping Rebellion and the Western Powers: A Comprehensive Survey),* Prof Ssu-yu Teng harps on an ambiguous note of Western sympathy mingling with Western aggression *vis-a-vis* the Taiping. In analysing the motives of the Western powers' ultimate renunciation of 'eutrality' and participation in the

Manchu suppression campaign against the Taiping, Teng itemises the following five considerations.

First, the primary motive was "protection of British commercial interests including opium, the import of which was then increasing." However, Teng considers it an imaginary fear on the part of Britain, because "up to 1862, the Taiping did not seriously disrupt trade." Secondly, Western powers wanted "to show a favourable response to Peking's conciliatory policy" after signing the Treaties of Beijing in 1863. Thirdly, Western powers wanted "to stop the destruction wrought by the Taipings." However, according to Teng, the reports about the Taiping destructiveness that circulated at that time were "somewhat exaggerated" and the fact was that Western troops in China were no less destructive than the Taipings. Fourthly, Western powers resented "the Taipings' attitude of superiority." Fifth, Great Britain's "political ambition" was "to carry out a third stage of intervention by fighting the rebels in Nanking and other areas in the interior, finishing the whole job of suppressing the Taipings for China" and to earn the gratitude of Prince Gong of the Manchu court.[22]

It may seem uncharitable if we dismiss all these as non-motives. But, it would be difficult to believe that after all the wanton military aggressions which Britain had committed against China during the First and Second Opium Wars (in 1840-42 and 1856-60), and after such shocking atrocities and destruction wrought by the British and French troops in Beijing in 1860, the Western powers, particularly Britain, were still so rational and humane as Teng describes them. Actually, Teng doubts his own analysis and keeps on qualifying and contradicting it. Throughout his book there is an unmistakable sympathy for the Taiping and on many occasions the author comes very close to demonstrating the Western or rather British aggressiveness against the movement. It is Teng's hesitation to describe it as "aggression" which resulted in the confusing analysis cited above.

Much as Teng has been reluctant to see, the facts were that the British government adopted an attitude of sham neutrality and was both openly and secretly helping the Manchu government to suppress the Taiping movement. Lindley, an eyewitness of the then Chinese scene, has disclosed that a number of important British officers. (Admiral Hope, Generals Staveley, Michael and Brown, Major Gordon, Captain Stack, Dr. Marcartney) actively supported the Manchu campaign against the Taiping.

Lindley also unmasked the true nature of British "neutrality" by pointing out the following fact: an Englishman, White, was sentenced by the British Consular Court of Shanghai for three years' imprisonment for helping the Taiping force and thus violating the "Ordinance of Neutrality" declared by Sir John Bowring, British plenipotentiary in China, in 1855. White died in prison. Later, when the House of Commons took up the case and some member of Parliament wanted to move for the prosecution of those British nationals who had equally violated the "ordinance of neutrality" by helping the Manchu side to fight the Taiping, the British government hurriedly passed an "Ordinance in Council" condoning all those who "may have assisted, or may hereafter assist, the Government of the Emperor of China", but rendering it liable to punishment those who "levy war, or take part in any operation of war against the Emperor of China."

Finally in 1864, the British Prime Minister, Lord Palmerston, the same leader who presided over Britain's interference policy in China during the First Opium War, blatantly justified the British attitude to help Manchu suppression of the Taiping. He declared in the Parliament: "We interfered in the affairs of China; and why? Because our treaty rights were endangered and our national interests were at stake." He added: "I say it is the duty of this country to endeavour by all the means in her power to extend her commerce."[23]

This makes it amply clear that Britain's China policies were motivated by her selfish interests, an important part of which was "commerce" including opium. Teng is wrong in saying that Britain should have had no ground to fear that her trade would be threatened by the Taiping activities. Fan Wenlan has cited some statistics which show that the imports of opium into Shanghai declined from 33,700 chests in 1859 to 28,400 chests in 1860 when the Taiping army extended their operations to the vicinity of Shanghai. Fan also points out that, because opium was prohibited in the Taiping Kingdom, the import of opium into Shanghai (which was meant to be distributed in the Yangtse valley, a part of which was under the control of Taiping) never reached 50 per cent of the previous level of import during the Taiping period.[24] Lindley has narrated additional evidence of the close link between British hostility towards Taiping and her opium interests. The notorious leading opium agency, Dent & Co. was one of the British institutions which cried vociferously against the Taiping regime for a good reason. Lindley himself saw the Dent Company's opium ship *Nimrod* anchoring at Wuhu, the important Taiping controlled port in Anhui along the Yangtse, for six months in the vain hope of expanding the Company's opium trade.

It may be relevant to mention here the infamous episode of the Lay-Osborn flotilla which was ordered in 1861 but was rejected by the Manchu government in 1863 shortly after its arrival from England due to the undue arrogance of both H.N. Lay and Captain Sherald Osborn. At a time when all the Western powers were pressurizing the defeated Manchu government and when the French ambassador, Baron J.B.L. Gros, had actually demanded an order for warships and armaments from the Manchu Foreign Office (known as Zongli Yamen or Tsungli Yamen) in his interview with Prince Gong, the British coaxing of the Chinese to order for a British fleet is a rare feat in the history of international relations. The purchase was initiated by Robert Hart, the famous British Inspector-General of China's Maritime Customs, who vividly described to Prince Gong how effectively the British warships could be employed against the Taiping amphibian force. When the Prince expressed the Manchu financial difficulties, Hart suggested that the Manchu government could issue licences to the opium dealers by levying 45 taels per licence, which could easily fetch the requisite amount, which ran into several hundred thousand taels of silver. The Chinese government gladly accepted the suggestion.[25] Hart's diplomatic mastery also exposed the British intentions in China at that time, viz. to expand the opium trade as well as to rescue the decadent Chinese government, so that not only all the existing concessions could be maintained, but

Britain could exact further advantages from Beijing's unpatriotic policies.

Though the Taiping leaders did not realize it, their challenge to the decadent and unpatriotic Beijing government indirectly threatened the "rights" and "interests" of the Western powers, particularly Britain. The "brave new world" now joined hands with China's *ancien regime* to work for the downfall of the unprecedented revolutionary movement. It was hard for it to survive, particularly when the leaders of the movement failed to size up the power of their foe.

The second point, arising from our previous discussion of the objective causes of the Taiping failure, concerns the real strength of China's old order which the Taiping heroes had challenged. This old order not only survived the Taiping challenge but was able to put down two equally widespread rebellions, the Nian and the Muslim rebellions which were virtually extensions of the Taiping movement. Not only that, the successful quelling of all these rebellions created a historical phenomenon (and this is also a matter of acadmic controversy) known as the Tongzhi Restoration. The post-rebellion Manchu dynasty emerged as an apparently strong power until its image was destroyed in the Sino-Japanese War of 1894-95.

This phenomenon provides food for thought to the historians. Professor Philip Kuhn of Chicago University (now at Havard) is one of the few scholars who have dwelt upon this topic. He thinks he has discovered the source of strength of China's old order. Kuhn observes: "the Chinese state, along with its Manchu overlords, was enabled to survive because significant segments of the elite identified the dynasty's interests with their own, took the lead in suppressing the dynasty's domestic enemies. The fact that the dynasty was thereby enabled to outlive its mid-century crisis by nearly fifty years points unmistakably to the toughness and resiliency of the Chinese social and political orders and further, to the persisting power and cohesion of the elite. The victory of the elite, can also be seen as an indication that the foundations upon which the traditional state rested were yet firm; and that the specific 'modern' factors that were to shake these foundations in later decades had yet to work a decisive change in the direction of Chinese history...we can reasonably seek the beginnings of the old order's decline no earlier than 1864, the year the Taiping Rebellion was destroyed."[26]

According to Philip Kuhn, although the Taiping army caught the Manchu rulers unawares and exposed their weaknesses, they were ultimately no match to Chinese gentry military forces founded by two talented elite, Zeng Guofan and Hu Linyi, after a mode originally invented by a Ming general Qi Jiguang in the 16th century. The characteristics of the gentry-led army were: (i) the entire rank and file were specially recruited and trained by the leadership: and (ii) the army infrastructure was built on clan relationship combining with the teacher-disciple formation among superior and inferior officer in the Confucian spirit. It was this combination which wrought the ruin of the Taiping.

Kuhn's premise has certain defects. First, he has over-emphasized the merits of the social militarization system and overlooked the fact that one of the decisive factors of Zeng Guofan's victory over the Taiping was the huge material resources under his control. At that time, the areas free from Taiping influence were still effectively controlled by the authorities. The landlord-dominated ruling elite was united in facing the Taiping threat to their existence. Zeng not only had generous support from the revenues of several provincial governments, but collected donations from the merchants of the treaty ports, particularly Shanghai. As a result, the anti-Taiping fighters were much better fed, clad and armed than their opponents. This material factor complemented by Zeng's indoctrination and propaganda created the high morale of his troops. It was a life-and-death struggle between the old order and its destroyer. When the old order grasped the urgency of the situation and staked its fortune to destroy its enemy, it gained an edge over the latter.

Secondly, Kuhn's dispensation of the class factor in his analysis diminishes the strength of his argument. Here, there are two allied questions: (1) who were the fighters in Zeng's army, and (2) for what were they fighting? Few landlords had enlisted themselves into the anti-Taiping ranks, which were filled up by the peasants and lumpen-proletariat and mostly from Zeng's home province, Hunan.

They followed Zeng in pursuit of the Taiping, partly because there was a regional affinity among themselves, but more importantly because they were mercenaries fighting for a reward. In the opposite camp, the Taiping soldiery also belonged to the peasantry and the lumpen-proletariat. They came from various provinces and were drawn together neither by regional affinity (although regional sentiments still existed among them) nor by any award.

They fought for a common ideology—a common goal. When these two camps of armed peasants met, the latter naturally were superior to the former in moral qualities. Had the Taiping mounted, like their Communist successors did, a psychological campaign aiming at explaining to their peasant brethren in the enemy camp what their purpose was in the war, they could have demoralized Zeng's army.

Ironically, it was Zeng Guofan who used the propaganda strategy against the Taiping camp. And the Taiping's internal strife in addition to discrimination against the non-Guangxi soldiers (the regional parochialism was a lapse but not by design) developed such a feud among the Taiping rank and file that some of them deserted to the enemy camp and fought their former comrades ferociously.

So, the resilience of China's old order cannot be overstressed. The Manchu dynasty had not yet reached the declining stage when the Taiping rose, and the socio-political structure of the ruling elite still had the vitality to mobilize resources to put down the rebellions. On the other hand the peasant movement of the Taiping had its weaknesses and could not fulfil its historical mission to destory the old order. There was a multiple combination of factors at work apart from the gentry militarisation institutions highlighted by Kuhn. Six decades later when these factors changed, the gentry militarization institutions' (including *tuanlian baojia* which Kuhn has specially commended) began to lose their effectiveness in the suppression of the Communist rebellion. Chiang Kai-shek tried to emulate Zeng Guofan and Qi Jiguang but in vain.

In this essay we have highlighted certain issues for discussion. We have chosen these issues because of divergent views about them in scholarly circles which not only provide scope for discusion but are areas of confusion, especially for the uninitiated.

There has been a tendency among the students of Taiping to divide their study of this event into separate compartments (such as the causes of Taiping uprising, its nature, the causes of its failure, its impact, etc.) without first understanding the event as an undivided whole. Such compartmentalization only restricts one's vision. *The Taiping Revolution* balances the piecemeal approach to the subject.

All historians need to have a framework of mind to develop their historical perspective in viewing all events of history. For understanding the Taiping movement, such a framework is all the more essential. After delving into existing historiography, students of Taiping, including this author, find a variety of frameworks in operation, which inevitably leads to complexity and confusion. The Taiping historians have not even agreed on terminology - some call Taiping a "rebellion," others call it a "revolution." It is important for each student to have his own perspective instead of adopting others' without critical analysis. The main aim of this essay in presenting divergent perspectives before the readers without elaborate discussion is to avoid conditioning the readers' minds.

To Indian students, the Taiping movement is not an entirely strange historical phenomenon. The issues involved in the Taiping event such as tenantry, sharecropping, land annexation, pauperization of peasantry, armed peasant rebellion, interpretations of religion, etc. have also existed in India's historical reality. The more important identity between India and China is that both the countries have, for thousands of years, been agriculture-oriented with the peasantry forming the foundations of the two societies. This makes it possible to evolve a proper Indian perspective on Taiping which should be different from both the Chinese and the Western perspectives.

We have mentioned, without spelling out the details, the Indian-inspired "little tradition" in China from which the Taiping movement took its birth. An investigation of the migration of folklore from India to China, and a good comparative study of the impact of the *dharma-defeating-evil* ideology in both India and China, will not only be fascinating in themselves but could enhance our understanding of the Taiping movement.

The rebellion-or-revolution issue is a new area for investigation. The significance of this issue is clearly linked with another prevailing issue, *i.e.* the dynastic cycle. Fresh ideas and new premises on these issues will help us diminish the Western prejudice about the changelessness of Chinese historical developments.

The Taiping ideology has embodied both the elements of Sino-Western cultural conflict and confluence. The Taiping's acceptance of Christianity, however perverted it might be, should be viewed in the light of the later anti-Christian feelings among the Chinese masses. To date there is no satisfactory study of the Sino-Western cultural interaction which is free from either the superiority-inferiority formula (*i.e.* the bankruptcy of the Chinese superiority-complex *vis-a-vis* Western culture turning into an inferiority complex) advanced by some Western scholars, or the teacher-attacking-student perspective (*i.e.* student China willing to learn from teacher West, but the teacher continuing to attack the student) propounded by Mao Zedang. A balanced theory in this respect should appreciate the positive side of both Western and Chinese cultures. This will lead to a healthier cultural exchange between China and the West.

In many ways, the Taiping movement was the precursor of the Chinese Communist movement. There is need for a good comparative study of the two. The comparison can extend to such issues like the borrowing of Western ideoloy, the mobilization of peasant power, the fighting organization and its life, the land and other economic programmes, egalitarianism, puritanism, and women's emancipation. The Taiping movement is regarded by some scholars as a model of a failed revolution, while the Communist movement is regarded as an established model of a successful revolution. The comparison between the "failure" and "success," and the inquiry about how the "success" has benefited from the "failure" is of academic value. When we close the book *The Taiping Revolution,* its concluding sentence (the voice of those who consider themselves as the descendants of the Taiping heroes) still lingers in the mind: "The martyrs of the Taiping Heavenly Kingdom will never be forgotten." (p. 178)

References

1. *Selected Works of Mao Tse-tung* (Peking, 1967), Vol. II, p. 243.
2. *Ibid.,* p. 237.
3. *Ibid.,* Vol. IV, p. 412.
4. *Ibid.,* p. 455.
5. *Selected Works of Mao,* Vol. II, pp. 308-309.
6. *Ibid.,* p. 308.
7. Shi Shaobin (ed.), *Zhongguo fengjian shehui nongmin-zhanzheng wenti taolun ji* (Collected Articles on the Problem of the Peasant Wars in Chinese Feudal Society), (Beijing, 1962), p. 405.
8. *Taiping Tian'guo geming wenwu tulu* (A Collection of Pictures of Documents and Objects of the Taiping Heavenly Kingdom), (Shanghai, 1952); Guo Ruoyu, (comp), *Taiping Tian'guo geming wenti wenwu tulu xubian* (Supplementary of the Above), (Shanghai, 1953).
9. Karl Marx in *New York Daily Tribune,* No. 3794, 14 June 1853, cited in *On Colonialism,* (New York, 1972), p. 19.
10. *The Times,* London, 30 August 1853, cited in Ssu-yu Teng, *The Taiping Rebellion and the Western Powers* (Oxford, 1971), p. 1.
11. See Bai Shouyi, "Guanyu Zhongguo fengjianshehui nongminzhanzheng xingzhi de shangque" (A Discussion on the Nature of the Peasant Wars in the Feudal Society of China) in Shi Shaobin (ed.), *op. cit.,* pp. 185-186.
12. Evidence by Jean Chesneaux, Marianne Bastid, Marie-Claire Berger, *China from Opium Wars to the 1911 Revolution* (New York, 1976).
13. Liu Da'nian, *Zhongguo jindai shi zhu wenti* (Problems About Modern Chinese History), (Beijing, 1965), p. 52.
14. Meng Xianzhang, *Zhongguo jindai jingjishi jiaocheng* (A Textbook of Modern Economic History of China), (Shanghai, 1951), p. 127.
15. Hubei University, *Zhongguo jindai guominjing jishi* (History of National Economy of Modern China), (Press of Higher Education, 1958), pp. 8-10.

16. *Marx on China: Articles from the New York Daily Tribune (1853-1860),* (London, 1968), p. 4.
17. *Taiping Tian'guo geming* (The Revolution of Taiping Heavenly Kingdom), (Shanghai, 1973), p. 9.
18. *Taiping Tian'guo geming,* p. 10.
19. *Lindley, op.cit.,* p. 154.
20. Fan Wenlan, *op.cit.,* pp. 151-154.
21. Vincent Shih, *op.cit.,* p. XVIII.
22. S.Y. Tens, *op.cit.,* pp. 312-314.
23. Lindley, *op.cit.,* pp. 700-702, 760, 766.
24. Fan Wenlan, *op.cit.,* p. 128.
25. Joint memorial by Yixin (Prince Gong), Guiliang, Wenxiang dated Beijing, 7 July, 1861, cited in Institute of Modern History (comp.), *Yangwu Yundong* (Source Materials for the Study of the Self-Strengthening Movement), (Shanghai, 1961), Vol. II, pp. 222-223.
26. Philip A. Kuhn, *Rebellion and its Enemies in Late Imperial China: Militarization and Social Structure, 1796-1864,* (Harvard University Press, 1970), pp. 7-8.

11

A New Look at Peasant Rebellions in China*

I

Often our pedantic approach to an earth-shaking event of our ancestor's time only exposes our callousness towards the faceless heroism of history. The Taiping Movement was a much more explosive and exciting epic than the French Revolution. But, unlike the French Revolution, it was an epic written by faceless heroes. The different fates met by the two movements can be spelt out. We often hear people say that if there had been no French Revolution, there would be no era of democracy today. Have we heard a similar assertion that without the Taiping Movement there could not have been China's present innings of revolutionary transformation?

No one can say for certain that the Taiping Movement has not contributed to the new China today as greatly as the French Revolution has contributed to the modern democratic era. So, Taiping's facelessness is not because of its failure; it could have gained the image of the French Revolution in Chinese history if contemporary academic attention had not been entirely absorbed by the dazzling achievement of China's second innings of peasant revolution by Mao Zedong. It is this second innings which has not only eclipsed the glory of the first (the Taiping) but has metabolised its image. The memory of Taiping, thus, fades in the absent-mindedness of the academics.

The rediscovery of the apparently lost power of the Taiping Movement is not an impossible task. It is already emerging from

*The article that was written in 1979 and published in *China Report*, Vol. XVI, No. 1 (Jan.-Feb., 1980) has been condensed for the present book.

two trends of studies, one in the Western world and the other in China itself. These two trends offer two perspectives which can enliven pedantic studies of 19th-century China's popular movements.

The first approach emerges from a general discussion of peasant rebellions in Asia by Donald S. Zagoria. In his article published not long ago and entitled "Asian Tenancy System and Communist Mobilization of the Peasantry"[1] Zagoria implicitly sees the inevitability of the peasant movement like that of Taiping through his very refreshing ecological analysis. He convincingly demonstrates that a peasant rebellion of the Taiping type was an inevitable outcome of "Monsoon Asia". For want of a better description, we call this approach the Monsoon Asia perspective. The second approach is the peasant war approach which has been a well-focused theme among the historians of the People's Republic of China.

Zagoria's Monsoon Asia perspective may be briefly summarised. China, the geographical theatre which staged the Taiping rebellion, is a part of Monsoon Asia, one of the wettest on earth. The wetness of the region which had given birth and sustained the Taiping Movement was irrigated by two of the best rivers of the world, the Yangtse and the Pearl, in addition to abundant rainfall. This made it possible for the cultivation of the world's famous "rice economy" which was highlighted by intensive utilization of farmland and a dense population. Then the vicious chain-reactions started. Increasing population resulted in increasing land hunger (land decreasing in the land-population ratio), which in turn led to fragmentation of land holdings. This brought about the weeding out process of the small holdings, and started the progression of proletarianization of the peasants.

On the other hand, land amalgamation in Monsoon China, coupled with a proto-capitalist development of urbanization, created widespread absentee or parasitic landlordism. Thus, the concentration of population in Monsoon China gave birth to the twin concentration of proletarianised peasant and parasitic landlords. Social relation between the two were maintained by the institution of tenancy and other forms of sharecropping marked by ruthless exploitation.

An ideal revolutionary crisis already existed. But, with the socio-psychological "peasant isolation", the tranquillity of Monsoon China was maintained like a lake of still water on top of an active volcano. Several potential factors could help overcome the peasant isolation and inject a demand for change among the socially and economically abandoned, included peasant radicalism or peasant revolutionary consciousness. Although Zagoria sees the validity of the triple aspects—physical, social and mental—of peasant isolation which hamper their mobilization into a revolutionary movement as postulated by Marx, he thinks it possible to end the isolation through impact of a combination of forces such as population pressure, developed communications, education and modern organization.

Zagoria also itemizes the social, psychological, political and technical conditions for organization of the peasantry for a successful revolutionary movement. The social conditions are: (*a*) a large class of landless and land-poor peasants in a tenancy system; (*b*) heavy pressure on land and (*c*) the existence of rural intelligentsia. The psychological conditions are: (*a*) peasants' dissatisfaction with the status quo and demand for change and (*b*) peasants awareness of parasitism of the landlords and the bankruptcy of the rural power structure. The political conditions are: (*a*) the role of midwifery revolutionary organisations (such as the communist party) and *(b)* weakening of the rural elite. The technical conditions are: *(a)* organisational skills of the peasantry and *(b)* organizational skills of the revolutionary movement. All these are the "prerequisites of conflict group formation" to realize the Marxist goal of transforming the peasantry from a "class in itself" to a "class for itself".

Zagoria, who believes in "a perfect correlation between economic grievances and peasant unrest" in Monsoon Asia, provides a good theoretical framework to understand the nature of the Taiping Movement. The framework greatly helps answer questions like: Was the Taiping Movement a revolution or, as some argue, a mere "rebellion"? Was it a peasants movement or a sham peasant movement? Where from came the magic power which, in a short span of a couple of years, suddenly transformed an originally pacific religious organisation (the God-Worshippers' Society) founded by a Confucian scholar (Hong

Xiuquan) into a political hurricane which dealt a fatal blow at the *ancien regime* and hit the Manchu Empire to a humpty-dumpty fall? How did it happen that the Taiping Movement that had shown such earthshaking power in the 1850s suddenly collapsed in early 1860s? What was its historical significance?

The Monsoon Asia perspective, of course, does not answer all these questions. We have to turn to the other alternative perspective for insight. In peasant war perspective, we have a rich stock of research works. In 17 years between 1949 and 1966, an impressive record was created by the academics of the People's Republic of China in their studies of the peasant wars in Chinese history. Three thousand research papers were written, fifty kinds of collections of source materials in addition to one hundred odd general books on the subject were published, and 70 to 80conferences and symposia at the national level were held to deliberate on the peasant wars.[2]

If the Monsoon Asia perspective, serves to widen our horizontal vistas by projecting on the panoramic canvas of the ecological and sociological background of the peasant rebellion, the peasant war perspective helps broaden our vertical vision by linking the Taiping Movement with both its predecessors and successors covering the long span of more than two thousand years from the first large scale peasant rebellion at the end of the 3rd century B.C. down to the Communist movement that overthrew the Kuomintang government in 1949. With the broadened historical vision, we are told to view the Taiping Movement not as an event of only fifteen years but as a part of the struggle of Chinese peasantry for hundreds and thousands of years and not merely as a happening of mid-19th century but as one of the runners of a long relay race. One Chinese historian, Mou Anshi, points out: "Viewing from the entire process of historical developments of the peasant wars in China over more than 2000 years, the Taiping Revolution was the highest peak of peasant revolution in Chinese history."[3] This observation highlights the perspective of the peasant war approach. By treating the Taiping Movement as the high tide of China's innumerable peasant wars in history, the study of all previous peasant wars becomes an integral part of the study of Taiping.

II

Unlike the Zagoria approach, a non-Marxist view emphasizing the organizational aspect of social development, the Chinese historical circles have by and large adopted the Marxist framework in their study of the peasant wars. However, the Chinese communist historical analyses in general and their studies of the peasant wars in particular, seem to show differences from the classical Marxist approach. People often brand the fresh Chinese approach as Maoist.

Maurice Meisner's remark about Mao standing Marx on his head should be taken with a sense of humour. Otherwise, there is the risk of exaggerating the Maoist deviation from classical Marxism. The Chinese communist historians basically employ Marxist methodology in studying the peasant rebellions in Chinese history. The starting point of their approach is the five-phased social evolution (from the primitive communist to the slave to the feudal, to the capitalist and to the socialist society) with the progressive productive forces struggling against the reactionary relations of production and finally elevating the mode of production from a lower to a higher stage. The historical stage set for the study of peasant wars was the feudal society.

Like all good Marxist analysts, Chinese historians follow the Marxist manual to examine the basic contradictions in the feudal society. Since the feudal mode of production dominated for 2000 years in Chinese history, this long span of history is viewed as three stages of an on-going course of very slow social and economic development. In the beginning and middle stages (which correspond to the time space between the Warring States period and the middle of Ming Dynasty, *i.e.* the 4th century B.C. to the 15th century A.D. with the beginning of Tang Dynasty or the 7th century as the dividing line), the feudal system was establishing, developing and consolidating itself in China. The feudal mode of production saw both harmony and conflict between the productive force and the relations of production. The peasants played a dual role in this historical stage. On the one hand, they did not represent a new mode of production. On the other hand, as the oppressed and exploited strata of the society, they were the fundamental revolutionary class. Their incessant wars and other forms of rebellion helped to regulate the relationship between the productive forces and relations of production, and thus inject vitality into the feudal socio-economic order.

In the last stage of China's feudal society (corresponding to the space between the 15th-16th century A.D. and 1840), the feudal mode of production was disintegrating along with a gradual growth of capitalist economic elements in China. There emerged the social force which represented the rudiments of capitalism, *i.e.* the town folks. But their influence was negligible and they were yet to distinguish themselves as a political force in Chinese society. The basic contradiction of the Chinese society at this stage remained that between the peasants and the feudal lords. The peasants remained the fundamental revolutionary class. The peasant wars during this period still belonged to the category of the traditional peasant wars and could not take the mode of production to a higher form of development. The task of destroying China's feudal order had to fall upon the bourgeois democratic revolution.[4]

The Taiping Movement broke out after the Opium War (1840-42) when China met with its semi-colonial fate and the task of China's revolution was complicated by the appearance of the new enemy of imperialism. It was against this socio-political background that Mao Zedong enunciated the new phase of democratic revolution in lieu of the classical Marxist formulation of bourgeois revolution as a solution to the basic contradictions within the feudal society. The latest opinion among Chinese historians is to place the Taiping in the category of China's democratic revolution, while still viewing it as the high tide of the historical development of peasant wars. In a speech addressed to the seminar on Taiping (held at Shanghai/Nanjing in 1979?) Liu Da'nian, Director of the Institute of the Study of Modern History in the Chinese Academy of Social Sciences, Beijing, observed that the Taiping should be examined through the spectrum of democratic revolution which lasted one hundred and ten years from the Opium War till the founding of the People's Republic of China. Although the old democratic revolution (marked by the absence of proletarian leadership), consisting of the Taiping, the Boxer and the 1911 Revolution, failed to deliver China from the clutches of feudal and imperial forces, its successor—the new democratic revolution—from the May original Movement (1919) onwards (after the emergence of the proletariat on the political stage) achieved the deliverance within the short period of thirty years. But the victory of 1949 belonged to both the old and new democratic revolutions. "By putting all the struggles of one hundred and ten years together, we solved the problem of anti-imperialism and anti-feudalism."[5]

According to the peasant war approach, one cannot understand the nature of the Taiping Movement without gaining an insight into the nature of Chinese feudal society. Once again, in consonance with the textbook Marxist postulation, the Chinese historians tell us to look at the Chinese feudal society from the angles of the ownership of the means of production, relationships between different social strata and distribution of social wealth. The nature of Chinese feudal society was highlighted by three ingredients: (*i*) the feudal land-ownership, *(ii)* the personal appendage of the peasants to their feudal lords and *(iii)* the exploitation of both the peasants necessary labour and surplus labour by their feudal lords through various forms of taxation and exaction. These three basic parameters varied in the three different stages of the 2000 year old Chinese feudal society.

In the initial stages of Chinese feudal society (4th century B.C. to 7th century A.D.), there was a high degree of concentration of land in the hands of feudal gentry lords who enjoyed political, social and economic privileges through their hereditary possession of government positions and land-ownership in addition to overlordship *vis-a-vis* the peasant labour. Within this ruling elite there was fierce struggle leading to further amalgamation of land and intensification of exploitation and repression. This phenomenon disturbed the balance between the three traditional land-ownerships of the state (imperial family), the landlords and the peasants—with the fast expansion of the landlords' ownership at the cost of the peasants' ownership. Many peasant families were rendered landless and homeless, and became the floating population. It was this floating population which organized and participated in large-scale peasant wars.

The appendage of the peasants to their feudal lords was no less a social evil. The law of the state protected the feudal lords' domination over the personal freedom of the peasants under their control. Exploitation, centred around the share-cropping institution, was compounded by innumerable additional forms of exaction, reducing the peasants socio-economic status to semi-serfdom.

Against such a social background, the peasant wars during this period always spear-headed against the bad and cruel feudal lords and the infinite infringement of individual liberty and rights. The peasants demanded alleviation from feudal repression and exploitation and rights and opportunities for livelihood. By the beginning of the Tang Dynasty (7th century), the dominating hereditary gentry feudal-lord families began to decline, as the famous lines of a Tang poem testify:

No longer flocking the eaves as of old
Of the rich, distinguished and noble household
Are the happy swallows in the springtide.
Nowadays they find it much merrier
To enter the house of a commoner.

In the middle stage of the feudal society (7th to 15th century) in China, barbarous repression and ruthless exploitation had given way to a comparatively moderate feudal order. The peasant families found a place in the government registers in their own right (while they had been registered as appendages of the families of feudal lords earlier). The lord-slave relationship in the society was transformed into the relationship between landowners and tenants. There was punishment for landlords who beat the tenants to death. There was also a reduction of exaction on the peasantry. Of course, the personal liberty and rights of the peasants were hardly sacrosanct. And the peasants remained constant targets of exploitation and repression.

The period was marked by increased social mobility, which in turn generated a popular desire for equality and equitable share of privileges. This desire inspired some of the leaders and followers of the peasant wars during this period. Towards the end of the Tang Dynasty, two famous leaders of peasant wars, Wang Xianzhi (who rose in 874 and died in battle in 878), and Huang Chao (who rose in 875 and died in battle in 883 after occupying the imperial capital, Chang'an, for three years in 880-82) used the terms of *"junping"* (equality), "tianbu" (literally, "Heaven amends") and "Chongtian" (literally "breaking the Heaven") in their self-proclaimed honorific titles. The emergence of the ideal of equality marked a significant enhancement of the Chinese peasants' revolutionary consciousness.

In the last stage of feudal society (15th century to 1840), the domination of the feudal lords over the personal liberty of the peasants diminished further and the imperial government further rationalized the system of taxation. The peasants' enthusiasm in productivity enhanced and there was a gradual development of the rudiments of capitalist economy. The feudal order had passed its prime in China but was far from dying. On the contrary, the landlords were attracted by the new standards of material life created by urbanization and improved handicraft skills and became ever more greedy and parasitic. This, in turn, sharpened the basic contradictions between the landlords and the peasants and infuriated the latter to rise in arms.

The progress of the times gradually taught the Chinese peasantry the importance of landownership to their well-being. Their rebel leaders finally addressed themselves to the task of revolutionizing the landownership system, and hit the nail of the peasant rebellion on the head. When Li Zicheng (1605-45) rose with his peasant army to tumble down the Ming Dynasty in 1643, he raised the slogan of' "juntian mianliang" (equal distribution of land and exemption of grain-tribute). The Chinese peasantry had advanced to the verge of becoming a "class for itself".[6]

We have just summarised the peasant war perspective. Before we probe the Chinese historians' analytical mind *vis-a-vis the* Taiping Movement, it may not be out of place to introduce the focal points which figured in academic debates among Chinese scholars pertaining to the peasant wars. There were three hotly debated questions:

(1) Whether the peasant wars were consciously anti-feudal in nature?

(2) Could the peasant wars lead to the establishment of a genuine regime of, by and for the peasants?

(3) What was the peasant rebels understanding of the imperial power?

Opinions were divided among Chinese historians on these questions. The most debated question over the years was that of the nature of the peasant wars. There were three schools of thought. The first school was of the opinion that in the feudal society, no peasant war could be consciously opposed to the feudal order. This was because :

(*a*) The peasantry was a "class in itself" unable to understand its own class interest;

(*b*) The peasants were small owners and small producers who were not hostile to the private ownership of land.

(*c*) The peasant rebels had no other than the feudal ideology to fall back upon when they had to deal with political issues.

The second school thinks that only in the last stage of the feudal society, when the peasants raised the demand for equal distribution of land and social wealth, did peasant wars become consciously opposed to the feudal system. The third school which represents the majority opinion of Chinese historians opines that the peasant wars in Chinese history were always anti-feudal in nature, because their anti-feudalness was decided primarily by their antagonistic class contradiction with the forces of feudalism. There are two other sections within the third school. The first thinks that the peasant wars were aimed at the revolutionization of the land ownership system, the replacement of the landlord's economy with the peasant's small farming economy and the destruction of the feudal hierarchical order. The dissenting section is of the opinion that the peasant revolutionary struggles could not go beyond the boundaries of the feudal economy. They were at best aiming at the establishment and consolidation of the small-holding system.

Could the peasant wars establish their own peasant regime? Three different opinions again emerged in the debate of this issue. To some scholars the answer is negative, again because of the peasants being small producers unable to comprehend the feudal superstructure. The peasants' involvement in revolutionary struggles was spontaneous, but not the result of heightened consciousness. In practice the peasants' armies in Chinese history only established temporary fighting organisation, never any political regime. Some scholars have challenged this view to say that the peasant rebels did establish their political regimes. But such regimes were feudal in nature and should not be regarded as "peasant regimes". Some other scholars think that the short-lived regimes as those established by Huang Chao, Li Zicheng and the Taiping were genuine peasant regimes.

About the peasant rebels understanding of the imperial power, there has been a division of scholarly opinion. Some scholars agree with Stalin's general observation that the peasants are supporters of imperial power. They think that the Chinese peasants had the same weakness as their counterparts in other countries had. The contenders of this view hold that the Chinese peasants have waged the largest scale and most numerous armed rebellions ever witnessed in the world. They have provided ample proof that their wars were unique as compared with peasant wars of other countries, that they were not enthusiastic supporters of the imperial power. Many rebel leaders in the Chinese peasant wars were opposed to imperial power.[7]

These controversies raged in Chinese historical circles during the 17 years before the Cultural Revolution (1949-66). Thereafter, particularly after the Spring of 1974, Chinese historical studies were under the impact of the anti-Confucian campaign. There emerged a central theme of "Ru-fa douzheng" (struggle between the Confucian and Legalist schools). This campaign was short lived. (It died a natural death after the exit of the "Gang of Four" in 1976 and the subsequent exposure of its sinister aim to cast a dark shadow around the bright image of Premier Zhou Enlai). But scholarly thinking on historical events has been considerably confused by the theorem of Confucian-Legalist struggle. This confused thinking also reflected on the discussions about peasant rebellions.

The advocates of the Confucian-Legalist struggle attempted to depict it as the constant dynamic force in China's historical development. Although the peasant wars retained the place of importance in their historical analyses, the antagonistic contradictions between the feudal power and the peasantry became obscured. The result of this, as pointed out in a recent exposition, is the distortion of the aims and nature of the peasant wars. For, some of the feudal rulers like Cao Cao (155-220, an eminent statesman and writer, father of the first ruler of the Wei Dynasty), Wu Zetian (624-704, who had the distinction of being the first and only female "Son of Heaven" in Chinese history in 684-704), became either "the spokesmen of the peasants" or "leaders supported by the peasants" because they were branded as great exponents of legalism.

Another obvious distortion was to depict the internal dissensions within the peasant movements as ramifications of the Confucian-Legalist struggle. As a result, the basic contradictions within the Chinese feudal society gained the appearance of a two-tier Confucian-Legalist struggle within the feudal political camp and the peasant political camp respectively.

Lastly, the exaggeration of the dark spot of Confucianism along with the accompanying beautification of the Legalist tradition constituted a great distortion of historical facts. Both Confucianism and Legalism were a part and parcel of China's feudal superstructure which helped to uphold the feudal order. In their opposition to the feudal order, the Chinese peasantry was both anti-Confucian and anti-Legalist. But many writings published under the influence of the anti-Confucian campaign not only singled out Confucianism as the target of peasant rebellions, they even twisted and fabricated facts to support their point of view.[8]

An even more serious confusion in Chinese communist ideology resulted from the Cultural Revolution and the ascendancy of the "Gang of Four" relates to the historical role of the development of productive forces *vis-a-vis* class struggle. Before the death of Mao (in September 1976) there was clearly an over-emphasis of class struggle to the extent of placing the development of productive forces in a secondary and subordinate role. This theoretical line has been abandoned now that China has embarked on the Four Modernizations by the end of this century. The Chinese communist theoreticians have been deeply involved in an intra-party debate for the last couple of years on the basic theoertical problems concerning the communist revolution and China's road to the goals of socialism/ communism. This debate is bound to influence the study of peasant wars among Chinese historians.

Liu Da'nian has already carried the above mentioned debate into the Seminar on Taiping to which we have alluded earlier. He said: "Nowadays we are discussing theoretical problems [inside the Communist Party]. Is there any issue which has a direct connection with the deliberations on the history of Taiping Heavenly Kingdom in our seminar? I think yes. One issue pertains to the role played by the productive forces and class struggle in the evolution of history. Whether only one of them is the locomotion of historical progress, or both can be? If only one is, then, which one, productive forces or class struggle? If both can be, then, what are their interactions?" Liu offered his own thinking about the issue. He thought that the development of productive forces was the prerequisite of social evolution. He quoted Engels that the economic force would always ruthlessly find its way to development. He also held that class struggle was the locomotion of historical development, quoting Marx's dictum that revolution was the locomotive of history and violence the midwife to the old society to deliver the baby of the new society. He also quoted the famous observation in the *Manifesto of the Communists* : "The history of all hitherto existing society is the history of class struggle."[9]

However, Liu cautioned his colleagues who were participants in the Taiping seminar that this adage of the *Manifesto* should not be taken as a label but should be understood in the full view of the historical facts which it represents. They were also asked by Liu to sharpen their sensitivity with the adage to detect academic approaches which do not give cognizance to class struggle. He cited the views of Jian Youwen (Jen Yu-wen)[10] on Taiping as an example. Jian, who had studied Taiping for many decades and written and spoken volumes on Taiping, had basically not understood the movement. For, he depicted the

Taiping land programme as an administrative measure and the difference between the Taiping leaders and the leaders who had suppressed Taiping as merely the difference between the new and old feudal lords. And as the vanquishing army was manned by peasants exactly like the vanquished Taiping army, there was no question of any class struggle or peasant revolution, according to Jian.[11]

One good news is that the themes of Taiping and peasant wars have once again attracted the disciplined attention of the Chinese historical circles. With the restored enthusiasm for historical research and the reiteration of the "Two Hundred" policy (i.e., "Let hundred flowers blossom and hundred schools contend"), we may expect not only clarification of the confused thought on peasant wars but also new perspectives and insights after the follow-up of the old debates and the initiation of new discussions on the subject.

III

The two new perspectives about peasant rebellion can be adopted and adapted for our study of the Taiping Movement.

The two perspectives can be used to answer the questions about the Taiping. The first series of questions relate to the rise of the Taiping War. How did it happen? Where from came the earth-shaking power? From its appearance, the movement started in a low key. The founder of the movement, Hong Xiuquan (Hung Hsiu-ch'uan—1814-64) was, according to many commentators, quite a mediocre school master.[12] The God-Worshippers' Society formed by him in 1843 was a peaceful organization to begin with. Even when Hong and his comrades were forced to take up arms in 1850 at Jintian they had only about three thousand followers. On top of it, China at that time, to borrow an expression from Marx and Engels, was wallowing in "the idiocy of rural life".[13] The modern and progressive classses, i.e. the bourgeoisie and the proletarians, according to Marx's reckoning, had hardly made their existence felt in the political scene in China. How was it that in a couple of the years Hong's followers suddenly struck the heartland of China like a bolt from the blue and shocked the whole world with its earth-shaking power?

With the help of our newly acquired perspectives, the question can be clearly answered. The feudal society that was Monsoon China was no ordinary land of rural idiocy. It was an active volcano. Monsoon China was another name for Volcanic China—a country which had seen in more than 2000 years (right from the 4th century B.C. down to the year 1949) several tens of eruptions of large-scale peasant wars, not to mention the small-scale peasant unrests which were as much a daily routine as traffic accidents in a modern city. The Taiping Movement was but one of the periodical eruptions.

Hong Xiuquan and his followers only played the role of midwife to the maternity patient of Monsoon China who was in her advanced stage of pregnancy with the baby of revolution. Owing to the process of proletarianization, a large number of land-hungry peasants became "bare sticks" *(guanggun)*—people who had no property, nor family because they were too poor to marry. If the status-quo-conscious people living in "peasant isolation" in Marx's terms could be called "stable peasants", in Volcanic China every stable peasant lived in the midst of a couple of "de-stabilized peasants", like the "bare sticks" or, in the terminology of Marx and Engels, the "lumpen proletariat" or the "social scum". The portrait of some of them was penned by a British traveller in China on the eve of the Taiping rising. The following depiction of Evariste-Regis Hue is about the famine-stricken peasants of Zhejiang in 1849: "...they began to assemble in great bands and wander about the provinces with bags on their backs, begging here and there for a little rice. They were hideous to look at; half covered with rags, their hair bristling, their features contracted, their lips livid and these but lately peaceful and industrious peasants were evidently driven by despair to be ready for every excess."[14]

As they were wandering about the neighbouring provinces, and as the area of their wandering was infested with Taiping activi ties after 1853, this depiction might as well be that of the Taiping fighters prior to their jumping into the fray. Marx and Engels, of course, had no high opinion of these people, and called them the "dangerous class" and thought them ready "for the part of a bribed tool of reactionary intrigue".[15] Mao Zedong, on the other hand, thought some of them "may join the revolution". But there were many more behind them, the land-hungry and landless peasants on the road of proletarianization, whom Mao deemed "the semiproletariat of the countryside" and "the biggest motive force of the Chinese revolution."[16]

Two of these de-stabilized peasants were actually the architects of the Taiping Movement. Yang Xiuqing (Yang Hsiu-ch'ing—about 1823-56), who was Commander-in-Chief of the Taiping Army and Prime Minister of the Taiping Government in Nanjing till his death, was a "bare stick" in his boyhood, after his peasant parents had departed from him very early. His adventurous spirit led him to Canton to transport goods to be exported to Britain and elsewhere. He lost his job after the hectic foreign trade had moved from Canton to the newly opened treaty ports of Shanghai and other cities. He soon joined the God-Worshippers. Xiao Chaogui (Hsiao Ch'ao-kuei—about 1820-52), one of the five top commanders of the Taiping army before he was killed in battle at Changsha, was originally a de-stabilized peasant. He earned his living by providing armed escort to travelling merchants before leading the Taiping uprising.[17] Both Yang and Xiao (and other innumberable Taiping fighters) could be picked from the crowd of the livid-lipped and rag-clad beggars of Hue's description, who were "driven by despair to be ready for every excess". And what an excess the Taiping Movement was! Here is at once the link between de-stabilisation and revolutionization of the Chinese peasantry and we have the following formula:

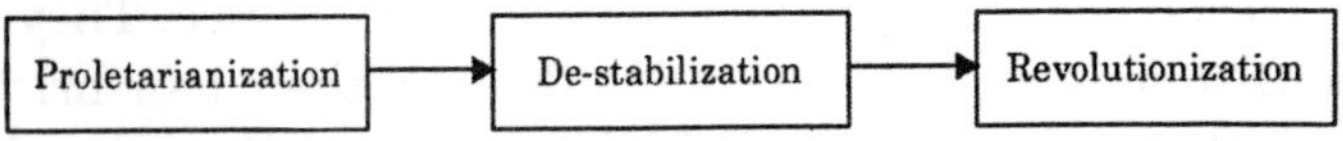

Fig. 1 : Transformation of Monsoon Chinese Peasantry.

In addition to this built-in process of peasant revolutionization in Monsoon China, the Chinese peasants in the Taiping era had already had two thousand years of peasant war experience behind them. The Taiping peasants were born not only in a socio-economic revolutionary *milieu,* but also a cultural revolutionary *milieu.* The rich heritage of peasant revolutionary tradition was not only handed down from generation to generation through folklore and other forms of information dissemination in the Little Tradition, but was carried forward from strength to strength by a succession of peasant rebellions. The peasant wars formed a vertical chain-reaction in history, with each rebellion echoing the war cries of its predecessors. It was in this way that the Chinese peasant rebellions progressed gradually from a lower to a higher form of struggle.

Immediately before the Taiping Movement there were a series of peasant uprisings launched by the "White Lotus Society" *(bai lian she)* between 1796 and 1835. It is worth noticing that the White Lotus rebels were the first Chinese peasants to raise categorically anti-Confucian slogans. They cried: "Censure Master Kong [Confucius] and discard the Four Books and Five Canons [Confucian classics]." They also raised the slogan: "Tongxiang tianfu." (Let everyone share the heavenly bliss and prosperity.)[18] It would be difficult to deny the fact of White Lotus influence on the Taiping ideology in which anti-Confucianism and egalitarianism formed an important part. The Taiping Movement which followed on the heels of the White Lotus rebellions, exactly reiterated the revolutionary slogans of the latter.

An additional evidence of the Taiping Movement being inspired by a rich revolutionary tradition was the choice of the term "Taiping" for the revolutionary regime. In my earlier essay, I have conceived the "Taiping" idealism as a borrowed concept from the Indian (Buddhist) culture.[19] I have a hunch that the real meaning of the term "Taiping" in the minds of the Taiping rebels was not "Grand Peace" as generally interpreted by scholars. There is no difficulty in identifying the Chinese concept "tai" as the English equivalent of "grand". But "ping" has two connotations: "peace" as well as "equality". In fact, "Taiping" was a favourite and auspicious concept of China's Great Tradition, meaning "trouble free". All the Chinese feudal rulers had a strong desire for "Tianxia taiping" (a reign free from wars, famines and other forms of troubles) and never ceased to reiterate this desire in their pronouncements. This hope was so frequently rendered into South Sea bubbles by the peasant uprisings. Why should the Taiping revolutionaries choose to associate their movement with such an illusory idea of feudal lords so incompatible with a revolutionary ideology?

Hence my hunch is that the peasants' "Taiping" idealism had nothing in common with "grand peace" which was the feudal rulers' anti-peasant-war illusion. As the Taiping ideology had such a strong accent on equality, the choice of "Taiping" served to reiterate the Taiping idealism of grand or perfect equality, which, at once, sounds like the Sanskrit term *Maha-samata*. There is reason to believe that the Indian Buddhist idea of *Maha-samata* (perfect equality) had spoken out the inner voice of Monsoon China's teeming millions who strongly desired a share of the "Heavenly bliss" as expressed by both the White Lotus and Taiping rebellions. So, "Taiping" was the Chinese peasants' echo of *Maha-samata*. Incidentally, in the Taoist tradition, which was closer to the peasants' Little Tradition than the Confucian Great Tradition, there was also a frequent usage of the term "Taiping", the origin of which could be traced to the Buddhist concept of *Maha-samata,* in case documentary evidence could be found.

Let us come to the second series of questions relating to the nature of the Taiping Movement. Was it a revolution or a rebellion? Was it a peasants movement or otherwise?

It is meaningless to go into semantics to prove, or rather produce, the nuances between the concept of "revolution" and that of "rebellion". The two are synonyms. There could not have been any qualitative difference between the two propositions: "Taiping was a revolution" and "Taiping was a rebellion", just as there is a little difference between 49% and 50%. When we say that 49% is not 50%, we also agree that 50% is not 49%. No sensible scholar will insist on a "revolution" not being a "rebellion", while we do hear some one say that a "rebellion" may not be a "revolution". The observation that "Taiping was a rebellion but not a revolution" can make sense only when it would mean that "Taiping was less-than-a-revolution". So the answer to any such formulation should actually indicate whether the Taiping Movement qualified the description of a revolution.

We have already hinted at the outset of this essay that the Taiping Movement was no less a revolution than the French Revolution or any revolution in history worth its name, and there was no. deficiency of *revolutionariness* in the Taiping

Movement itself. That some deficiency has been felt is actually caused by the deficiency of empathy on the part of the commentator. It is this deficiency of empathy which has resulted in the deficiency of perspective in many of the scholarly studies of the Taiping Movement.

Much as those who have posed the question would not like it to be so summarily dismissed, there is no other way that we can deal with the question. When we view the Taiping Movement in different perspectives, we are on different wave lengths. Both the Monsoon Asia perspective and the peasant war perspective have clearly demonstrated the nature of the Taiping Movement. Here was a mass movement waged by the most abandoned to challenge the seemingly most powerful in the same society. In the process of challenge the most abandoned actualized their innate supreme power. Here we see the meaning of a revolution just as the hero of the French Revolution, Danton, sees it.

Some scholars might like to link Taiping's want of revolutionariness with its want of success. This linkage seems to have fallen into the trap of the Chinese great tradition, which says:

Cun ze wei wang, bai ze wei kou.
(Those who vanquish become kings;
Those who are vanquished become bandits.)

Indeed the Chinese Great Tradition (the imperial ruling circles) had already branded the Taiping fighters as "Long-hair bandits" *(changmao zei)*. Should we say that the Taiping Movement deserved this historical evaluation because it was vanquished?

But no one can even categorically say that the Taiping Movement was a failure. Here, again the question of perspective arises. What would be the highest criterion to judge the success of a historical event? There cannot be any higher criterion, in the judgement of modern social sciences, than the advancement of the productive force—hence the elevation of civilization to a higher level. The Chinese historical mind has actually been preoccupied by the question whether the Taiping Movement did push social productive forces forward.

By viewing the Taiping Movement in the peasant war perspective, Liu Da'nian told the Taiping scholars that Taiping, along with the Boxer Movement, the 1911 Revolution and the May 4th Movement, should share with communist revolution the success of pushing China's social productive force to a higher level. Besides, the Taiping Movement also achieved the following (*i*) mobilizing and organizing the scattered struggle of the people to sweep off the authority and order of the patriarchal society, *(ii)* accelerating the pace of decline and collapse of the Manchu Empire and the entire feudal order, *(iii)* smashing the dream of the imperialist powers to colonize China, and (iv) providing an example for emulation for future mass struggles.[20] Liu's assessment suffices to place the Taiping Movement at par with revolutionary movements.

The crux of the issue relating to the discussion of the nature of the Taiping Movement is whether the movement can be deemed as one of, by and for the peasants. In one recent study on Taiping by Chinese historians, two scholars hold that by taking a peasant-qua-peasant proposition the Taiping was the highest peak of all peasant revolutionary movements. "It not only inherited and enhanced the ideological tradition of the peasant revolution in Chinese history which was characterised by chaste idea of equality and democracy, but also developed it and injected in it fresh contents to create a more perfect peasant revolutionary democracy."

The Taiping ideology was reflected from the three famous "Edicts" issued by the Taiping government on behalf of the "Heavenly King" (they were actually the Taiping revolutionary manifestoes), in addition to the writings of Hong Xiuquan. These became an important treasure in the history of the peasant revolutionary ideology. The Taiping ideology which served to enlighten contemporary thinking had these progressive ingredients: *(a)* the creation of the symbol of the absolute truth in God to declare war against the value system of the feudal and patriarchal society, *(b)* the propagation of the ideas of human rights and equality to attack the feudal divine monarchical power and all kinds of idol worship, (c) the establishment of the opposition between "God" *(huang shangdi)* and "Yamaraja devils" *(yanluo yao)* to bring the dichotomy down to earth to sharpen the class and national contradictions in real life.

The proclamation of the "Land Programme of the Heavenly Dynasty" *(Tianchao tianmu zhidu)* was a landmark in China's socio-political evolution, the scholars hold. It was the general outline of Taiping's social reform programme. It completely negated the Manchu feudal autocratic rule and provided a complete alternative order in the political, economic, cultural and military arenas.

For the first time in history, the scholars continue, the peasant masses not only heard the clarion call from the Taiping leaders to fight the reactionary, decadent and rotten feudal autocracy, but also breathed the fresh air of democracy and equality from the declarations of the Taiping government. The three "Edicts" spelled out the "Taiping" idealism of Chinese peasants. "Land is for everyone to till, food is for everyone to eat, clothes are for everyone to wear and money is for everyone to spend. Let nowhere be there inequality. Let no one suffer from the want of food and warmth."

The new government measures of Taiping are itemised by the scholars. First, it launched a campaign in the capital and other cities to suppress counter-revolutionaries, who included Imperial officials, landlords, spies and traitors. Secondly, it announced the nationalization of vegetable farms and shops, and gold, silver and other properties were to be surrendered to the "Sacred Treasury". Thirdly, it imposed a control over commercial activities. Fourthly, it organized handicrafts production to enable trades and skills to give the best account of themselves. Lastly, it implemented the policy of allotting duties and jobs according to each person's ability without any consideration of personal wealth or social status. They would be provided with food and clothing without discrimination. Food-grains were distributed according to population registers. Sixth, it abolished footbinding, prostitution, buying and selling slaves and other ugly customs which had persecuted women. It also organized women to participate in public activities, defence and production work.[21]

The list is long and impressive enough to prove that Taiping was a movement attacking the enemies and promoting the interests of peasants. It was of, by and for the peasants.

The same scholars offer an explanation about the Taiping government's order asking law-abiding citizens to remit revenues according to the practices of the Manchu government. This is regarded as a measure of expediency, not to be interpreted as the revolutionary regime's bowing before the propertied classes as scholars often make it appear.[22]

Both Zagoria's "prerequisites of conflict group formation" and the Chinese communist historical analyses are not blind to the shortcomings of the Taiping Movement. While the Zagoria perspective lays the blame mainly on the unfavourable political and technical conditions for the failure of the movement, the Chinese communist view emphasises the limitation of the times. The proletarian class had not yet arrived on the political scene to lead the movement, peasantry alone could not overthrow feudalism and imperialism.

By and large, the Chinese historians have been conscious of their duty to avoid taking the absolutist view in evaluating the Chinese peasant wars and the Taiping Movement. According to Marxist education, absolutist analysis is a metaphysical tendency alien to dialectical materialism. However, there have been, at times, deviations from the materialist approaches in recent Chinese historical studies of the Taiping Movement. For instance, certain Taiping leaders, like Hong Xiuquan, have been depicted as spotless and perfect revolutionaries, while others who had shared with Hong both the sacrifices and responsibilities in building up the Taiping Movement have not been given their due. Two outstanding examples merit mentioning. Wei Changhui (1823-56), one of the six leading lights of the movement received the most uncharitable treatment just because he had come from a landlord's family. Li Xiucheng (1823-64), who had played a decisive role in resurrecting the Taiping power and giving the movement the second lease of life after the disastrous internal rift in 1856 resulting in the departure of all the survivors of Hong's top lieutenants, was black-listed because he had written a confession during his captivity in the hands of the Manchu. This unfair historical assessment has recently been pointed out by leading historians.[23] One could expect some partial, if not full, rehabilitation of these heroes in the future Chinese historical studies.

A more heartening development is the reiteration of the methodology of historical materialism in recent Chinese historical writings. In the light of historical materialism, no human being could be a perfect and spotless person. It should be conceded that all the Taiping heroes suffered serious shortcomings. Both their merits and demerits should be viewed according to their historical and class background and the "manifestations in them of the limitations of their classes and their times."[24]

One manifestation of such limitation was the unsound foundation of the Taiping fighters' internal unity. In the first place, the conception of equality, which was the very cornerstone of their unity, arose from "the backward, isolated and scattered mode of production of small land-holdings". Such a mode of production bred the demand for an equality of "the uniform level" *(qi yi de shuiping)*. In the second place, the isolated and scattered state of the small farmers created the inherent difficulty in uniting them politically into one revolutionary force. In achieving this aim, the Taiping Movement had to resort to "the appeal of god" and "the [bigotry of] parentalism". The bigotry of parentalism was fundamentally incompatible with the principle of equality.

There was a negative element in the Taiping ideology or superstition about "the Heavenly Father's descent to earth". For one thing, it affected the unity of the top leadership. Yang Xiuqing, who shared with Hong Xiuquan the exclusive privilege of personification of the Heavenly Father's descent and enjoyed the maximum opportunity to play the game of "descent" (by falling into a trance and speaking the Heavenly Father's voice), became the victim of the corrupting influence of feudal ideology and individual authority. His chastening the leader, Hong, with merciless flogging on 24 December 1853, deaf to the entreaties of other top leaders, only betrayed his selfish desire for absolute authority and sowed the seed of the tragedy of 1856 in which he himself lost his life. On the other hand, Hong Xiuquan himself was also not free from tyrannical attitude towards his subordinates, often subjecting them to physical violence.

The Taiping's levying revenues from the propertied classes according to the Manchu practice was once considered in Chinese study circles as the pursuance of a "revisionist" line on the part of Yang Xiuqing in collusion with Wei Changhui and Shi Dakai (1831-63) in opposition to Hong Xiuquan's correct line. This premise is consigned to the cold storage now. A realistic appraisal thinks that, although the measure should not be interpreted as a compromise of the Taiping revolutionary principle, it was a manifestation of the limitation of the Taiping movement.

For, it gave *de facto* recognition to the landownership of the landlords who had remitted government revenue. This served to weaken the economic foundation of the peasants' regime. By and by, following the development of class struggle and the usurpation of leadership power by the degenerates at the regional level within the Taiping kingdom, the landlords' exploitation of the peasants received a kind of protection, while the peasant's struggle against excessive rent was suppressed. "This was not infrequent an occurrence in Jiangsu (Kiangsu) and Zhejiang (Chekiang) after 1860." The Taiping leaders "could neither anticipate it, nor escape it", due to their peasant limitations.

It is also felt by many scholars that while the Taiping leadership was launching a frontal attack on Confucianism - the bastion of feudal ideology—it also unwittingly followed the feudal ideological track, since it possessed no advanced ideological weapons and was ignorant of the scientific world view.[25]

This takes us back to the classical Marxist proposition that in the scale of historical materialism and social evolution the bourgeoisie was a more advanced class than the peasantry. With the return of Chinese study circles to an impassionate realistic mood the allegiance to this tenet is now openly professed in the discussion of the Taiping. Listen to this commentary: "Peasants constitute the major revolutionary force in the feudal society. They have been the major force of revolution in the modern history [of China].

However, looking towards the direction of social evolution, the bourgeoisie is after all, more advanced than the peasantry. Not only were the outline of the *Tongmenghui* (Alliance Society) and the Three People's Principles of Sun Yat-sen much more advanced than the 'Land programme of the Heavenly Dynasty' of the Taiping, but, in certain sense, even the reform proposals mooted by the reformists during the period of reform and modernization were more advanced than the Taiping revolutionary programme."[26]

All this serves to answer another series of questions posed at the beginning of this essay, *i.e.* how did such a powerful movement suddenly collapse, and what were the cause of the failure of Taiping? The peasant war perspective seems to argue that the fate of Taiping Movement was predetermined by its innate historical limitations. This, however, is not to ignore the other objective factor—the counter-attack by the combined strength of the Manchu army, the Hunan army led by Zeng Guofan (1811-72), the Anhui (Anhwei) army led by Li Hongzhang (1823-1901), and the foreign mercenary troops.

The above discussion of the shortcomings and the lesser advancement of the Taiping peasant war should not mislead us into believing in the accuracy of the less-than-a-revolution assessment. The dialectical position of the peasant war perspective is to see both the great achievement and great shortcomings of the Taiping Movement. In a recent Chinese study, the historical significance of Taiping is lifted up to the canvas of the historical developments of the world.

First, as the Taiping Movement broke out at the juncture of fierce scramble for world markets on the part of European capitalist powers, the Taiping Movement created a commercial and financial crisis among these powers.[27] Secondly, the Taiping revolution echoed with a number of anti-imperialist revolutions all over the world, including the 1857 revolution in India.

Here, the significance of Taiping becomes prominent: "Compared with the national liberation struggles in Asia and Africa, the peasant wars in modern Chinese history, especially the Taiping revolution, lasted the longest duration, had the largest scale and were more clearly anti-feudal and anti-aggression in their programmes. They [the Chinese peasant wars] enriched the contents of the national struggles in Asia and Africa and at the same time dealt the imperialists a heavier blow. Hence Engels viewed the Taiping as 'the opening day of a new era for all Asia'."

Thirdly, the Taiping and other peasant wars inspired the old democratic revolution led by the Chinese bourgeoisie. Sun Yat-sen, who was nick-named "Hong Xiuquan No. 2", styled himself as a successor of the Taiping fighters. Fourth, as we have already referred to, the Taiping was a part and parcel of the peasant revolution for one hundred and ten years ending in 1949. This premise is based on Mao Zedong's observation that "the Chinese revolution is essentially a peasant revolution", paraphrasing Stalin's earlier observation that "*in essence,* the national question is a peasant question".[28] There is even more concrete affinity between Taiping and the 1949 communist victory.

This is spelt out thus: "In their long revolutionary course of sixty years [1850-1911], the peasant wars in modern Chinese history had laid the foundation stone for the victory of the New Democratic Revolution [in 1949] judging from their achievements of the anti-feudal and anti-revolutionary tasks, from their earth-shaking and indomitable spirit of revolutionary struggle and from the historical experiences and lessons learnt from their successes and failings."[29]

This is, indeed, a high tribute to the Taiping Movement. Yet, the indebtedness of the Chinese communist revolution to the Taiping Movement cannot be exhaustively dealt with even in a long essay. To borrow Zagoria's "prerequisites of conflict group formation", in many aspects in the social, psychological, political and technical conditions for organizing a successful movement of peasant revolution, the Taiping Movement was like a prototype of Mao's new democratic peasant rebellion.

Of course, the Maoist revolution had one asset which was wanting in the Taiping revolution, *i.e.* Marxist revolutionary ideology. But even in the ideological field, the Taiping had contributed its share. What was it? It was the perspective, the Monsoon Asia perspective, the peasant war perspective, the perspective that the most abandoned faceless creatures in the oblivion of rural idiocy could summon such supreme power as to dazzle and puzzle the whole industrial world.

Mao's assuming leadership in the Chinese communist movement from 1935 onwards signified the victory of the peasant war perspective. What happened afterwards was like a cake-walk in comparison to the uphill tasks in search of a proletarian solution of China's revolutionary problem. Only through such a spectrum can we really grasp the inner rhythm of China's historical development. Until China smells the chemicals blown out of the chimneys of her Four Modernizations, her history would remain one of, by and for the peasants.

References

1. In John Wilson Lewis (ed.), *Peasant Rebellion and Communist Revolution in Asia* (Stanford, 1976), pp. 29-60.
2. Liu Zhongri and Zhou Shaoquan, "Shiqinian Zhongguo nongmin zhanzheng de yanjiu" (Studies on the history of Chinese peasant wars during seventeen years) in *Zhongguo nongmin zhanzheng shi luncong* (Symposia on the history of peasant wars in China), Vol. I, (Shanxi, 1979), pp. 33-34.
3. Mou Anshi, "Lun Zhongguo jindai nongmin geming zhanzheng de lishi zuoyong" (On the role of peasant wars in China's modern history) in *Zhongguo nongmin zhanzheng shi luncong.* Vol. I, p. 92.
4. Tong Chao, "Cong Zhongguo fengjian shehui jiben maodun de bianhua kan nongmin geming zhanzheng de lishi zuoyong" (Viewing the historical role of peasant wars through the spectrum of the changes of basic contradictions in China's feudal society) in *Zhongguo nongmin zhanzheng shi luncong,* Vol. I, pp. 50-53.
5. Liu Da'nian, "Guanyu lishi qianjin de dongli wenti" (On the motive forces of historical progress) in *Jindaishi yanjiu* (Studies of modern history), No. 1 (1979), pp. 62-63.
6. *Tong* Chao, *loc cit.,* pp. 54-67.
7. Liu and Zhou, *loc cit.,* pp. 35-39.
8. Bai Gang, "Ping 'sirenbang' zai nongmin zhanzhengshi lingyuli suo zhizao de hunluan ji qi fan'geming benzhi" (On the distortions created by the "Gang of Four" in the arena of history of peasant wars and the anti-revolutionary nature of such distortions) in *Zhongguo nongmin zhanzheng wenti luncong,* Vol. I, pp. 1-25.
9. Opening sentence of Section I: "Bourgeoisie and Proletarians". See *Karl Marx and Frederick Engles: Selected Works* (Moscow, 1969). Vol. I, p. 108.
10. See my previous article, *antea,* pp. 451, 472-473.
11. Liu Da'nian, *loc cit.,* pp. 58-67.
12. Fan Wenlan (1893-1969), eminent Chinese communist historian and Director of the Institute of Modern History of the Chinese Academy of Sciences, was one such

commentator. See his *Zhongguo jindai shi* (History of Modern China), (Beijing, 1954), pp. 99-100.

13. In the "Manifesto of the Communists" in *Marx and Engels, op cit,* p. 112.
14. Evariste Regis Huc, *The Chinese Empire: Forming a Sequal to the Work entitled Recollections of a Journey Through Tartary and Tibet,* (London, 1855), Vol. II, pp. 324-25 cited in Kung-chuan Hsiao, *Rural China; Imperial Control in the Nineteenth Century* (Seattle, 1960), p. 403.
15. From "Manifesto" in *Marx and Engels, op. cit.,* p. 118.
16. Mao Zedong, *Selected Works,* (Beijing, 1967), Vol. II, pp. 324, 326.
17. Fan Wenlan, *op. cit.,* pp. 100-101.
18. Wang Yuxin, "Qingdai zhongye bailianjiao qiyijun de jieji jieceng fenxi" (An analysis of the class components of the White Lotus rebellion army in the middle of the Manchu Dynasty) in *Zhongguo nongmin zhanzheng shi luncong,* Vol. I, p. 497.
19. See my previous review article, *antea,* pp. 451, 472, 473.
20. Liu Da'nian, *loc. cit.,* p. 62.
21. Ye Guisheng and He Zhiqing, "Guanyu Yang Xiuqing pingjia de jige wenti" (Several issues relating to the appraisal of Yang Xiuqing) in *Zhongguo nongmin zhanzheng shi luncong.* Vol. I, pp. 501-507.
22. *Ibid.,* pp. 515-525.
23. Ding Shouhe and Chen Wengui, "Shishi qiu shi he lishi kexue" (Seeking truth from facts and the science of historical studies) in *Jindaishi Yanjiu,* Vol. I, p. 77.
24. Ye Guisheng and He Zhiqing, *loc cit,* p. 532.
25. All the above are the views of Ye and He. See *ibid.* pp. 512, 526-528.
26. Ding Shouhe and Chen Wengui, *loc cit,* p. 87.
27. Borrowing the analysis of Karl Marx. See Marx, "Revolution in China and in Europe" in Marx and Engels, *On Colonialism,* (New York, 1972), p. 26.
28. Mao Zedong, "On New Democracy" in *Selected Works,* Vol. II, p. 366.
29. Mou Anshi, *loc cit,* p. 107.

12

Yi He Tuan Movement : The Most Heroic Boxing on Earth*

Our focal book *The Yi Ho Tuan Movement of 1900(Yi Ho Tuan* for short)** opens with a clear perspective: "The Yi Ho Tuan Movement, which broke out in China in 1900, shook the whole world. It was a patriotic anti-imperialist uprising, mainly of peasants. It was the climax of the Chinese people's struggle against aggression and partition following the Sino-Japanese War of 1894." (p. 1)

I

A proposition seemingly hard to dispute, but it is not so simple. Victor Purcell (1896-1965), author of the best English language book written so far on *The Boxer Uprising,*[1] had no hesitation in expressing his reservations on the above premise.

The relevance of Purcell to our discussion is best explained by him in the following words which appear in the opening paragraph of his book : "To the West in general the Boxer Uprising of 1900 is a half-forgotten episode in the history of China's resistance to progress; to the historians of People's China it is the heroic resistance of the Chinese peasantry to foreign imperialism..." (p. vii). Between these poles-apart opinion worlds, Purcell tried to build a bridge. His book has an even sprinkle of source materials taken from both worlds. To be sure, Purcell's book has had a sobering effect on the violent Sinophobic Western mood which had partially resulted from the equally violent xenophobic Chinese mood exemplified by the Boxer Movement.

---

*The article that was written in 1979, and published in *China Report,* Vol. XVI, No. 2 (March-April, 1980) has been abridged for this edition of the book.

** Foreign Language Press, *The Yi Ho Tuan Movement of 1900* (Peking, 1976).

Purcell has travelled a long way from the commentaries of the old China hands and other Western eye-witnesses of the event. Prominent among the early Western writings on the Boxers are: W.A.P. Martin's *The Siege in Peking: China Against the World* (New York, 1900); Rev. Roland Allen's *The Siege of the Peking Legations* (London, 1901); Marshall Broom Hall's *Martyred Missionaries of the China Inland Mission* (London, 1901); Arthur H. Smith's *China in Convulsion, 2* Vols. (New York, 1901); Nigal Oli-phant's *Diary of the Siege of the Legations in Peking During the Summer of 1900* (London, 1901); Harry Craufuird Thomson's *China and the Powers: A Narrative of the Outbreak of 1900* (London, 1902); Gordon Cassery's *The Land of the Boxers, or China Under the Allies* (London, 1903); J. J. M. de Groot's, *Sectarianism and Religious Persecution in China* (Amsterdam, 1903); and Paul Henry Clements' *The Boxer Rebellion : A Political and Diplomatic Review* (New York, 1915).

Matching with the rich corpus of Western literatures on the Boxer Movement is its still richer counterpart in the Chinese language. A good part of it is now included in two source material series compiled by the historians of the People's Republic of China. They are : *(a) Zhongguo jindaishi ziliao congkan : Yi he tuan,* or in brief *Yihetuan ziliao* (Source Materials of the Boxer Movement) compiled by the famous Chinese historian Jian Bozan (1898-1968) in collaboration with four other leading members of the Chinese History Society *(Zhongguo shixue hui)* in four volumes published in Shanghai in 1957; *(b) Yihetuan dang an shiliao* (government files pertaining to the Boxer Movement) in two volumes published in Beijing in 1959.

Preceding Purcell's work were two serious studies in English which had their Chinese connections. The first modern research work on the Boxers in English is George Nye Steiger's *China and the Occident : The Origin and Development of the Boxer Movement* (New Haven, 1927). Chester C. Tan, a U.S. scholar of Chinese origin, has considerably improved upon Steiger's treatise in *The Boxer Catastrophe* published by Columbia University in 1955.

Mention should also be made about a commemoratory volume of Victor Purcell edited by Jerome Ch'en and Nicholas Tarling entitled *Studies in Social History of China and South-East Asia* (Cambridge, 1970) in that Jerome Ch'en has contributed an article "The Origin of the Boxers" (pp. 57-84). In all these works Purcell's mastery of the sources from both Chinese and English literatures stands out prominently.

Yi Ho Tuan, the book is an English rendering of a Chinese book. A comparison of the English and Chinese versions reveals that there is considerable omission in the English translation to the extent of reducing its informative value. In the Chinese version there are detailed descriptions of the Boxer organisation some of which are left out in the translated version. A few examples:

On page 20 of *Yi Ho Tuan* there is a discussion of the "grass-root unit" of the Boxers along with a mention of Red and Blue Lanterns. But it omits other organisational details set out in the original.

On page 21 of the same book there is another omission in connection with the battle formation of the Boxers. The Chinese original says: "During fighting all the formations were distinguished by their standards. The squad of ten had a small triangular flag, while the brigade of one hundred held out a big square flag bearing the word 'Ling' [order]. The general standard [of the Boxers] had saw-toothed border, bearing three broad characters of Yi He Tuan."[2]

On page 24 in the first paragraph we miss a significant passage of the original which reads "They [the Boxers] raised the militant slogan of 'exterminate the foreigners and kill the corrupt officials. They sang : 'The Eldest Brother cuts off the foreign heads, while Second Elder Sister slays the imperial brutes. After striking down the foreigners and the imperial officials there is future for the common people'."[3] The passage elucidates an important point which both versions of the book have reiterated, viz. : "... the iron fist of the uprising falling on imperialism, also hit hard at its appendages, the feudal forces." (*Yi Ho Tuan,* p. 24)

Yi Ho Tuan and its Chinese version have given a refreshing account of the Boxer Movement with a clear perspective. Recently an even more refreshing and significant study of the Boxer Movement has been published by the Institute of Modern History of the Chinese Academy of Social Sciences, Beijing. In its journal No. 1 (1979), there is an article entitled "Yihetuan de xingqi he shibai" (The Rise and Fall of the Yihetuan).[4] The author is Hu Sheng who is familiar to the students of history in India and other countries because of the wide circulation of the English translation of his book *Imperialism and Chinese Politics* (Peking, 1955; Chinese version published in Beijing, 1948). The article marks the premature publication of two chapters of a book of history of modern China under preparation by the author. Although it has been written in the survey style of a textbook, Hu Sheng's grasp of vast data and deep insight in China's modern development have made it a very scholarly and weighty document for the study of the Boxer Movement.

Anothor Chinese communist commentator of the Boxer Movement similar to Hu Sheng was Fan Wenlan (1893-1969) whose unfinished book on modern Chinese history, *Zhongguo jindai shi* (History of Modern China) (Beijing, 1958) has an important chapter on the Boxer Movement.

Victor Purcell and Hu Sheng respectively represent the mainstreams of Western and Chinese scholarly assessments of the Boxer Movement. It is interesting to compare them. Western scholarly assessment of the Boxer Movement as represented by Purcell shows a sophisticated understanding. The Western mind is objective and compromising, trying to sail away from the age-old Sinophobia and to keep a balance between the diametrically pitched Occidental and Oriental prejudices. Chinese scholarly view on the subject as represented by Hu Sheng, Fan Wenlan and also *Yi Ho Tuan* is strongly affected by revolutionary passion, with empathy for the unknown Boxer heroes on the one hand and hatred for China's foreign aggressors as well as her own decadent rulers on the other. While Victor Purcell, Jerome Ch'en, Chester Tan and George Steiger have excelled in interpretation, their studies lack the clear-cut perspective as shown in Fan Wenlan's chapter, Hu Sheng's article and *Yi Ho Tuan's* text.

II

The framework of our discussion has already been provided by Purcell who thought no fruitful inquiry into the Boxer Movement would be possible without answering three questions: (*i*) whether the Boxer organisation was a militia or a heretical sect; (*ii*) whether the Boxer Movement was pro- or anti-dynastic; and *(iii)* whether it was anti-foreign or anti-Christian. To these might be added two other questions : whether it was an epic or a catastrophe, and whether the Boxer's was a peasant or plebeian movement.

To understand the nature of the Boxer Movement *vis-a-vis* the hated Manchu regime, it is necessary to join the fray of the Steiger-Tan contention on whether the Boxers were a militia or a heretical sect. The origin of the controversy, one might say, lies in the last syllable of the name Yihetuan. In the first place, it was a newly acquired name. Not until 1898 had the Boxers claimed to be "tuan" which connotes "militia". Secondly, the change of name did have a political significance involving a change in the relationship between the Boxers and the imperial authorities. The question is rather complex.

We can agree with Jerome Ch'en that it is not very important to arrive at a categorical yes-or-no conclusion with respect to the question whether the Boxers had any connection with the White Lotus and its later ramifications. This, however, does not get us away from Purcell's and the Chinese communist historians' perspective because the more we set our eyes on the White Lotus rebellion, the greater we feel its affinity with the Boxer Movement. In fact, a linkage between the two helps us to gain historical perspective in our study of the Boxer uprising.

In a nutshell, we can treat the Boxer Movement as a continuation and follow-up of the White Lotus and the Nian (Nien) rebellions. This is because all three were major revolutionary movements launched by the North China peasantry along with a broad united front at a time when a rudimentary capitalist economy was fast growing in China, and new social strata emerged from Chinese society. The Boxer Movement, like its two predecessors launched by the forefathers of the Boxers, was essentially a peasant movement—a struggle of the rural and urban social strata against the feudal force. In this context, the entire 19th century, from 1876 (the outburst of large-scale White Lotus rebellion) to 1900 in North China, was a century of furious peasant uprising challenging the feudal authorities. The Boxers, from the beginning, despised the feudal authorities, were never deterred by Manchu suppression. If they raised pro-government slogans, it was more a consequence of the Manchu ruling elite yielding to their pressure rather than their timidity before the brutal force of the Manchu dynasty.

We are already on the controversy of whether the Boxer Movement was pro- or anti-dynastic, largely provoked by an observation of George Steiger: "Whatever the Boxer movement may have become—by the spring of 1900, it was, in the beginning, neither a revolutionary nor an heretical organization; it was a lawful and loyal volunteer militia, whose existence was fully justified by the reasonable apprehensions of the government and the people."

III

The pro- or anti-dynasty question defies an either-or answer due to the complexity of relationship between three involved parties—the infuriated underdogs of North China, the aggressive Christian churches and the Manchu government caught between the devil and the deep sea. While many Western scholars have tended to overlook the complexity in this triangular relationship, *Yi Ho Tuan* maintains a clear vision of it. The book clearly indicates that in the confrontation between the people and the church, the Manchu government was basically pro-church and anti-people, because "the Ching [Manchu] rulers had all along followed a capitulationist line in foreign affairs, selling out China's sovereign rights to the imperialists in exchange for the latter's support of their own rule and bloody suppression of the masses." (pp. 10-11) It was this basic pro-church and anti-people stand which decided the basic anti-dynastic nature of the Boxer Movement. "What could the Chinese people do but take up arms against the imperialists and their [Manchu] lackeys?" (p. 19)

The book also sees the other side of the contradiction, viz. conflict of interests between the Manchu regime and the imperial power, (p. 11) The authors have brought out the duality of the Manchu government policy in suppressing the Boxers on the one hand and appeasing them on the other. This duality is highlighted by a quotation of the later reminiscence of the Empress Dowager Cixi : "At that time [of Boxer Movement] I could not make a decision on my own... If I had not compromised on... [adhering to the policy of suppressing the Boxers], on the one hand humouring them [the Boxers] somewhat so as to steady the popular mind and on the other restraining them to a considerable degree... nobody can tell what catastrophe would have resulted once the paper tiger [of the Manchu authorities] was punctured..." (p. 59)

In *Yi Ho Tuan,* we have a reminiscent description by the Empress Dowager about the actual siege of the imperial capital in 1900 by the Boxers: "At that time they had become more powerful with a larger following. In and out of the palaces there was great confusion with groups of men, hair tied up in red cloth, entering and leaving. Nobody could tell who was a 'bandit' [Boxer] and who not, and nobody bothered to ask. But the eunuchs and guards on duty were actually mixing with them." (pp. 58-59) The book also says: "[Beijing] was then controlled by the Yi Ho Tuan contigents 200,000 strong, which would at once topple her [Empress Dowager's] rule if provoked." (p. 58)

On pages 33 to 37 in *Yi Ho Tuan* there are graphic descriptions of how the Boxers actually controlled the twin cities, Beijing and Tianjin. In Beijing the Boxers guarded the imperial palaces, goverment offices, residencial areas and street crossings day and night and also demonstrated at night. In Tianjin, Boxer patrols ordered government official to step down from their sedan-chairs or dismount from their horses, stripping the "last shreds of prestige from those who had ridden roughshod over the people." (p. 35) They even made the fierce Tianjin military commander scurry for shelter in a street encounter. In the triangular equation between the Boxer, the imperial authorities and the foreigners, the Boxers were really on top. Why, then, did they not take advantage of the situation and overthrow the Manchu authorities?

Hu Sheng has provided answers to this paradox. First, the greatest weakness of the Boxer Movement was its want of desire to seize political power. In this respect, it differed sharply from all other peasant wars in Chinese history which had demonstrated a keen desire to fight their way into the imperial capital and take over the government. The Boxers were neither ideologically nor organizationally prepared for such a take-over. Secondly, decentralization was another weakness of the Boxer Movement. Even after their entry into Beijing, they still had no central leadership. Anyone could form a Boxer unit. With such a loose organization it was difficult to put seizure of political power on the agenda. Third, although the Boxers did raise the slogan of exterminating "one dragon" and "two tigers" whom they considered as traitors (with Emperor Guangxu being the "dragon" and the Prime Minister, Prince Qing, and the leading modernist among (he courtiers, Li Hongzhang, being the "tigers"), they also identified many important Manchu courtiers as their friends and supporters. Hence the issue of overthrowing the Manchu regime got obscured. Fourth, the Empress Dowager who was the *de facto* ruler succeeded in deceiving the Boxers. Through Prince Zhuang she awarded the Boxers with 100,000 tales of silver and twenty thousand piculs of rice and set up a "shrine" *(tan)* in Prince Zhuang's office to "register" the Boxer organizations. After being "registered" and receiving the awards, the Boxer units styled themselves as "Fengzhi yihe shentuan" (Sacred organization for righteousness and harmony with royal mandate). This created the impression that the Boxers were pro-dynasty. (pp. 119-121)

The Boxer Movement has given rise to many a Western theory of the innate anti-foreignism of the Chinese culture. However, almost all modern Western scholars who have closely examined the nature of the movement—from Steiger to Purcell—have unanimously put the blame on Western powers and Christian missionaries.

The observation of Lenin in 1900 on the Boxer Movement which is quoted in *Yi Ho Tuan* and deserves to be quoted once more: "It is true the Chinese hate the Europeans, but which Euporeans do they hate and why? The Chinese do not hate the European people, they hate the European capitalists and the European governments obedient to them." (p. 126, citing V. I. Lenin: *Collected Works,* Moscow, 1960, Vol. IV, p. 373)

IV

Touching upon the controversy whether the Boxer Movement was "anti-foreign" in a general sense or was specifically "anti-missionary", once again Victor Purcell was most thoughtful. His conclusion is: "The Boxer movement was anti-foreign and therefore anti-Christian." (p. 263) He thinks it meaningless to apportion blame among Western governments, diplomats, merchants and missionaries, but rather it was the sum total of all these elements united under the broad design of imperialism which was the target of the Boxer wrath.

Besides Purcell, many Western scholars have made significant studies of the Chinese cultural interaction with Christianity *vis-a-vis* the anti-Christian movements in China. Their analyses of the genesis of Chinese anti-foreignism[5] as demonstrated in the late 19th century cover the following broad aspects:

First, the Chinese did not relish the demonstration of cultural and racial superioritv by Western Christians in China.

Secondly, the Western Christian drive to destroy China's cultural identity also invited strong anti-Western and anti-Christian feelings.

In *Yi Ho Tuan,* the charges against the Christian missions are even more sharply pronounced : "[F]oreign missonaries who wore the cloak of religion had for some time been penetrating China's cities and countryside, building churches, lording it over the people and committing many crimes." (p. 12) Fan Wenlan further spells out the crimes committed by foreign missionaries against Chinese people : *(a)* occupying land properties and yet evading government revenues, shifting the tax burden onto the peasants; *(b)* using treaty privileges to shield the converts in their litigation against the people; (c) encroaching upon China's sovereign rights and pressurizing the Manchu government to punish the officials whom they disliked; *(d)* encouraging the converts to commit atrocities on the people; and *(e)* blackmailing the people and exacting money from them. Fan observes : "The hypocritical missionaries were generally abominable rascals and the ace spies for the capitalist countries to plunder the colonies, committing all kinds of crimes. The Chinese people who had been victimized by them were justified to attack them and drive them away." (pp. 336-368).

Justifications for attacking the foreigners there were plenty, but driving them away did not materialize. Was the Boxer attack wise or foolish? Was it fanaticism or heroism? Was the movement an epic in the history of China's anti-imperialist struggle or a fiasco? Academic opinions are divided on these questions.

Victor Purcell agrees with Chester Tan that the Boxer Movement was a "catastrophe". "Not only did it entail slaughter and suffering, but it resulted in the imposition of crippling taxation on the already impoverished Chinese people to pay indemnities imposed by the Powers." (p. 271) The indemnity amounted to 450 million taels, *i.e.* one tael of silver to be paid by every Chinese citizen. And the Manchu government was simply reduced to "a debt-collecting agency for the Powers." (Purcell, p. 261, quoting Tan).

Yet Chester Tan and Victor Purcell have not missed the silver lining. The Boxer Movement fully exposed the "ignorance and folly of the Manchu rulers", hence it became "the last struggle of the Chinese people against foreign imperialism under the rule" of the Manchu Dynasty, says Tan. (p. 241) Purcell thinks the Movement not only stopped the foreign powers' attempt to partition China, but also "signalized the birth of Chinese Nationalism." (p. 271)

These positive achievements of the Boxers were reiterated by Chinese communist historians with much greater emotion and enthusiasm. In the concluding words of *Yi Ho Tuan* we read : "Not in vain did the Yi Ho Tuan heroes shed their blood. Their patriotism and dauntless courage will inspire the Chinese people forever. In the annals of the Chinese nation, the anti-imperialist and anti-feudal exploits of the Yi Ho Tuan will always be a lustrous chapter." (pp. 127-128)

That the Boxer Movement was a revolutionary epic, instead of a catastrophe, is the message of Chinese historians. The Yi He Tuan hymn has been jointly sung by Fan Wenlan, Hu Sheng, *Yi Ho Tuan* and Mou Anshi, whose article highlighting the historical role played by both the Taiping and Boxer movements entitled "Lun Zhongguo jindai nongmin geming zhanzheng de lishi zuoyong" (On the historical significance of peasant revolutionary wars in modern China) is included in No. 1, *Zhongguo nongmin zhanzheng shi luncong.*

The first great historical significance of the Boxer Movement, in the view of Chinese historians, is that it scared the imperialist aggressors out of their wits and put the brakes on imperialist designs to partition China. As *Yi Ho Tuan* says : "It [Boxer Movement] gave the invaders a taste of the people's heavy fist and shattered their fond dream of partitioning China. Earlier, they had arrogantly boasted that with 10,000 soldiers carrying modern arms they could subjugate all China. Clamour for partition had filled the air. But after the Yi Ho Tuan mounted the political stage, this claptrap was no longer heard..." (p. 124).

The book quotes the German General and Commander-in-Chief of the Allied Forces, Alfred Waldersee (1832-1904), in suppressing the Movement and the British under-secretary of foreign affairs, William Broderick. While Broderick advised his countrymen to respect the national feelings of the Chinese people who occupied "a quarter of the world's population", Waldersee echoed: "The partitioning of China is therefore the least feasible policy." (p. 124) Fan Wenlan quotes many more such comments of Western statesmen to make the same point. A revealing quotation is from Robert Hart depicting China's waking up from a sleep of several thousand years. (Fan, p. 400) Hart is also quoted by Mou Anshi to have worried about the Western powers' fiasco in China as compared to Napoleon's debacle in Moscow. (p. 96) All this drives home the conclusion of Fan Wenlan that the Boxer Movement made "the imperialist understand the Chinese people." (p. 398)

The second great historical significance of the Boxer Movement lies in the awakening of the Chinese people's patriotic consciousness. As *Yi Ho Tuan* clearly spells out, the Movement not only educated the Chinese people about the true nature of imperialist aggression, but also "exposed the treasonous character" of the Manchu authorities. (p. 125) Fan Wenlan observes that the "Yi He Tuan Movement, indeed, shook the entire China". Even the coolies and domestic servants of the foreigners in Shanghai felt that the hour of finally settling the score with the foreigners had arrived. (p. 383) In the words of Hu Sheng the Chinese people never looked back after the Boxer Movement. Their revolutionary movement surged forward wave after wave till they achieved complete victory over feudalism and imperialism, (p. 157)

Third, both *Yi Ho Tuan* and Mou Anshi have treated the Boxer Movement as a cornerstone of the victory of the Chinese communist revolution. This assessment originated from a speech of Zhou Enlai (1898-1976) in 1955 : "For more than one hundred years (till recently), the people of China had suffered the ruthless aggression, oppression, pillage and slaughter by the imperialist powers. During this period, the Chinese people ceaselessly waged heroic struggles against the aggression of the imperialists and oppression of the feudal forces... The Boxer Movement of 1900 exemplified the Chinese people's tenacious strugele against the imperialist aggressor. Their heroic struggle laid one of the cornerstones for the great victory of the Chinese people fifty years thereafter." (Mou Anshi, pp. 107-108, citing *Renmin Ribao* or *People's Daily,* 12 December 1955).

V

Centering around the Boxer Movement there took place the unprecedented demonstration of xenophobia by Chinese people on the one hand and Sinophobia by the Western powers on the other. After that both the Chinese and Christian civilizations began to appreciate each other. The Boxer Movement had the distinction to be a series of lasts. Apart from being the last Sino-Western conflict. It was the last earth-shaking event of the 19th century. In addition, as Chester Tan says, it was the last countryside popular movement during the Manchu dynasty.

To study such an event obviously involves errors of commission and omission in appreciation, sympathy and empathy. Many aspects of the Movement have received comparatively exhaustive scholarly treatment as we have shown. Conclusions have not yet been conclusive. While old controversies are kept alive, new ones appear.

The paradox of the Boxer Movement lies in two realms. First, being an upsurge of youthful enthusiasm and heroic will power, dauntlessly challenging the European automatic killing machines with their bare fists and holding the two thousand year ruthless, autocratic and repressive imperial authorities in great contempt, it had all the ingredients of a revolutionary mass struggle. Yet, paradoxically, it neither defeated imperialist aggression nor marginally diminished the authorities of the decadent feudal regime. Secondly, having erupted like a volcano, catching all internal and external reactionaries unawares and having staged a demonstration of unison, discipline and conscious assertion of the ordinary people's political rights and sung a hymn of patriotism with both fanciful ideology (however primitive it might be) and resolute action, it unmistakably promised a great revolutionary struggle. Yet not only no reliable leadership emerged from the movement to offer a strategy and programme, but it remained throughout decentralized, disunited and headless, allowing opportunities to lapse and even falling a prey to the conspiracy of the Empress Dowager.

To take the Western and Chinese studies of the Boxer Movement as a whole, there have emerged certain broad perspectives about the nature of the Movement. First, in the opinion of the Chinese communist historians and also to some extent in the view of Victor Purcell, the Boxer Movement was a resurgence of revolutionary fervour of the peasantry of North China in the true tradition of heretical sects, particularly that of the White Lotus. This perspective sees the White Lotus, Nian, and Boxer rebellions which had taken place in the span of one century (1796-1900) in totality and not in isolation. This is an advantage. As Jerome Ch'en says, any categorical assertion, including Ch'en's own, on whether the Boxers were or were not heretical sects and whether the White Lotus were organizationally involved in the Boxer Movement or not, is immaterial. Even a simple yes or no answer to these questions should not obscure the perspective that the Boxer, Nian, and White Lotus belonged to a single current of peasant movement. All three sprang from the volcanic socio-economic -political background of North China which could be characterised by the existence of three infrastructures : (*i*) of feudal exploitation and repression, *(ii)* the north Chinese peasants' infrastructure of rebellion embedded in the White Lotus movement and its various ramifications and *(iii)* the Western imperialist infrastructure of semi-colonization of China which was limited to opium imperialism before 1840 and extended to territorial, treaty-port and finance imperialism after the Opium War. The Boxer Movement marked the manifestation of the peasant-rebellion infrastructure challenging the other two infrastructures.

Secondly, the triangular equation between the three infrastructures, as emerged from Hu Sheng's study, provides us with an insight into the Boxer paradox that after moving so close to seizure of imperial power it did not seize it. Does this mean that the Boxers were not revolutionary, or, in Purcell's terminology, not "anti-dynastic"? Purcell's analysis that the Movement was essentially anti-dynastic, but was dominated by pro-dynastic elements is not as convincing as Hu Sheng's analysis that while the Western imperialist powers outsmarted themselves by driving the Manchu government into the united front of the Boxer Movement, the Manchu *de facto* ruler, Empress Dowager, and her courtiers outsmarted the Boxer braves in fanning their anti-foreign fury to cool their anti-dynastic zeal.

In this game of wits, the peasant masses of North China who exhibited such heroic revolutionary bravery and conscious will power ultimately lost the golden chance of assuming political leadership of the country to gain a vantage position in their overall struggle for liberation from the clutches of feudalism and imperialism.

Chinese historians, after highlighting the vital shortcomings of the Boxer Movement (forgetting the fundamental revolutionary task of overthrowing the Manchu authority which was the culprit of all the miseries of 19th-century China), have not lost sight of the greatness of the Boxer uprising. "The world-shaking Yi Ho Tuan Movement", says *Yi Ho Tuan,* "is the glory and pride of the Chinese people." (p. 124) Hu Sheng adds : "Although the Yi Ho Tuan Movement did not properly tackle the relationship of these twin struggles [of anti-feudalism and anti-imperialism], its power gushed out from beneath the earth like a turbulent current, which forced the Manchu imperial court to do what it had never dared to imagine—declaring war against the external (aggression)." (p. 157) Hu Sheng and his colleagues have seen in the Yi He Tuan Movement the most heroic boxing on earth— the turbulent bare-bodied human wave dauntlessly challenging the aggressive bullets of the Western powers.

However, times have changed, as Hu Sheng sees. Spontaneous peasant movements like the Taiping and the Boxer could no longer shoulder the revolutionary task of anti-feudal and anti-imperialist struggle, hence could no longer be the focal point of historical development of the 20th-century With the proletarian class entering the stage of history as a conscious "class for itself" the Chinese peasants no longer needed to box their class enemies with bare fists, along with their fanciful but totally unreliable spirit of invulnerability. Though the 19th-century was one of national humiliation and economic misery for the Chinese people, yet it witnessed such great popular movements like the Taiping and Boxer. Furthermore, from the stepping stones of these movements the Chinese people marched in bigger strides to catch up with the progress of the new era of democracy and modernity. On this happy note, we may bid farewell to our excursions into the nineteenth century.*

References

1. Victor Purcell, *The Boxer Uprising: A Background Study* (Cambridge University Press, 1963).
2. Yihetuan Yundong (The Yihetuan Movement). (Shanghai, 1972), pp. 11-12.
3. *Ibid,* p. 13.
4. *Jindaishi yanjiu* (Studies of Modern History), (Beijing), 1979, No. 1, pp. 96-163.
5. P.A. Cohen, *China* and *Christanity : The Missionary Movement of the Growth of Chinese Anti-Foreignism* 1860-1870 (Harward, 1953).

* This was the last of four articles, along with "Opium War", "Taiping". "Reform", in the series "Nineteenth-Century China Revisted" in *China Report.*

13

Buddhist Incense to Chinese Mass Rebellion : A Case Study of the Boxer Uprising of 1900*

Our thoughts go back to the most heroic boxing on earth which is also the most maligned historical event known as the "Boxer Uprising" in Western circles. To me this mass movement was worthy of its Chinese name "Yihequan", *i.e.* "Boxing for Righteousness and Harmony". No single event in Chinese history has created greater anti-Chinese sentiments in the Western world than the doings of these self-righteous Boxers. Yet, it was their heroism which served as an eye-opener for the Western colonial powers that no one should attempt conquering or partitioning a people who could generate such an anti-foreign and anti-Christian fury as what had been wrought by the Boxers.

The Boxer uprising of 1900 eloquently demonstrated to the whole world that the Chinese cultural tradition was the unity of two opposite trends: (1) the force which strove for social harmony, and (2) the force which struggled against social injustice. There is no denying the fact that the cultural force for social harmony had all along been inspired by the teachings of Confucius and cemented by the followers of the Confucian school of thought. In other words, this is the cultural force of Confucian harmony-ethics. As for the cultural force of social struggle, this was the age-old weapon of China's down-trodden masses against a hierarchical order which was well protected by the Confucian harmony-ethics. The leaders of the Yihe

*The article that was published in *Bodhi-Rasmi,* (Souvenir of the First International Conference on Buddhism and National Culture, New Delhi, October, 10-15, 1984) has been abridged for the present volume. For the full text see Tan Chung, *Triton and Dragon,* (Delhi, 1986).

Boxers (and indeed all their predecessors who had engaged in similar pursuits) were condemned by the custodians of Chinese culture as "bu ren bu yi" (anti-human-kindness and anti-righteousness) "wu fu wu jun" (father-forsaking and ruler-forsaking). There could be no greater crimes than these charges in the Confucian order. I have named this anti-Confucian cultural force as that of "Buddhist struggle ethics".

It would be over-simplification for me to describe Buddhism as a "struggle-ethics" alone. There are many ideological thrusts in Buddhist philosophy. Some of these thrusts, like the quest for a happy world, the Buddha's awards for the suffering and the concept of equality among all men had the ingredients for an ideology of mass rebellion. Buddhism also carried to China the eternal Indian aspiration of Truth *(dharma)* overcoming Evil *(mara),* and the Buddhist iconography vividly depicted the Great Divide between the celestial warriors and demons. The Buddhist theory of *samsara* (transmigration) evoked hope from despair and encouraged strife for better fortunes. The Mahayana Bodhisattva tradition provided legitimacy to rebel leaders in power struggles and enriched the struggle-ethics.

The vigorous preaching of Buddhism among Chinese masses through vivid and interesting visual and auditory media like frescoes and sculptures in temples and caves, story-telling and dramatic performances sponsored by Buddhist monasteries over the centuries (particularly from the 7th to the 10th century) created a deep imprint on Chinese folklore. The cosmos of the pre-scientific and illiterate minds of Chinese peasants and town-folks was filled with "tianbing tianjiang" (celestial soldiers and generals) and "moluo" (Chinese corruption of *mara).* The Chinese masses firmly believed in their existence. In other words, they were indoctrinated by the Buddhist struggle-ethics and were ready to pursue the course of struggle by invoking the protection and aid of the celestial warriors when the demons and their human reincarnations had made their life miserable.

However, the elite of Buddhist community who had indoctrinated the Chinese masses with the struggle-ethics befriended the high-ups and maintained a distance from the down-trodden of the country. The Taoist priests, on the other hand, loved to stay away from the urban life and had a greater rapport with Chinese peasants. Taoism had borrowed heavily from Buddhism both in theory and practice. The intimate interactions between the Taoist priests and Chinese masses did not result in neutralising the Buddhist influence, but only sinicised many of the Buddhist legends and deities without totally erasing their original identity.

Occurring at the turn of the century, the Boxer Uprising is a part of the modern era. The elite of China had already started realizing the backwardness of the nation not only from the point of science and technology, but also from the point of social evolution. On the other hand, the presence of modern European civilization in China had been expanding day after day. This presence was not only manifested in the form of industrial products, which included cotton textiles and steel arms, but also in the form of Christian churches and missionaries—the cultural emissaries of the advanced world. Against this modern trend, what the Yihe Boxers did in burning the churches, destroying the railway lines, boycotting imported goods and even killing the foreign missionaries and their families and the Chinese converts apparently represented a retrogression. Most of those who have condemned the Boxer movement have condemned this hostility against modern civilization and its representatives.

Even among the modern Chinese historians there exists a regretful feeling that such a patriotic anti-imperialist movement which the Yihe Boxers represented should have drawn its inspiration from religious superstition and backwardness, sacrificing lives of innocent youth and teenagers as gun-fodders. And the highly commendable discipline of the Boxers was maintained by "feudal superstition and death".[1]

The Boxers seemed to have left a deep impression about their "anti-Christian" and "anti-foreign" fanaticism. They also seemed to have never made up their minds whether they should overthrow or support the hateful, corrupt and incompetent Manchu regime. These apparent drawbacks gave rise to academic controversies about their genuine patriotism and revolutionariness.

The post-Opium War period of Chinese history showed an unmistakable tendency of downward movement in the country's political, social, economic life. Western (plus Japanese) imperialism was obviously the root cause of China's deteriorating fortune. The Manchu government knew it clearly, but had been given enough beatings to remain subservient. The upper classes on the whole had no mood to break their heads against the new alien dominating forces which were much more formidable than the Manchu domination. The illiterate peasants in their simple wisdom put two and two together and realized the harm done to them and their country by the newly arrived foreigners whom they regarded as representatives of foreign imperialism, and rightly so. Their anti-foreign and anti-Christian wrath must be understood in this perspective.

The logical identification of Christian churches with the fortresses of Western imperialism in the eyes of Chinese Boxers can find no better testimonial than the following observation of Sir Robert Hart (1835-1911), a British national who had been the founding father and head of Chinese customs office for more than forty years from 1861 to 1906:

> "He [the Westerner] is a Christian—therefore it is a sacred duty to attack every other Cult and preach the Gospel; he finds consumers keep alive a demand for opium—therefore it is right, if not his duty to supply; he learns that China has an immense population—therefore he inveighs against every restriction...; he is told by some one that China has no laws, that Chinese judges are corrupt...therefore he demands and obtains extra-territoriality; he finds that China is not a military nation—therefore he pushes aside discussion, asserts his superiority, sees right in might, and has his own way...he knows that such is the way of doing things at home—therefore he condemns all Chinese otherness..."[2]

It is well known that the areas of Boxer activities in the end of the 19th century were the areas infested by the White Lotus Rebellion a century ago. Although by 1835 all the rebellions inspired by the White Lotus had been destroyed by the Manchu government, the secret society of the White Lotus still survived among the masses. Many scholars rightly hold the opinion that the Boxer Movement actually marked the revival of the White

Lotus Rebellion.[3] But there has been another school of thought viewing the Boxers as a militia quite different from the White Lotus and other heretical sects and the debate between these two schools has continued.[4]

The White Lotus was a secret society having nearly one thousand years of history, which fact made it an important embodiment of China's Buddhist struggle-ethics. The symbol of "white lotus" came from the Buddhist "pundarika" which was the very symbol of *Buddhadharma.* Bright *dharma* vanquishing dark evil was the tenet of this sect. Every time when it launched a rebellion, it advocated that Maitreya Buddha had reincarnated and Mingwang (Enlightened Raja), the messenger and manifestation of Vairocana Buddha's wrath had been born. A famous White Lotus rebel leader in the past was Han Shantong (7-1351) who proclaimed himself as "Kongque mingwang" (Enlightened Raja of Peacock), and kindled the anti-Mongol revolutionary fire in the country. Incense burning was an important ritual of the White-Lotus. Han's rebel army was famous for its incense-burning and thus nick-named "incense army" *(xiangjun). Dhupana* (incense-burning), an originally Indian ritual, thus became quite stimulating in Chinese politics after its introduction to China along with the importation of famous Indian perfumes.

Interestingly, not only the White Lotus stream was present in the Boxer Movement, but there was a similar sect known as "Wenxiang jiao" (Incense-smelling sect).[5] True to this Buddhist tradition, many Boxers believed that there was magic power in the incense smoke which provided a communication line with their deities. They also inherited the Indian Buddhist (also Hindu) belief that fire could be sent afar to burn the evil spirits, and set the European oceanliners ablaze at sea. This was known as the Red Lantern Cult *(Hongdengzhao).*[6] Non-vegetarian food was regarded by the Boxers as profane,[7] which further strengthened the kinship between the Boxer Movement and Buddhism. There was a secret chanting of some Boxers which they had sworn not to share even with parents, wife and children. The secret chanting was: "Guanshiyin pusa" (Bodhisattva Avalokitesvara).[8] Some Boxers wore a red turban emulating the fourteenth century White Lotus rebel group, the

"Red Turban Army" led by Liu Futong. The only innovation made by the Boxers was to have each red turban bear the Chinese character "Fo" (Buddha).[9] There was another Boxer magic which bore evidence of Chinese folk adaptation of the Indian legend of churning the ocean, which had originally been a Brahmanical story but was later shared by the Buddhists. One of the Boxer leaders was a Buddhist monk named Haigan, meaning "dry sea", suggesting his possession of the magic power of churning the sea dry. The Boxer followers congratulated each other that the emergence of Monk Haigan signified the doom of the foreigners (who had thrived on sea).[10] The Boxers were also fascinated by the supernatural power of Buddha's "endless light" *(Amitabha),* and had among their deities "Heavenly Light", "Earthly Light", "Solar Light" and "Lunar Light". They also had the Buddhist "Dragon King" *(Nagaraja)* as their protector.[11]

There is evidence that the Boxer Movement was inspired by the two classics of Chinese struggle-ethics. *Shuihu zhuan* and *Xiyou ji.* Among the slogans raised by the Boxers were "titian xingdao" (implementing justice for the Heaven), "shafu jiping" (killing the rich to help the poor), "da zangguan, weimin chuli" (punishing the corrupt officials and doing service for the people).[12] These slogans echoed the norms of alternative ethics propounded by *Shuihu.* When the Boxers first grouped themselves, every unit *(tuari)* had exactly 108 members. And the period for mastering the magical boxing was exactly 108 days.[13] This number of 108 which is that of the *Shuihu* heroes, seems to have cast a spell on the Boxers. "Seeking *dharma* from the Western Heaven" *(xitian qujing),* an important theme of *Xiyou ji,* was revived by the Boxers in a different form. One of the secret chantings of the Boxers reads: "Wo qui xifang shengmu Amituofo" (I invoke the protection of the Holy Mother of the West, Amitabha Buddha).[14] The monkey king, Sun, of the novel was one of the most popular deities among the Boxers. Another hero of the novel, Pig Zhubajie, also became a holy protector of them.[15]

The Chinese struggle-ethics belonged to the down-trodden masses who were traditionally described as "shou wu cun tie" (without not even an inch of iron in their hands). For such people to rise in rebellion against the heavily armed opponents, they were much in need of extraneous reinforcement, be it real or imaginary. No real reinforcement from outside their social strata would come. The only available reinforcement was the illusory supernatural power dangled by Buddhism and Taoism. The Boxers were not day dreamers. As a famous Chinese historian, Jian Bozan, observes: "the Boxers did not embrace religion to lead people to the paradise after death, but to lead them to wrest from the enemy the real world which they had lost, to fight for their own destiny and for the freedom of their motherland."[16] They were not really blinded by superstition. Superstition was just the means not the end. The spiritual power kindled by superstition transformed hundreds of thousands of isolated individual weaponless peasants into a united, disciplined, courageous and righteous fighting force and also transformed every member of the fighting force into an indoctrinated, high-moral fighter. The Boxer leaders spread the story of the Jade Emperor's (Taoist counterpart of Indra) sending down eight million celestial troops to fight the foreign intruders.[17] The spread of this story virtually resulted in so many docile peasants being transformed into anti-imperialist fighters, who bravely faced foreign bullets with their bare bodies. Although the Boxers were physically vanquished, the moral force which they had exhibited ultimately terrified and daunted the evil spirit in the foreign powers who, with the exception of Japan, finally respected China's existence as an independent and sovereign people. In this sense, the Boxer Movement triumphed, which was also the triumph of the Chinese struggle-ethics—the triumph of the Indian tradition of dharma overcoming mara.

From a materialist view-point this discussion may sound unconvincing. Yet in a sense, the approach of the Boxers was materialistic. Their quest was for a material power which could neutralize the foreign superiority in weaponry. Instead of sitting idly praying for the descending of the celestial saviours, the Boxers practised the martial art and strived to perfect the skill of transforming the celestial warriors into themselves (concentrating their minds during their meditation and secret chanting to be possessed of the spirit of their deities). To a scientific modern mind this process of transformation was novel and self-deceiving. Given the available information and facilities of the homeless peasants at that time it was highly progressive and rational. It was, indeed, the only available avenue left for those who did not wish to see the perpetuation of foreign imperialist domination and Chinese helplessness in the face of foreign aggression. In the long process of social evolution, the shedding of the Boxers' heroic blood and the loss of the Boxers' valuable lives (although in the contemporary market, twenty of them were worth only one U.S. dollar) seem to belong to Karl Marx's "realm of necessity". The Boxer's idolization of the traditional martial art of Sino-Indian progenitor by their various cults of "shenquan" (godly boxing), "hongquan" (red boxing), "dahongquan" (great red boxing), "meihauquan" (plum-blossom boxing) and their uniting all the cults under the banner of "yihequan" (righteous and harmonious boxing)[18] represented a highly realistic approach of resurrecting the strength and vitality of China's cultural tradition at a moment when the very existence of Chinese culture was threatened seriously. This provided a sharp contrast to the Chinese high-ups' approach of buying weapons from the imperial powers to strengthen China which proved futile.

The Boxer Movement invited the charge of xenophobia against Chinese culture which she has not been able to wash clean with tons of holy water from the Yangtze and Yellow rivers. Yes, certain foreigners were identified by the Boxers as demons. But, on the side of celestial warriors of the Boxer's Great Divide, there were also foreigners—who in their consciousness were very much their own—whom we have already mentioned: Maitreya, Valocana and Amitabha Buddha, and Bodhisattva Avalokitesvara. Two more Indian names of the same category deserve further notice. One is Bodhidharma who was affectionately and reverentially called by the Boxers as "Damo laozu" (Reverend Patriarch Bodhidharma).[19] As this ancient Indian monk was regarded as the founding father of martial art in China, it was but natural that he became the most popular deity among the Boxers. Another Indian name was Vaisravana who was the famous "tuota tianwang" (the Deva-king who bears a pagoda on his palm) in Chinese Buddhist legend. The Taoists and the entire Chinese folklore owned him, changed his Indian name into Chinese, as "Li tianwang" (Deva-king Li). He was a popular Boxer deity.[20] One Boxer leader, Li Daliang, has become a legendary figure whose story is still vividly retold among the peasants of his native place, Hebei Province. Li who had assassinated a wicked magistrate, was hiding behind the mud-image of Deva-king Li inside a dilapidated temple of the Jade Emperor for safety. A fellow-peasant helped him to come out of his hiding with a trick. The two made a one-metre tall iron pagoda with the inscription on its bottom that Li Daliang was "Deva-king Li" sent to the world by the Jade Emperor. One night, the temple caught fire and was razed to the ground. The only thing remained on the ruins was this iron pagoda. When people examined it and discovered the inscription, the legend of Li Daliang became wide-spread. He, then, emerged from underground to become a mass leader. The story says that even after the defeat of the Boxers, Li Daliang escaped arrest because of the magic pagoda on his palm, making him truly the immortal Vaisravana.[21]

The Boxer Movement also supplied additional evidence for accusing Chinese culture for "Sinocentric culturalism", meaning her intolerance of foreign cultural influence. Yet it was ideologically a Buddhist oriented struggle-ethics against the preachers of Christianity, which was naked Western imperialism *not* even in disguise. If the Chinese culture had a blind anti-foreign Sinocentric tendency, it would have been hard to explain that an ideology inspired by a foreign religion—Buddhism—could make millions of people (including the Boxers) sacrifice their lives against injustice and repression, that the Chinese corruption of the Sanskrit word *"Amitabha"* was the secret spiritual linkage between Chinese masses (including the Boxers and their celestial protectors, and that the Indian invention of incense-burning was held by the Boxers as so vital a practice in their grim struggle against the entire European world. There was also the Indian national flower, the lotus, which occupied an important place in the Boxer legend. Not only the Boxers were torch-bearers of the idealism enshrined in the White Lotus symbol—the idealism so popularly spread in China by the Buddhist classic, *Saddharmapundarika-sutra*—but the Boxers had another lotus-inspired deity in "Huanglian shengmu" (Holy Mother of Yellow Lotus Flower).[22] Among the four varieties of sacred lotus flowers *(utpala, padma, kutnuda* and *pundarika)* in Buddhist tradition, there was no place for the Yellow Lotus, which was obviously the Chinese adaptation. Any way, the Lotus was as sacred in China as it had been in India—its natural habitat. Lotus and incense added not only colour and aroma to China's ecological environment, but also had significance in China's political, social and cultural history. Even though Christianity also attempted to offer equally marvellous materials and ideas to China as Buddhism had done in the past, there was a great difference in the two. While Buddhism was brought to China with folded hands accompanied by the colours of lotus and fragrance of incense, Christianity was brought to China (in the second half of the 19th century) by gunboats, cannons and rifles, accompanied by the colour and poison of opium. If the Boxers had not appreciated the good things of Christian civilization, it was certainly not due to Sinocentrism.

One last controversy to be ironed out is that between the "heretical" and "militia" schools. Each school has apportioned some blame to the Boxer Movement. After retrieving it from the "militia" schools' criticism of collusion with the reactionary Manchu regime, the "heretical" school, led by Victor Purcell, blamed it for mystic obscurity in its objective and direction.

Some years ago, two Chinese scholars have advanced a theory which has escaped international attention. While recognising the pivotal role played by members of the heretical sects within the Boxer Movement, they feel it incorrect to pin the Movement to the heretical sects first and then, explain the process of its transformation into open mass organizations. In their opinion, the majority of the Boxers had nothing to do with the heretical sects. They were attracted into the Movement only because of its anti-imperialist thrust which was the embodiment of the revolutionary aspiration of the times.[23] Indeed, the "heretical" theory has been proved inadequate to explain the lack of central leadership of the Movement (if it was under one single heretical sect) on the one hand and the absence of serious factional strife within the Movement (if it was under several sects on the other). All signs point to the fact that this was a spantaneous mass movement, the involvement of and participation in which witnessed few parallels in history. It was the confluence of the traditional struggle-ethics with the modern anti-imperialist current. Dr. Sun Yat-sen (1866-1925), "Father of Modern China", once likened the Boxer Movement to the Meiji Restoration of Japan.[24] We can very well conclude that the Boxer Movement has demonstrated before the whole world the inner strength and vitality of China's cultural tradition and the existence of the other China which was non-Confucian but Buddhistic, non-stagnant and dynamic.

References

1. Lu Yao, "Yihetuan yanjiu pingshu" (Comments on the study of Boxer Movement), *Jindaishi yanjiu* (Study of modern history), No. 2, 1982, p. 143.
2. Robert Hart, *These from the Land of Sinim* pp. 123-124, cited in P.A. Varg, *Missionaries, Chinese and Diplomats* (Princeton Univ. Press, 1958), p. 36.
3. See Victor Purcell, *The Boxer Uprising: A Background Study* (Cambridge Univ. Press, 1963).
4. The debate was revived in recent years by Tai Hsuan-chih, a scholar of Taiwan, and Prof. Jerome Ch'en of York University. See Jerome Ch'en, "The Origin of the Boxers", in Jerome Ch'en & Nicholas Tarling (ed), *Studies in the Social History of China and South-East Asia* (Cambridge Univ. Press, 1970), p. 348.
5. Jiang Kai. "Pingyuan quanfei jishi" (An account of the Boxer bandits in the Northern Plain) cited in *Yihetuan* (hereafter *YHT)* (A collection of contemporary accounts about Boxer Movement compiled by Jian Bozan, *et al,* publish by the China Historical Society, Shanghai, 1957), Vol. I, p. 354.
6. The Red Lantern Cult was one of the highlights of the Boxers, particularly at Tianjin city. One of the well-known Boxer leaders was Zhu Hongdeng, whose name means "red lantern". Under the impact of the Boxers, every household at Tianjin lit a red lantern at night in the hope that the holy fire would help to destroy the "Ocean Devils".
7. Liu Mengyang, "Tianjin quanfei bianluan jishi" (Record of event of the Boxer bandits' rioting at Tianjin) *juan* 1, in *YHT,* Vol. II, p. 11.

8. Guan He, "Quanfei wenjian lu" (Eye-witness account about Boxer bandits), in *YHT,* Vol, I. p. 470.
9. Liu Yitong, "Min jiao xiangchou dumen wenjian lu (Eye-witness account of fighting between Boxers and Christians at the city gate). in *YHT,* Vol. II, p. 183.
10. Liu Mengyang, *loc cit,* pp. 26-27.
11. *YHT,* Vol. I, p. 299, citing Japanese eye-witness, Atsusuke Sahara's "Miscellaneous notes about Boxing."
12. Lu Yao, *loc cit,* p. 152.
13. Liu Yitong, *loc cit.*
14. *YHT,* Vol. I, pp. 238-239, citing Atsusuke Sahara's "Miscellaneous notes".
15. *YHT,* Vol. I, p. 299.
16. Lu Yao, *loc cit,* p. 144.
17. Anonymous, "Tianjin yiyue ji" (A month at Tianjin) *YHT,* Vol. II, p. 141.
18. Lu Yao, "Yihetuan yundong chuqi douzheng jieduande jige wenti" (On the issues relating to the initial stage of the Boxer Movement) in *Zhong-guo jindaishi lunwen ji* (A collection of papers on modern Chinese history), (Compiled by China people's University, Beijing, 1979) Vol. II, pp. 673-678.
19. Liu Mengyang, *loc cit,* p. 8.
20. Guan He, *loc cit,* p. 468.
21. *Lidai nongmin qiyi chuanshuo xuan* (Selection of legendary stories about peasant uprising in history), (Compiled by the Institute of Literary Studies of the Chinese Academy of Social Sciences, published in Sanghai, 1979), pp. 337-437, story "Tuota Li Tianwan" (Deva-king Li who bore a pagoda on his palm).
22. A woman, said to be a former prostitute, became one of the leaders of the Boxers and was projected as the "Holy Mother of Yellow Lotus", See Guan He, *loc cit,* p. 487.
23. Jin Chongji & Hu Shengwu, "Yihetuan yundong shiqide ge jieji dongxiang" (Activities of various classes during the Boxer Movement), in *Zhonogguo jindaishi lunwen ji,* Vol. II, p. 696.
24. Sun Zhongshan (Sun Yat-sen), "xinli jianshe" (Psychological reconstruction), cited in Lu Yao, *loc cit* in *Jindaishi yanjiu,* pp. 159-160.

Part–IV
Reformation

14

The Reformers' Non-Violent Path to Modernisation 1898*

I

The 1898 Reform Movement in China is no hot cake for the historians. The English publishing world has not offered a single title before the appearance of the book under review.** The Chinese publishing circles are just as indifferent. There is no famous Communist Chinese historian who can be called a specialist either on the Movement or on Kang Youwei.

One reason why the topic is not the communist historians' cup of tea is that reformism does not fit into the Marxist intellectual framework. In the concluding chapter of *The Reform Movement of 1898* it is uncharitably asserted: "A reform movement is at the outset reactionary by nature, for it always opposes the revolution and attempts to ameliorate social contradictions." Lenin is quoted to say that every reform is introduced in order "to stem, weaken, or extinguish the revolutionary struggle in order to fragment the strength and energy of the revolutionary classes, to befog their consciousness, etc."

In his famous essay "On New Democracy" (1940), Mao has made an observation about the guiding ideology of the reform which contains a dichotomy in appraisal: "At the time, the ideology of the new learning played a revolutionary role in fighting the Chinese feudal ideology and it served the bourgeois-democratic revolution of the old period. However, because the Chinese bourgeoisie lacked the strength and the world had

* The article that was written in 1978 and published in *China Report*, Vol. XIV, No. 4 (July-August 1978) has been abridged for the present edition of the book.

** Foreign Languages Press, *The Reform Movement of 1898* (Peking, 1976).

already entered the era of imperialism, this bourgeois ideology was only able to last out a few rounds and was beaten back by the reactionary alliance of the enslaving ideology of foreign imperialism and the 'back to the ancients' ideology of Chinese feudalism; as soon as this reactionary ideological alliance started a minor counter-offensive, the so-called new learning lowered its banners, muffled its drums and beat a retreat, retaining its outer form but losing its soul."[1]

What we feel disturbed about is the uncharitable views of Mao about the weakness and cowardice of an ideology which he himself considers progressive and revolutionary in character which had played a positive role in history.

This dichotomy in Mao's appraisal of the Reform Movement has infected other Chinese commentators as well. In *The Reform Movement* we see a similar dichotomy and for the same reason. It offers a bouquet for Tan Sitong's philosophical work entitled *A Study of Benevolence.* "It pointed out the need to 'break all trammels', that is, to smash the feudal fetters. Permeated with such democratic spirit, the book played an active role in the intellectual circles of that period." This positive appreciation is, however, neutralised by the following observation: "Tan Ssu-tung, however, failed to free himself from the feudal 'trammels... He opposed feudal ethics, yet dared not break with Confucianism. He cursed autocratic monarchy but at the same time pressed for reforms...to bolster the position of Emperor Kuang Hsu. This shows how the bourgeois reformists, however fervent and energetic their left-wing may have been... were impotent to extricate themselves from the dragnet of feudal forces."

Another dichotomy in the book is with reference to Yan Fu's translation of T.H. Huxley's *Evolution and Ethics* which introduced to the Chinese mind Charles Darwin's theory of evolution. *The Reform Movement* hails it as an important landmark in history. It says: "... the introduction to China of the aforesaid theory helped to awaken the Chinese people to the fact that, unless China roused itself to action, it would sink under the jungle law of the capitalist world. In fact, progressive-minded people were steadily coming forth with vocal demands for China's self-strengthening through reform." (p. 53) Having said this, the book does not acknowledge China's indebtedness to either Yan Fu or T.H. Huxley or Charles Darwin. Instead, it condemns Darwin's theory as "thoroughly reactionary" because it has not only debased man "to the level of all other living creatures" and accepted "the trampling underfoot by the strong of the weak as fated", but also "tends to justify the capitalist powers' aggression against weak nations." (p. 52) Crowning its denunciation of bourgeois Western learning is this assertion: "The law of history, that a weak nation can defeat a strong one and a small nation can defeat a big one, has utterly smashed the reactionary view of vulgar evolutionism."

Yet another self-contradiction in the book's assessment of the Reform Movement *vis-a-vis* the foreign powers is that, on the one hand, it acknowledges the fact that: "In striving for national salvation through reform by imperial decrees the bourgeois reformists meant to save China from the threat of imperialist partition and further, to transform semi-colonial China into an independent nation." (p. 67) On the other hand, it blames the reformers for their failure "to see its [imperialism's] hidden, velvet-gloved aggression." (p. 67) Then it tries to give a rational explanation to this self-contradiction: "But there was really nothing strange in Emperor Kuang Hsu and Kang Yu-wei looking upon the British and Japanese imperialists as their 'saviours.' For these imperialists had long been thinking of grooming Kuang Hsu to their needs and Kang Yu-wei and his colleagues were the very ones they intended to use to this end."

It is a harsh accusation that the nineteenth-century reformers were unwittingly playing the imperialist game. This is not only in contrast with Mao Zedong's view of the positive historical role of the Reform Movement, but also contradicts what the book itself has conceded, viz. the reformers' intention to save China from imperialist aggression.

It is in consonance with this Maoist perspective that The *Reform Movement* treats the Reform Movement as an intended solution to "the grave national crisis and acute class contradiction." (p. 4) However, the book has to say something different from the Maoist intellectual authorities. The authors think that an additional motivation behind the Reform Movement was the reformers' apprehension that "the Ching government should go down in the mounting storms of mass resistance", and the reform was "designed to lull and mislead the people with pronouncements of loyalty to the nation and of saving it." So we shall not consider this point as a part of the Maoist perspective.

II

Almost in all academic discourses on the 1898 Reform, the great intellectual movement of 1895 has not been given its due. This was the famous event known as "Gongche shangshu" (presentation of memorial by the riders of public carts). Two thousand years ago, during the Han Dynasty, public servants (who were selected scholars) used to travel by bullock-carts provided by the imperial government on their first journey to the imperial capital to report for duty. In 1895 there were neither bullock-carts nor cart-riders in the limelight. But 1,200 provincial graduates, holders of the title of academic distinction of "Elevated Man" (modern scholars often equate it with the academic degree of Master of Arts), who were the distant descendants of the Han Dynasty bullock-cart riders, signed *en masse* a memorial to the throne at the moment when the Manchu government was about to ratify the Treaty of Shimonoseki between China and Japan, which was the most unequal among all unequal treaties signed between China and any foreign government. *The Reform Movement* furnishes a gist of this 14,000-character memorial on pp. 23-25, but totally omits its fireworks.

The authors of *The Reform Movement,* like many Chinese and foreign commentators of the 1898 Reform, have failed to grasp the historical significance of this Public Carts Representation of 1895. First, although mass demonstrations before imperial authorities are not unknown in Chinese history, it was unprecedented that more than a thousand eminent scholars from all over China, among whom were hundreds of prospective imperial officers, made a verbal demonstration before the imperial court in the imperial capital. Being an autocracy, the Manchu government and its imperial predecessors used to persecute, even put to death, scholars who were critical of the emperor and his government in an implicit and disguised manner in their writings. The twelve hundred signatories of this open remonstration had taken a great risk in associating themselves with the daring document drafted by Kang Youwei for whom it was his second daring memorialization. Kang did it with full awareness of the serious consequences of his own action—he was liable to not only a death sentence but the total liquidation of his kith and kin on the charge of rebellion against his ruler and instigating others to rebel. Judging from the historical circumstances of their situation, the scholars' mass representation in 1895 was no less a heroic demonstration than the May Fourth Movement in 1919.

Secondly, the memorial itself was a daring document. It almost spelt out the charge of treason against the imperial ruler who would endorse the cession of Chinese territory to Japan—an act, says the memorial, tantamount to "the betrayal of Your Majesty's ancestors above and the abandonment of Your Majesty's subjects below." The memorial thus requests that the emperor should castigate himself most severely and with utmost sincerity to move the righteous officials to tears and to put "complacent generals and coward soldiers" to shame. It also recommends stringent punishment of "those responsible courtiers who are in favour of appeasement and bringing humiliation to the nation, those generals who not only did not fight sincerely and fled the battlefield along with the whistling wind, losing territories and armed forces under their command, but also deduct and detain payment to the officers and men and pocket it, those diplomatic envoys who, of their own volition, sign treaties which cede territories and bring humiliation to the country and those responsible officers guarding our territory who are bad at commanding their subordinates and slacken in the defence of the land." The memorial also lashes at the imperial government's impotence in mobilising the four hundred million people of China.

Third, in this memorial, Kang Youwei and his colleagues demonstrated their political vision in sizing up the international situation, pin-pointing the malaise of the country and its remedy, and professing a dynamic political philosophy. The document is charged with patriotic sentiments and has an undertone of anti-foreign-imperialism. It emphasizes "bian" (change). "If we don't change our laws and institutions, we shall let the territories of our ancestors be cut asunder till we extinguish as a nation. If we change our laws and institutions, we shall reinvigorate the might and effectiveness endowed by our ancestors and become great and strong. The pros and cons of reform are clear for everyone to see." The memorial harps on the theme of galvanising the vitality of the country. The memorial candidly points out the ruler's intellectual alienation from the masses. The hierarchy of the government was like a pagoda of a hundred storyes and made it more and more difficult to get to the higher echelons. The vastness of the country was like a huge mansion of thousands of tightly sealed rooms, difficult to communication. A province of thousands of miles had only a couple of viceroys and governors to communicate with the centre. The court of hundreds of officials had only three to five key personalities who had access to the emperor.[2]

In this memorial was written the manifesto for reform, which anticipated the reform programme of 1898. It was this memorial which moved the emperor, won Kang Youwei the imperial recognition and paved the way for the growth of the forces of reform both within and outside the imperial government, culminating in the hundred days reform in 1898. Underlying the triumph of the 1895 "public carts" memorial was an intense struggle between the progressive and conservative forces in the ruling elite. The intensity of the struggle could be compared with a small-scale mass armed rebellion.

Kang Youwei's persistent appeal for reform and submission of seven strongly worded, sentiment-changed memorials (the first one was submitted in 1888, the second, third and fourth in 1895, and the fifth, sixth and seventh in 1898) finally resulted in Emperior Guangxu's dramatic assertion as an unprecedented active reformist-ruler for a short period of 102 days from 11 June to 20 September 1898. In those few days, the emperor issued on an average two reform edicts a day which is a world record in administrative diligence.

Scholars generally think that the reform measures underlined by the massive imperial directives were actually mild and moderate. First of all, as late Professor Victor Purcell of Cambridge University comments, the driving spirit behind the Reform Movement, Kang Youwei, was himself a conservative.[3]

On top of it, almost before every major reform decision was taken, the emperor would pay a visit to the empress' chamber in the Summer Palace at Yiheyuan to ask for the assent of his aunt and god-mother, the ultra-conservative and notorious Empress Dowager Cixi (Ts'u-hsi) who, although had formally ceased to be the Regent as the emperor had already become an adult, actually continued to hold the reins of power. According to a contemporary account, the Empress played a double game *vis-a-vis* the reform. While she instructed the Grand Council and Grand Secretariat to stall the implementation of the reform orders from the Emperor, at the same time, she affected an expression of indifference whenever the Emperor broached the subject of reform before her. She had even a stock answer to the Emperor: "As long as you don't burn the ancestral tablet[4] and cut off the braid,[5] I won't care what you do."[6]

Rumour, however, floated around in the imperial capital that drastic changes of social customs and living habits were to take place. The braids would be cutoff, costumes changed and traditional etiquette abolished. There was even a rumour that the emperor had been drugged by Kang Youwei to become a fanatic Catholic and that Buddhism and Taoism and all traditional ways of worship would be banned so as to popularize Catholicism. A large number of tradition-minded people as well as Buddhist monks (many of whom had enjoyed immense royal patronage) got panicky.[7] The seemingly smooth, moderate and peaceful reform movement actually generated a lot of tension among the high-ups of Chinese society. It was nothing short of a social war within the ruling classes.

The Reform Movement has grasped the intensity of this social struggle. It says: "Tension gripped the Ching court in the summer of 1898. Backed by Empress Dowager Tzu Hsi, the diehard high officials of her faction, who feared that the reform movement would shake their ruling position and the whole feudal order, were using every possible means to suppress it... On the other hand, Emperor Kuang-Hsu, emboldened by the intense activities of his faction and the reformists, wished to use the reform to shake off Tzu Hsi's control and gain the real power for himself... " (p. 85).

The book also quotes Chairman Mao to say that in old China one could talk about reform only at the risk of imprisonment and decapitation. Then, it describes how Tan Sitong died heroically as a martyr. He declined to flee to Japan by saying: "If no one is ready to lay down his life, how can the sacred, illustrious Sovereign's kindness be repaid?" (p. 118) After this description, the book comments: "But the question remained: for whom, for what, was he 'holding' his 'sword'? The answer could only be: for bourgeois reformism, for his 'sacred, illustrious Sovereign' whose 'kindness' he was ready to repay with his own blood. This was dictated by his class nature. The shedding of his blood symbolized not the commencement but the abortion of the political reform movement, revealing the reformist road as a blind alley." (p. 118)

This brings us to the difficult task of assessing, with fairness and historical objectivity, the nature of the 1898 Reform. At the outset, we could agree with the contention of the book and other Chinese Communist discourses of the event that this Reform Movement was of, by and for the ruling elite of late Manchu China. Its ultimate aim was to reinvigorate China's existing sociopolitical system so as to extricate the ruling elite from the internal and external crises they had fallen into. The Reform Movement mobilized strength well within the ruling elite and did not in the least involve the masses.

However, we must give the reformers, at least some of them, credit for not only having grasped the dynamism of social progress but also for having dedicated their energy, even their lives, to the realization of political and social progress in China. The reformers, each in their own ways, had entered into a new universe much larger than their social system and their education and upbringing would normally have led them to. Their intellectual outlook and emotional involvement had moved away from the narrow confines of personal or even group interest to larger problems of the sad plight of the country and its future.

By any criterion, they were the people who were thinking, speaking and doing things in a progressive manner and in an advanced direction. The positive character of the Reform Movement can be spelled out.

First, it symbolized China's national awakening. "The awakening of our country", wrote Liang Qichao (1873-1929), Kang Youwei's disciple and one of the pillars of the Reform, "from a long dream of four thousand odd years, began actually from the defeat in the 1895 war, the cession of Taiwan and the stipulation of an indemnity of two hundred million [taels]."[8] There is more dramatization than exaggeration in this statement.

Over the long years of her history, China had innumerable experiences of national crises. But her agony in the last decade of the nineteenth century was unprecedented. China was like a lamb surrounded by hungry wolves eager to tear her apart. National survival was the loudest slogan in the Reform Movement. It was the trumpeters of Reform that really woke up China to strive for survival in the international jungle of "might is right."

Secondly, the Reform Movement was, as Kwang-ching Liu has implied, the first conscious national movement in China to modernize her social and political institutions, many of the ideas and ideals of which have only been realised by later political movements, including the Communist movement. Victor Purcell has ably summed up the aims of the 1898 Reform: "[The 1898 Reform] had the following aims—to abolish the old examination system together with the 'Eight-legs essay', to convert the temples and out-moded institutions of learning into new-type colleges and high schools; to reduce the number of the Green Standard troops and to intensify the training of the army on modern lines; to do away with sinecure offices; to establish a national bank; to grant all subjects the right to memorialise the throne; to provide a general administration for mining, railway, agriculture, industry, and commerce; to found a national Peking university; to promote new publication and translation bureaus."[9]

Two main themes of the Movement were: *(a)* modernizing and rationalizing administration and the larger system involving governance of the country like recruitment of government officials and training of armed forces; *(b)* democratizing political life. In the first aspect, the 1898 Reform gave a thundering start to a long-drawn process of administrative reform which, in a sense has not ceased till today. Kung-ch'uan Hsiao uses the term "gradualism" to highlight the Reform strategy of Kang Youwei and his colleagues.[10] Maribeth Cameron thinks that from the "Hundred Days" onwards till its end, the Manchu government had undertaken a "programme of gradual reform."[11] This gradualness is a significant historical phenomenon. There has always been a feeling in India that her political and legal system ill fits Indian ethos as it was abruptly imposed on the country by a foreign power. In comparison, it seems the Chinese experience was a gradual voluntary progress towards aids modern institutions of governance. If this should be regarded as a merit, part of the credit goes to the 1898 Reform.

Kang Youwei's programme of democratization which was accepted by the emperor was spelt out by him thus: (*i*) to invite suggestions and criticisms from all walks of life and grant royal audience to people who had substantial opinions; (*ii*) to convene conferences of people's deputies (one deputy for ten thousand families) to discuss important affairs of the country and immediately implement the decisions taken by the two-thirds majority of the conference; *(iii)* to open a special house of books and consultants so that the emperor could go and consult everyday in his leisure hours; (*iv*) to print newspapers to gather information and wisdom and translate news from *The Times of London* and other foreign papers; and (*v*) to search for talents in the country and appoint them to assist the emperor.[12] The viability and effectiveness of these measures may be questioned, but not Kang's sincerity and determination for democratization.

Third, although the reformers were ultimately driven away from political power by the conservative forces, the reform spirit survived and even won over such obscurantists as Empress Cixi, who faithfully implemented most of the measures initiated by Emperor Guangxu during the "Hundred Days." The reformers had made a deep impression on China's political fabric with their idea of "bian" (change). They rightly emphasised that the spirit of change and reform had existed in Chinese tradition in Confucius' teachings and in the national ethos. In their ideological struggle with the conservatives, the reformers succeeded in refuting the charges of their opponents that modernization and adoption of Western institutions amounted to betraying the Chinese tradition. As a movement for political transformation and for changing the Chinese situation for the better, the 1898 Reform had set the pattern of political development in China.

This pattern was enunciated by Kang Youwei and Xue Fucheng (1838-94), a reform-oriented scholar. Kang Youwei urged the emperor in his memorials thus: "We should not conserve the old and must reform our institutions. We should not reform slowly, but must change fast. Small changes will not do, we must transform totally." Again, "Changes in arrangements and not in the system, or changes in the system and not in personality would amount to no change."[13]

Xue Fucheng observed "Buddhadhamma originated from India but prospered in the East. Mathematics started in China but reached perfection in the West... Alas! The world changes endlessly, which offers endless scope for the sages to grasps the change. We who live in the modern world...must adapt ourselves to modern changes..."[14]

However, realising the tempo of the changing world is one thing and keeping abreast of it is another. The tempo of change in the Chinese political situation was fast at the turn of the century. After China made the first stride towards modernization during the "Hundred Days", she never looked back. Close upon the heels of the Reform Movement came the Boxer Uprising which shook the Western world. In another ten years, the seemingly eternal imperial system crumbled.

Another four decades later China became the home of an ultra-modern political ideology— Communism. Sun Yat-sen, father of Chinese republicanism, received encouragement and beneficial influence from the 1898 Reform, while Mao Zedong, father of Chinese Communism, was one time a great admirer of Liang Qichao the Reform hero. Some of the Reform leaders like Tang Caichang became participants and supporters of the republican revolution. Ironically, Kang Yuwei himself, the locomotive of Chinese political dynamism in the 1890s failed to keep pace with the times and slipped into the camp of the opponents of republicanism.

III

It is difficult to regard the 1898 Reform as a failure. Failure and success, in fact, are relative concepts. It is worth pondering how under the autocratic rule of Manchu-China, an insignificant Chinese scholar initially without any imperial backing (*i.e.* Kang Youwei) could create such a historic event and powerful political movement just by wielding his pen. If the Manchu court could be so easily influenced by sensible and rational, emotional and outspoken memorials, China would not have come to such an impasse as she did during the 1890s. The ardent appeal of the reformers was only one of the multiple factors which had fermented the Reform Movement. Another crucial factor was Emperor Guangxu. This monarch was placed on the throne (his predecessor and elder cousin had no heir) in his boyhood because his mother happened to be the real sister of Empress Cixi, who was the real kingmaker. When the emperor came of age and became conscious of his legitimate right as a ruler, there developed a personal conflict between the aunt and the nephew over the issue of who should reign the country. Under the highhanded Empress Dowager the Emperor grew increasingly impatient and developed the feeling of rebellion. His personal ambition complemented his patriotism to make him desperate, in the spring of 1898, to proclaim: "If the Empress Dowager still refuses to give me power, I would rather abdicate than become the monarch of a dead state."[15] By sheer accident, the political agitation led by Kang Youwei coincided with the climax of the inner-palace conflict between the Empress Dowager and the Emperor. The Emperor embraced the reform ideology partly out of his youthfulness and patriotism and partly because the ideology could add respectability to his personal struggle with his aunt for power. The third crucial factor of the event was Empress Cixi, who by 1898 had been addicted to political power. In her thinking the emperor was just her pawn. The emperor's growing intransigence not only irked her, but also put her in a quandary. She had a strong desire to depose the emperor, but was wise enough not to do so because of the dignity of the imperial system and public (including external) pressure. The same pressure forced her to renounce her regency, and apparently gave the Emperor a free hand to run the government. One of her calculations in retiring into political hibernation was her anticipation that the emperor would run into trouble in managing the country's affairs and would thus offer her an opportunity to come back.

It is clear that the factors which contributed to the success of the Reform Movement were also factors which foreshadowed its failure. First, the pen-pushers without the backing of the guns could not make much of a fuss under the contemporary political circumstances. Second, the position of the emperor on which the reformers had staked all their hope, was actually untenable. Third, the Empress Dowager was lurcking in the shadow for a kill. The end of the "Hundred Days" drama was not entirely unexpected.

Chinese Communist historians, as shown in *The Reform Movement,* attribute the failure of the Reform Movement to the reformers' lack of confidence in the common people. Hence their inaction in mobilizing the masses. This point is well and legitimately taken. Even when discussing the 1898 events with a hindsight Liang Qichao made an interesting observation which truly betrays the limitations of the reform ideology: "That people's government can be established in Western countries is because the people's wisdom there has blossomed... Although it is an universal truth that every person has his right of self determination, this cannot be applied to children who need the protection of the parents. China today is a child... Thus, to advocate people's government in China, today, amounts to invite trouble. People are ignorant and outlaws are at large. Once trouble starts, there will be insurgencies here and there. The country will fall apart and the people will be victimised."[16]

This observation helps substantiate *The Reform Movement's* sharp criticism of the reformers' fear of revolutions in China. "This alienated them from the masses of the people, so much so that they could not obtain an ally truly capable of defeating the old forces." (p. 121) This erroneous approach, says the book, pushed the reformers to rely on (1) "the reform-inclined intellectuals and scholar-officials of the landlord class", and (2) "some imperialist countries", mistaking "the imperialist Britain, Japan and the United States for 'friendly countries' ready to help China in its reform." (pp. 121-122)

The Reform Movement's laying blame squarely on Western imperialism reiterates a typical Maoist proposition which has been brought out by Mao Zedong himself in a lucid manner in his famous essay "On the People's Democratic Dictatorship" which he wrote on 30 June 1949 to commemorate the twentyeighth anniversary of the Chinese Communist Party. In this essay Mao mentions Kang Youwei and Yan Fu, the two leading reformers, as "representatives of those who had looked to the West for truth before the Communist Party of China was born." Here Mao has at once established a teacher-pupil relationhip between the West and the Chinese intellectuals. Mao recalls that he himself, during his student days, was involved in the wave of "the new learning": "For quite a long time, those who had acquired the new learning felt confident that it would save China... Only modernization could save China, only learning from foreign countries were then progressive, as they had successfully built modern bourgeois states. The Japanese has been successful in learning from the West, and the Chinese also wished to learn..."

This also depicts exactly the scene of the Reform Movement. Mao continues: "Imperialist aggression shattered the fond dreams of the Chinese about learning from the West. It was very odd—why were the teachers always committing aggression against their pupils? The Chinese learned a good deal from the West, but they could not make it work... Day by day, conditions in the country got worse and life was made impossible. Doubts arose, increased and deepened."[17]

Here is, clear and simple, the theory of "bad teachers" to explain the failure of the Reform Movement, and of similar movements aimed at saving China from ruin by means of emulating the Western road to modernisation. In Mao's opinion, the Chinese were not bad pupils at all. They learnt a good deal from the West. They had all the knowledge about national salvation. They started as the Western teachers taught, industries, railways, telegraph office and what not. They switched over to Western education. They left no stone unturned in their rage for Westernization. Only the result evaded them. The reformers, of course, could be blamed for relying on outmoded monarchy to carry out modernization. But, how to explain the want of success in China's modernization efforts even after the overthrow of the monarchy in 1911? So, in Mao's theory, Western imperialism is blamed for having charmed China to emulate them, but actually sucking out China's vitality through the instruments of Westernization. And it was foolish for China to regard as her teachers those who were actually bleeding her white. The real culprit who sabotaged China's Reform Movement was Western imperialism.

IV

In the last part of the treative Prof Tan Chung has analysed the assessment both Chinese and Western of Kang Youwei. Among the Western scholars is included, in the main, Professor Kung-chuan Hsiao, among the communist scholars are included the studies of Hou Wailu and Fung Yu-lan along with the works of Yang Rongguo and Dr K.P. Gupta. On the basis of a detailed historiographical Sketch of their views and the revised assessment of Kang Youwei, Prof Tan Chung has concluded the discussion with the following observations.

We cannot conclude our discussion without dwelling on the scholarly appraisal of Kang Youwei who was not only the locomotive of the Reform Movement, but also represented a distinct stream in the new tide of modern Chinese thought.

We shall close our discussion and bid farewell to Kang Youwei and his reform colleagues, who have, both during their lifetime and afterwards, received more bullets and brickbats than garlands and bouquets. They did not deserve such unkind treatment. History is often merciless, and the reformers had the misfortune to be born in a country which, during the last one hundred thirty years, has been seized by the rage of violent revolution. Now that the rage is cooling off, there is hope that more academic attention and appreciation would befall the Reform Movement and its heroes. As we have seen, even the worst critic of the Reform Movement has implictly admitted the significance of the Reform Movement in bringing about China's modern awakening, similar to the epoch-making effect of the Enlightenment in Europe during the 18th century. And this admission alone qualifies the 1898 Reform as a memorable event.

References

1. *Selected Works of Mao Tse-tung* (Peking, 1959), Vol. II, p. 371.
2. For the full text of the memorial of 1895, see *Wuxu bianfa,* Vol. II, pp. 131-154.
3. Victor Purcell, *The Boxer Uprising*: A Background Study (Cambridge Univ. Press, 1936), p. 104.
4. Instead of idols, every Chinese family had a wooden tablet on the altar for worship. The first thing the Taiping leader, Hong Xiuquan, did as a token of rebellion was to burn the tablet.
5. The braid was a part of hair style which the Manchus had imposed on their subjects. The first act of rebellion by Sun Yat-sen was to cut off hits braid and those of others.
6. Su Jizu "Qingting wuxu chaobian ji" (An Account of the Manchu Palace Coup in 1898) in *Wuxu bianfa,* Vol. I, p. 342.
7. *Ibid.,* pp. 337, 338, 342-343.
8. Liang Qichao, "Wuxu zhengbian ji" (An Account of the Political Coup D'etat of 1898) in *Wuxu bianfa,* Vol. I, p. 249.
9. Purcell, *op. cit.,* p. 104.
10. Kung-ch'uan Hsiao, *A Modern China and a New World: K'ang Yu-wei, Reformer and Utopian, 1858-1927* (University of Washington, 1975), p. 194.
11. Meribeth E. Cameron, *The Reform Movement in China, 1898-1912* (reprint, New York, 1963), p. 199.
12. *Wuxu bianfa,* Vol. II, pp. 184-185.
13. Cited in Liang Qichao, *loc cit.,* p. 277.
14. Xue Fucheng, "Chouyang chuyi" (Suggestions in Sea Defence) in *Wuxu bianfa,* Vol. I, p. 161.
15. Liang Qichao, "Wuxu zhengbian jishi benmo" (Events of the 1898 Coup D'etat) in *Wuxu bianfa,* Vol. I, p. 381.
16. *Idem,* "Wuxu zhengbian ji" *loc. cit.,* p. 294.
17. *Selected Works of Mao Tse-tung,* Vol. IV, pp. 412-413.

Bibliography

In English

Aird, J.S., *The Size, Composition and Growth of the Population of Mainland China*, Washington D.C., 1961.

Allen, G.C., and Donnithrone, A.G., *Western Enterprise in Far Eastern Development : China and Japan,* London 1954.

Allen, Nathan, *An Essay on the Opium Trade,* Boston, 1850.

Allen, Roland, *The Siege of the Peking Legations,* London, 1901.

Andors, Stephen, *China's Industrial Revolution,* New York, 1977.

Appleton. W.W., *A Cycle of Cathay. The Chinese Vogue in England,* Columbia Univ., 1951.

Ayers, William, *Chang Chih-tung and Educational Reform in China,* Harvard, 1971.

Banister, T.R., *A History of the External Trade of China, 1834-81,* Shanghai, 1931.

Banno, Masataka, *China and the West 1858-1861 : The Origins of Tsungli Yamen*, Harvard, 1964.

Beckmann, G.M., *The Modernization of China and Japan,* New York, 1962.

Bennett, A.A., *John Fryer, The Introduction of Western Science and Technology into Nineteenth-Century China,* Harvard, 1967.

Berard, Victor, *British Imperialism and Commercial Supremacy,* London, 1906.

Biggestaff, Knight, *The Earliest Modern Government Schools in China,* Cornell Univ., 1961.

Blythe, W., *The Impact of Chinese Secret Societies in Malaya,* Oxford, 1969.

Boar, R.P., *Famine in China and the Missionary : Timothy Richard as Relief Administrator and Advocate of National Reform 1876-1884,* Cambridge, 1972.

Boardman, E.P., *Christian Influence upon the Ideology of the Taiping Rebellion,* Madison, 1952.

Booker, H.S., *The Problem of Britain's Overseas Trade,* London, 1948.

Bowley, A.L., *A Short Account of England's Foreign Trade in the Nineteenth Century,* London, 1922.

Broomhall, Marshall, *Islam in China : A Neglected Problem,* London, 1910.

— —, *Martyred Missionaries of the China Island Mission,* London, 1901.

Cady, J.F., *The Roots of French Imperialism in Eastern Asia,* New York, 1954.

Cameron, M.E., *The Reform Movement in China 1898-1912,* Stanford, 1931.

Campbell, C. J. Jr., *Special Business Interests and the Open Door Policy,* Yale, 1951.

Cary-Elwes, Columba, *China and the Cross. Studies in Missionary History,* Longmans Green, 1957.

Cassery, Gordon, *The Land of the Boxers* or *China Under the Allies,* London, 1903.

Chan, Wellington K.K., *Merchants, Mandarins and Modern Enterprise in Late Ching China,* Harvard, 1979.

Chang, Chung-li, *The Chinese Gentry : Studies on their Role in Nineteenth Century Chinese Society,* Seattle, 1955.

Chang, Hao, *Liang Ch'i-ch'ao and Intellectual Transition in China, 1890-1907,* Harvard, 1971.

Chang, Hsin-pao, *Commissioner Lin and the Opium War,* Harvard, 1964.

Chaudhuri, K.N., *The Economic Development of India Under the East India Company,* Cambridge Univ., 1971.

Ch'en, Gideon, *Lin Tse-hsu, Pioneer Promoters of the adoption of Western Means of Maritime Defence in China,* Peiping, 1934.

— —, *Tseng Kuo-fan : Pioneer Promoter of the Steamship in China,* Peiping, 1935.

— —, *Tso Tsung-t'ang, Pioneer Promoter of the Modern Dockyard and the Wooden Mice in China,* Peiping, 1938.

Chen Han-seng, *Agrarian Problems in Southern most China* Shanghai, 1936.

— —, *Industrial Capital and Chinese Peasants,* Shanghai, 1939.

— —, *Landlord and Peasant in China,* New York, 1936.

— —, *The Present Agrarian Problem in China,* Shanghai, 1933.

Ch'en Jerome, "The Nature and Characteristics of the Boxer Movement—A Morphological Study" in the *Bulletin of the School of Oriental and African Studies,* London Univ. Vol. XXIII, No. 2, (1960).

— —and Tarling, Nicholas eds, *Studies in the Social History of China and South-east Asia,* Cambridge Univ., 1970.

Cheng, J.C., *Chinese Sources for the Taiping Rebellion, 1850-1864,* Hong Kong, 1963.

Cheng Tien-fong, *A History of Sino-Russian Relations,* Washington, 1957.

Cheng, Ying-wan, *Postal Communication in China and Its Modernization, 1880-1896,* Harvard, 1970.

Chesneaux, Jean, *Peasants' Revolts in China 1840-1849,* (tr. C. Curwen), London, 1973.

— —ed., *Popular Movement and Secret Societies in China 1840-1950,* Stanford, 1972.

— —, *Secret Societies in China in the Nineteenth and Twentieth Centuries* (tr. G. Wettle), London, 1971.

— — and Bastid, Mariance and Berger, Marie-Chaire, *China from Opium War to the 1911 Revolution* (tr. Anne Destony), New York, 1976.

Chi, Ch'ao-ting, *Key Economic Areas in Chinese History,* London, 1936.

Chiang Siang-tseh, *The Nien Rebellion,* Univ. of Washington, 1954.

Chien Po-tsan, Shao Hsun-cheng, and Hu Hua, *Concise History of China,* Peking, 1964.

Chien Yu-wen or Jian Youwen (see Jen Yu-wen).

Chinese Customs, *Decennial Reports, 1882-1911,* Shanghai.

— —, *Reports on Trade and the Treaty Ports and Trade Reports 1882-1919,* Shanghai.

Chu, S.C., *Reformer in Modern China : Chang Chien, 1853-1926,* Columbia Univ., 1965.

Ch'u T'ung-tsu, *Law and Society in Traditional China,* Paris and the Hague, 1961.

— —, *Local Administration in China under the Ch'ing,* Harvard, 1962.

Chu, Wen-djang, *The Moslem Rebellion in Northwest China 1862-1878,* Leiden, 1966.

Clement, P.H., *The Boxer Rebellion : A Political and Diplomatic Review,* New York, 1915.

Clyde, P.H., and Beer, B.F., *The Far East, A History of the Western Impact and the Eastern Response 1830-1965,* New York, 4th edn. 1966.

Coble, P.M. Jr., *Shanghai Capitalists and the National Government,* Harvard, 1977.

Cochran, Cherman, *Big Business in China : Sino-Foreign Rivalry in the Cigarette Industry, 1890-1930,* Harvard, 1980.

Cohen, P.A., *Between Tradition and Modernity : Wang T'ao and Reform in Late Ch'ing China,* Harvard, 1974.

— —, *China and Christianity : The Missionary Movement and the Growth of Chinese Antiforeignism 1860-1870,* Harvard, 1963.

Cohen, W.I., *America's Response to China : An Interpretative History of Sino-American Relations,* New York, 1971.

Collis, Maurice, *Foreign Mud,* London 1946, reprint, 1967.

Costin, W.C., *Great Britain and China, 1833-1860,* Oxford, 1937.

Cowan, C.D. ed., *The Economic Development of China and Japan,* London, 1964.

Cranmer-Byng, J.L., *An Embassy to China : Lord Macartney's Journals,* Longmans, 1962.

Crow, C., *Four Hundred Million Customers,* London, 1937.

Crowley, J.B., ed., *Modern East Asia : Essays in Interpretation,* Harcourt, 1970.

Curbon, E.C., *The Kaiping Mines (1877-1912),* Harvard, 2nd edn. 1971.

Curwen, C.A., *Taiping Rebel: The Deposition of Li Hsiu-ch'eng,* Cambridge Univ., 1977.

Dawson, Raymond, *The Chinese Chameleon: An Analysis of European Conceptions of Chinese Civilization,* Oxford, 1967.

— —, *Imperial China,* Penguin, 1972.

Dean, B., *China and Great Britain : The Diplomacy of Commercial Relations, 1860-1864,* Harvard, 1953.

Dennet, Tyler, *Americans in Eastern Asia,* New York, reprint, 1963.

Douglas, R.K., *Europe and the Far East, 1506-1912,* Cambridge Univ., 1913.

— —, *Li Hungchang,* London, 1895.

Dulles, Foster R., *China and America,* Washington, 1967.

Dunham, B., *Man Against Myth.* New York, 1962.

Dunne, G.H., *Generation of Giants, The Study of Jesuits in China in the Last Decades of the Ming Dynasty,* Notre Dame, 1962.

Edwardes, Michael, *The West in Asia 1850-1914,* New York, 1967.

Elvin M.J., *The Pattern of the Chinese Past,* Stanford, 1972.

— —and Skinner, G.W., *The Chinese City between Two Worlds,* Stanford, 1971.

Endacott, G.B., *A History of Hong Kong,* Oxford, 1958.

— —, *Government and People in Hong Kong, 1841-1962, A Constitutional History,* Hong Kong, 1964.

Epstein, Israel, *From Opium War to Liberation,* Hong Kong, 3rd edn.1980.

Fairbank, J.K., *China Perceived : Images and Policies in Chinese-American Relations,* New York, 1974.

— —, ed., *Chinese Thought and Institutions,* Chicago, 1957.

— —, *Ch'ing Documents: An Introductory Syllabus,* 2 Vols., Harvard, 3rd edn. 1970.

— —*New Views of China's Tradition and Modernization,* Washington, 1968.

— —, ed., *The Cambridge History of China* Vol. X, Cambridge Univ., 1978.

— —, ed., *The Chinese World Order,* Chicago, 1957.

— —, ed., *The Missionary Enterprise in China and America,* Harvard, 1974.

— —, *The United States and China,* Harvard, 4th edn. 1979.

— —, *Trade and Diplomacy on the China Coast: The Opening of Treaty Ports, 1842-1854,* Harvard, 1953.

— —and Banno, Masataka, *Japanese Studies of Modern China ; A Bibliographical Guide to Historical and Social-Science Research in the 19th and 20th centuries,* Rutland, 1955.

— —and Liu, Kwang-ching, *Modern China, A Bibliographical Guide to Chinese Works, 1898-1937,* Harvard, 1950.

— —and Reischauer, E.O. and Craig, A.C., *East Asia: The Modern Transformation,* Boston, 1965.

Fay, C.R., *Imperial Economy and Its Place in the Formation of Economic Doctrine, 1600-1932,* Oxford, 1934.

Fay, P.W., *The Opium War, 1840-1842,* Chapel Hill, 1975.

Fei Hsiao-tung & Chang Chih-yi, *Earthbound China,* Chicago, 1947.

Feuerwerker, Albert, *China's Early Industrialization : Sheng Hsuan-huai and Mandarin Enterprise,* Harvard, 1958.

— —, ed., *History in Communist China,* M.I.T., 1968.

— —, *The Chinese Economy ca. 1870-1911,* Ann Arbor, 1969.

— —, Murphey, Rhoads, and Wright, Mary C. eds., *Approaches to Modern Chinese History,* Berkerley, 1967.

Fevour, Edward le, *Western Enterprise in Late Ch'ing China. A Selective Survey of Jardine, Matheson and Company's Operations, 1842-1895,* Harvard, 1968.

Fishel, Wesley R., *The End of Extraterritoriality in China,* Berkeley, 1952.

Folsom, K.E., *Friends, Guests and Colleagues : The Mufu System in the Late Ch'ing Period,* Berkeley, 1968.

Fong, H.D., *Cotton Industry and Trade in China,* 2 Vols. Tientsin, 1932.

Foreign Languages Press, Peking :

The Opium War (1976);

The Reform Movement of 1898 (1976);

The Taiping Revolution (1976);

The Yi Ho Tuan Movement of 1900 (1976).

Forsythe, S.A., *American Missionary Community in China, 1895-1905,* Harvard, 1971.

Foster, William, *England's Quest of Eastern Trade,* London, reprint, 1966.

Fox, G., *British Admirals and Chinese Pirates, 1832-1869,* London 1940.

Franke, W., *China and the West* (tr. R.A. Wilson) London, 1967.

— —, *The Reform and Abolition of the Traditional Chinese Examination System,* Harvard, 1960.

Gallagher, John and Robinson, Ronald, "The Imperialism of Free Trade" in *The Economic History Review,* 2nd Series, Vol. VI, No. 1, (Aug. 1953).

Garrett, S.S., *Social Reformers in Urban China, The Chinese Y.M.C.A., 1895-1926,* Harvard, 1970.

Green, O.M., *The Foreigner in China,* London, 1942.

Greenberg, Michael, *British Trade and the Opening of China,* Cambridge Univ., 1951.

Gregory, J.S., *Great Britain and the Taipings,* London, 1969.

Griswold, A.W., *The Far Eastern Policy of the United States,* New York, 1939.

Groot, J.J.M. de, *Sectarianism and Religious Persecution in China.* Amsterdam, 1903.

Gulick, E.V., *Peter Parker and the Opening of China,* Harvard, 1973.

Hail, W.J., *Tseng Kuo-fan and the Taiping Rebellion,* New York, 1964.

Hao, Yen-p'ing, *The Compradore in Nineteenth Century China, Bridge Between East and West,* Harvard, 1970.

Hart, Sir Robert, *These from the Land of Sinim,* London, 1901.

Harmann, Albert, *An Historical Atlas of China,* Chicago, 1966.

Hibbert, Christopher, *The Dragon Wakes: China and the West, 1795-1911,* Longman, 1970.

Ho, Ping-ti, *Studies on the Population of China, 1368-1953,* Harvard, 1958.

— — *The Ladder of Success in Imperial China, Aspect of Social Mobility, 1368-1911,* Columbia Univ., 1962.

Ho, Ping-yin, *The Foreign Trade of China,* Shanghai, 1935.

Hobsbawn, E.J., *The Pelican Economic History of Britain,* Vol. III: *From 1750 to the Present Day,* Pelican, 1969.

Holeden, Reuben, *Yale in China : The Mainland, 1901-1951,* New Haven, 1964.

Holt, Edgar, *The Opium Wars in China,* Pennsylvania, 1964.

Hou, Chi-ming, *Foreign Investment and Economic Development in China, 1840-1937,* Harvard, 1965.

— —, ed., *Modern Chinese Economic History,* New York, 1979.

Hsia, Ching-lin, *Studies in Chinese Diplomatic History,* Shanghai, 1925, reprint, Arlington, 1976.

Hsiao, Kung-ch'uan, *A Modern China and a New World, K'ang Yu-wei, Reformer and Utopian, 1858-1927,* Seattle, 1975.

— —, *Rural China : Imperial Control in Nineteenth Century,* Seattle, 1960.

Hsu, I. C.Y., *China's Entrance into the Family of Nations : The Diplomatic Phase, 1856-1880,* Harvard, 1960.

— —, ed., *Readings in Modern Chinese History,* Oxford, 1971.

— —, *The Ili Crisis,* Oxford, 1966.

— —, *The Rise of Modern China,* Oxford, 1975.

Hu Sheng, *Imperialism and Chinese Politics,* Peking, 1955.

Hudson, G. F., *Europe and China : A Survey of their Relations from the Earliest Times to 1800,* London, 1931.

Hughes, E.R., *The Invasion of China by the Western World,* 2nd edn. London, 1968.

Hummel, A.W. ed., *Eminent Chinese of the Ch'ing Period, 1644-1912,* Washington D.C., Vol. I, 1943, Vol. II, 1944.

Hunt, M.H., *Frontier and the Open Door, Manchuria in Chinese-American Relations, 1895-1911,* New Haven, 1973.

Hunter, W.C., *The "Fan-Kwae" at Canton before Treaty Days, 1825-1844,* London, 1882.

Hurd, D., *The Arrow War : An Anglo-Chinese Confusion, 1859-60,* London, 1967.

Imlah, A.H., *Economic Elements in the Pax Britannica,* Harvard, 1958.

Jen Yu-wen, *The Taiping Revolutionary Movement,* Yale, 1973.

Joseph, Phillip, *Foreign Diplomacy in China, 1894-1900,* London, 1928.

Kang, Chao, *The Development of Cotton Textile Production in China,* Harvard, 1975.

King, F.H.H., *Money and Monetary Policy in China, 1845-1895,* Harvard, 1965.

Kuhn, P.A., *Rebellion and Its Enemies in Late Imperial China: Militarization and Social Structure, 1796-1864,* Harvard, 1970.

Kuo, P.C., *A Critical Study of the First Anglo-Chinese War, with Documents,* Shanghai, 1935.

Langer, William, *The Diplomacy of Imperialism,* New York, 1950.

Latourette, K.S., *A History of Christian Mission in China,* London, reprint, 1966.

— —, *The Chinese, Their History and Culture,* 4th edn. New York, 1964.

— —, *The Great Century in Northern Africa and Asia A.C., 1800-A.C. 1914,* New York, 1944.

Lattimore, Owen, *Inner Asian Frontiers of China,* Boston, 1962.

— —, *The Situation in Asia,* Boston, 1949.

— —and Lattimore, Eleanor, *The Making of Modern China, A Short History,* London, 1945.

Lee, Robert, H.G., *The Manchurian Frontier in Ch'ing History,* Harvard, 1970.

Lens, Sidney, *The Forging of the American Empire : A History of American Imperialism from the Revolution to Vietnam,* New York, 1974.

Levenson, J.R., *Confucian China and Its Modern Fate,* 3 Vols. Berkeley, Vol. I, 1958, Vol. II, 1964, Vol. III, 1965.

— —, ed., *European Expansion and the Counter-Expansion of Asia, 1300-1600,* New York, 1967.

— —, *Liang Ch'i-ch'ao and the Mind of Modern China,* Harvard, 1953.

Levy, Marion, "Contributing Factors in the Modernization of China and Japan" in *Economic Development and Cultural Change,* October issue, 1953.

Lewis, J. W. ed., *Peasant Rebellion and Communist Revolution in China,* Stanford, 1976.

Li, Chien-nung, *The Political History of China, 1840-1920* (tr. S.Y. Teng and J. Ingalls), Princeton, 1956.

Lindley, A.F, *Ti-ping tien-kwoh : The History of the Ti-ping Revolution,* London, 1886, New York, reprint, 1970.

Liu Kwang-ching, ed., *American Missionaries in China, Papers from Harvard Seminar,* Harvard, 1966.

— —, *Americans and Chinese : A Historical Essay and Bibliography,* Cambridge Univ., 1963.

— —, *Anglo-American Steamship Rivalry in China, 1862-1874,* Harvard, 1968.

— —, "Nineteenth-Century China : The Disintegration of the Old Order and the Impact of the West" in Pint-ti Ho and Tang Tsou, eds., *China in Crisis,* Chicago Univ., 1968, Vol. I, Bk. I.

Liu Shih-shun, *Extraterritoriality : Its Rise and Its Decline,* Columbia Univ., 1925.

Lo Jung-pang, *Rang Yu-wei: A Biography and a Symposium,* Turson, 1967.

Loewe, Michael, *Imperial China : The Historical Background to the Modern Age,* Allen & Unwin, 1966.

Lubbock, A.B., *The Opium Clippers,* Boston, 1933.

Mackenzie, Compton, *Realms of Silver, One Hundred Years of Banking in the East,* London, 1953.

MacNair, H. F., *Modern Chinese History, Selected Readings,* Shanghai, 1923.

— —and Lach, Donald, *Modern Far Eastern International Relations.* Van Nostrand, 2nd edn. 1955.

Mallory, W. H., *China, Land of Famine,* New York, 1926.

Mao Tse-tung (Mao Zedong), *Selected Works,* Peking, Vols. I-III, 1967, Vol. IV, 1969, Vol. V, 1977.

Martin, W.A.P., *The Siege in Peking, China Against the World,* New York, 1900.

Maverick, L.A., *China, A Model for Europe,* San Antonio, 1946.

McCordock, R.S., *Britain's Far Eastern Policy, 1894-1900,* New York, 1931.

McCormick, T.J., *China Market—America's Quest for Informal Empire,* Chicago, 1967.

Meadows, T.T., *The Chinese and their Rebellions,* London, 1956, reprint, Stanford, 1954.

Meijer, M.J., *The Introduction of Modern Criminal Law in China,* Batavia, 1950.

Meng, Ssu-ming, *The Tsungli Yamen : Its Organization and Functions,* Harvard, 1962.

Michael, Franz, *The Taiping Rebellion : History and Documents,* Seattle, Vol. I, 1966, Vols. II & III, 1971.

Michie, Alexander, *The Englishman in China, during the Victorian Era,* 2 Vols, London, 1900, reprint, Taipei, 1966.

Moon, P.T., *Imperialism and World Politics,* New York, 1926.

Moore, Barrington Jr., *Social Origins of Dictatorship and Democracy : Lord and Peasant in the Making of the Modern World,* Boston, 1966.

Moore, C.A., *The Chinese Mind : Essentials of Chinese Philosophy and Culture,* Honolulu, 1967.

Morse, H.B., *The Chronicles of the East India Company Trading to China,* Oxford, Vols. I-IV, 1926, Vol. V. 1929.

— —, *The International Relations of the Chinese Empire,* 3 vols, London, 1910-18.

— —and MacNair H. F., *Far Eastern International Relations,* New York, 1931, reprint, New York, 1967.

Moulder, F.V., *Japan, China and Modern World Economy,* Cambridge Univ., 1977.

Murphey, Rhoads, *The Outsiders,* Ann Arbor, 1977.

— —, *The Treaty Ports and China's Modernization : What went wrong*? Ann Arbor, 1970.

Myers, H., *The Chinese Economy, Past and Present,* Belmont, 1950.

— —, *The Chinese Peasant Economy, Agricultural Development in Hupei and Shantung, 1890-1949,* Harvard, 1970.

Nye, Gideon Jr., *Tea and Tea Trade,* 3rd edn. New York, 1980.

— —, *The Opium Question and the Northern Campaigns,* Canton, 1875.

Oliphant, Nigal, *Diary of the Siege of the Legations in Peking During the Summer of 1900,* London, 1901.

Owen, D. E., *British Opium Policy in China and India,* New Haven, 1934.

Parry, J.H., *The Age of Reconnaissance,* London, 1963.

Pelcovits, N. A., *Old China Hands and the Foreign Office,* New York, 1948, reprint, 1969.

Pelissier, Roger, *The Awakening of China, 1793-1949,* G.P. Putnam's Sons, 1967.

Perkins, D.H. ed., *China's Modern Economy in Historical Perspective,* Stanford, 1975.

Powell, R. C., *The Rise of Chinese Military Power, 1895-1912,* Princeton, 1955.

Purcell, Victor, *The Boxer Uprising. A Background Study,* Cambridge Univ. 1963.

Rawlinson, J. L., *China's Struggle for Naval Deevelopment, 1839-1895,* Harvard, 1967.

Remer, F., *The Foreign Trade of China,* Shanghai, 1926, reprint, Taipei, 1967.

Rowbotham, A., *Missionary and Mandarin : The Jesuits at the Court of China,* Berkeley, 1942.

Rozman, Gilbert, ed., *The Modernization of China,* New York, 1981.

Sargent, A.J., *Anglo-Chinese Commerce and Diplomacy,* Oxford, 1907.

Schurmann, Franz & Schell, Orvile, *The Chinese Reader : Imperial China, The Decline of the Last Dynasty and the Origins of Modern China, The 18th and 19th Centuries,* New York, 1967.

Schwartz, B.I., *In Search of Wealth and Power : Yen Fu and the West,* Harvard, 1964.

See Chong-su, *Foreign Trade of China,* New York, 1919.

Selby, John, *The Paper Dragon : An Account of the Wars,* Arthur Barker, 1968.

Shen Wei-tai, *China's Foreign Policy, 1839-1860,* New York, 1932.

Shih, V.Y.C., *The Taiping Ideology, Its Sources, Interpretations and Influences,* Seattle, 1967.

Smith, A.H., *China in Convulsion,* 2 Vols. New York, 1901.

— —, *Chinese Characteristics,* New York, 1894.

Smith, D. B. and Lumby, W. R., *The Second Chinese War, 1856-1860,* London, 1954.

Spector, Stanley, *Li Hung-chang and the Huai Army. A Study in Nineteenth Century Chinese Regionalism,* Seattle, 1964.

Spence, Jonathan, *To Change China: Western Advisers in China,* Boston, 1969.

Sprenkel, Sybile van der, *Legal Institutions in Manchu China, A Sociological Analysis,* London, 1962.

Steele, A. T., *The American People and China,* New York, 1966.

Swisher, Earl, *China's Management of the American Barbarians: A Study of Sino-American Relations, 1841-1861, with Documents,* New Haven, 1951.

T'an, Chester C., *The Boxer Catastrophe,* New York, 1955.

Tan Chung, *China and The Brave New World: A Study of the Origins of the Opium War 1840-1842,* New Delhi, 1978.

Tawney, R. H., *Land and Labour in China,* Boston, 1966.

Taylor, G.E. and Michael, F.H., *The Far East in the Modern World,* New York, 1956, rev. edn. 1964.

Teng, Ssu-yu, *Chang Hsi and the Treaty of Nanking, 1842,* Univ. of Chicago Press, 1944.

— —, *Historiography of the Taiping Rebellion,* Harvard, 1962.

— —, *New Light on the History of the Taiping Rebellion,* Cambridge Univ., 1950.

— —, *The Nien Army and their Guerrilla Warfare, 1851-1868,* Paris, 1961.

— —, *The Taiping Rebellion and the Western Powers: A Comprehensive Survey,* Oxford, 1971.

— — and Fairbank J. K., *China's Response to the West,* Harvard, 1954.

Thomson, H.C., *China and the Powers: A Narrative of the Outbreak of 1900,* London, 1902.

Thomson, J.C. Jr., Stanley, P.W. and Perry, J.C., *Sentimental Imperialists—The American Experience in East Asia,* New York, 1981.

Torgasheif, B.P., *China as a Tea Producer,* Shanghai, 1926.

Turner, F.S., *British Opium Policy and Its Results to India and China,* London, 1876.

Valk, M.H. van der, *Conservatism in Modern Chinese Family Law,* Leiden, 1956.

Varg, P.A., *Missionaries, Chinese and Diplomats: The American Protestant Missionary Movement in China, 1890-1952,* Princeton, 1958.

— —, *Open Door Diplomat: The Life of W. W. Rockhill,* Urbana, 1952.

— —, *The Making of a Myth: The U.S. and China, 1897-1912,* Michigan State Univ., 1968.

Vinacke, H. M., *A History of the Far East in Modern Times,* New York, 6th edn. 1961.

Vincent, J.C., *The Extraterritorial System in China: Final Phase,* Harvard, 1970.

Wakeman, F. Jr., *Strangers at the Gate, Social Disorder in South China, 1836-1861,* Berkeley, 1966.

Waley, Arthur, *The Opium War Through Chinese Eyes,* London, 1958.

Wang, Y.C., *Chinese Intellectuals and the West: 1872-1949,* Univ. of North Carolina, 1966.

Ware, E., *Business and Politics in the Far East,* New Haven, 1932.

Warren, Samuel, *The Opium Question,* London, 1840.

Wehrle, E.S., *Britain, China and the Anti-missionary Riots, 1891-1900,* Minnesota Univ., 1966.

Wilbur, M.E., *The East India Company and the British Empire in the Far East,* California, 1945.

Williams, S.W., *The Middle Kingdom,* London, Vol. I, 1848, Vol. II, 1883.

Williamson, J, A., *A Short History of British Expansion,* London, 1958.

— —, *Great Britain and the Commonwealth,* London, 1945, 3rd edn. 1965.

Willmett, W.E. ed., *Economic Organization in Chinese Society,* Stanford, 1972.

Willoughby, W. W., *Foreign Rights and Interests in China,* 2 Vols. Baltimore, 1927, reprint, Taipei, 1966.

Winks, Robin, ed., *Historiography of the British Empire-Commonwealth,* Durham, 1966.

Wolseley, Lt. Col. G.J., *War with China in 1860,* London, 1862.

Wong, J.Y., *Yeh Ming-ch'er, Viceroy of Liang Kuang (1852-8),* Cambridge Univ., 1976.

Wright, A.F. ed., *Studies in Chinese Thought,* Chicago, 1976.

Wright, M.C., *The Last Stand of Chinese Conservatism, The T'ung-chih Restoration, 1862-1874,* Stanford, 1957.

Wright, S.F., *Hart and the Chinese Customs,* Belfast, 1950.

Wu Wen-tsao, *The Chinese Opium Question in British Opinion and Action,* New York, 1928.

Yang, C.K., *Religion in Chinese Society: A Study of the Contemporary Social Functions of Religion and Some of their Historical Factors,* Berkeley, 1961.

Yang, I-fan, *Islam in China,* Hong Kong, 1969.

Young, L.K., *British Policy in China, 1895-1902,* Oxford, 1970.

Young, M.B., *The Rhetoric of Empire: American China Policy, 1895-1901,* Harvard, 1968.

Yuan Tung li, *China in Western Literature, A continuation of Cordier's Bibliotheca Sinica,* New Haven, 1958.

Zen Sun, E-tu, *Chinese Railways and British Interest, 1898-1911,* Columbia Univ., 1954.

Index

D

E

T